A Blogger's Guide to

JAPAN

Kristine Ohkubo

(Revised Edition)

A Blogger's Guide to JAPAN/Kristine Ohkubo. —Revised ed.

ISBN: 978-1-0880-6988-2

Contents

Tokyo-to: Tokyo Metropolis

Introduction

For many, the island country of Japan is a far distant place characterized by temples, shrines, kabuki, Noh, tea ceremonies, ikebana, kimonos, geisha, and samurai. They often dream about visiting this alluring nation, but few actually have an opportunity to do so.

However, for those who do travel to Japan, it becomes a destination that they visit over and over again. As a matter of fact, Japan received a record number 12 million visitors in 2014 and is seeking to increase tourism up to 20 million visitors by 2020. With the Olympic Games scheduled to take place in Tokyo in 2020, that number does not appear far-fetched.

I had the pleasure of traveling to Japan on several occasions, fell in love with the country, and vowed to return many times. I approached each visit with wide-eyed enthusiasm, immersing myself in the local culture and learning about the history and traditions of this magnificent place that once I only dreamed about. I fell in love with Japan and its people and wanted to share my experiences with others so that they too would carve out an opportunity to someday travel there. I found that the easiest way to reach people in this age of technology and social media was by creating a blog. Thus, *Traveldreamscapes* was born.

I published numerous blog posts and photos gathered from my travels, which was received with so much enthusiasm by my readers that several asked me whether I had intentions of writing a book about my travels to Japan. At first, the idea seemed daunting but the more I thought about it, the more I gravitated toward the notion.

Certainly, there are countless travel books about Japan but I wondered how many were actually written from a travel blogger's perspective. You will find that this book offers a different approach to introducing both new and seasoned travelers to Japan. I will give you the history and background of each place to help you develop a greater appreciation for the sites you visit. Not only will you learn about the popular destinations for tourists but you will also discover attractions off the beaten path. I will uncover festivals and traditions unique to each area and introduce you to local cuisines.

One of the best ways to immerse yourself in a culture is to sample its diverse cuisine. While traveling in Japan today, you will find many western chain restaurants as well as western-style eateries to choose among. Rather than settling for the familiar places, select a traditional restaurant frequented by the locals and sample some of Japan's regional cooking.

Japanese cuisine has a vast array of local specialties known as kyodo ryori (郷土料理). These dishes are typically prepared using local ingredients and traditional recipes. Although many local ingredients are available nationwide these days and it is not uncommon to find regional dishes throughout Japan, you can still find true kyodo ryori to fulfill your adventures in gastronomy. After all, your travels should be an adventure where you actively engage in the traditions and offerings of a country rather than just observing as a bystander.

The book is organized by region/prefecture so regardless of whether you are traveling for a week, a month or several months, you can use this book not only to plan your travels but also to explore further once you are there. Where available, the web page address, physical address, and travel tips will enable you to obtain current, detailed information for each venue.

It is my hope that this guide to Japan will awaken your curiosity about this beautiful country and encourage you to explore it on your own. To quote J.R.R. Tolkien, "Little by little, one travels far."

Wishing you happy and safe journeys to Japan!

Japanese Prefectures

The island country of Japan is divided into nine regions and forty-seven prefectures (ken). The Meiji Fuhanken Sanchisei Administration created the first prefectures to replace the provinces of Japan back in 1868. Technically, however, there are only forty-three actual prefectures, two urban prefectures (fu) consisting of Osaka and Kyoto, one territory (do) comprised of Hokkaido and one metropolitan prefecture (to) known as Tokyo.

The prefectures form the country's jurisdictional and administrative division levels, similar to U.S. states.

Starting from north to south, the prefectures are:

Region	Prefecture		Capital City
Hokkaido	(1)	Hokkaido	Sapporo
Tohoku	(2)	Aomori	Aomori
	(3)	Iwate	Morioka
	(4)	Miyagi	Sendai
	(5)	Akita	Akita
	(6)	Yamagata	Yamagata
	(7)	Fukushima	Fukushima
Kanto	(8)	Tokyo	Tokyo

Region		Capital City	
Region			**Capital City**
	(9)	Ibaraki	Mito
	(10)	Tochigi	Utsunomiya
	(11)	Gunma	Maebashi
	(12)	Saitama	Urawa
	(13)	Chiba	Chiba
	(14)	Kanagawa	Yokohama
	(15)	Yamanashi	Kofu
Chubu	(16)	Nagano	Nagano
	(17)	Niigata	Niigata
	(18)	Toyama	Toyama
	(19)	Ishikawa	Kanazawa
	(20)	Fukui	Fukui
	(21)	Gifu	Gifu
	(22)	Shizuoka	Shizuoka
	(23)	Aichi	Nagoya
Kansai	(24)	Osaka	Osaka

Region	Prefecture		Capital City
	(25)	Kyoto	Kyoto
	(26)	Shiga	Otsu
	(27)	Hyogo	Kobe
	(28)	Mie	Tsu
	(29)	Nara	Nara
	(30)	Wakayama	Wakayama
Chugoku	(31)	Tottori	Tottori
	(32)	Shimane	Matsue
	(33)	Okayama	Okayama
	(34)	Hiroshima	Hiroshima
	(35)	Yamaguchi	Yamaguchi
Shikoku	(36)	Tokushima	Tokushima
	(37)	Kagawa	Takamatsu
	(38)	Ehime	Matsuyama
	(39)	Kochi	Kochi
Kyushu	(40)	Fukuoka	Fukuoka

Region			Capital City
Region			**Capital City**
	(41)	Saga	Saga
	(42)	Nagasaki	Nagasaki
	(43)	Kumamoto	Kumamoto
	(44)	Oita	Oita
	(45)	Miyazaki	Miyazaki
	(46)	Kagoshima	Kagoshima
Ryukyu	(47)	Okinawa	Naha

Tokyo Special Wards

Although Tokyo is often thought of as a city, it is officially a "metropolitan prefecture," which combines elements of both a city and a prefecture, a characteristic that is unique to Tokyo alone.

There are twenty-three municipalities known as "special wards" that make up the core and the most populous part of Tokyo. These wards consist of:

1. Adachi
2. Arakawa
3. Bunkyo
4. Chiyoda
5. Chuo
6. Edogawa
7. Itabashi
8. Katsushika
9. Kita
10. Koto
11. Meguro
12. Minato
13. Nakano
14. Nerima
15. Ota
16. Setagaya
17. Shibuya
18. Shinagawa
19. Shinjuku
20. Suginami

21. Sumida
22. Taito
23. Toshima

Hokkaido Region

Introduction to Hokkaido (北海道)

Formerly known as Ezochi, Hokkaido is located in the northernmost region of Japan and is the second largest island next to Honshu, the main island. It represents 22 percent of Japan's total land mass, yet it is home to only five percent of the country's total population.

The area was exclusively inhabited by the Ainu (Japan's native people) until the Edo era (1603-1868) when mainlanders began moving into the southwest region of the province.

During the Meiji era (1868-1912), a period when Japan underwent a major transformation and emerged as the modern nation we know today, the Ezochi Province became known as Hokkaido (where "Hokkai (北海)" means north sea and "do (道)" denotes its prefectural status).

Travelers need to be aware that the region's weather can be rather harsh in the winter with heavy snowfalls and below zero temperatures. During the summer, however, Hokkaido is a welcome retreat from the hot and humid temperatures that are common throughout the rest of the country.

The largest city and the capital of Hokkaido is Sapporo which hosted the Olympic Winter Games in 1972 and is home to the Sapporo Yuki Matsuri (Sapporo Snow Festival), an annual festival held during February. The city is also where the Sapporo Brewery originated during the Meiji period.

Hokkaido's numerous national parks are a major draw for many visitors. Other notable attractions include flower gardens, hot springs, and some of the best powder skiing opportunities available in Japan.

The regional dishes that characterize Hokkaido include: Genghis Khan (barbecued lamb and vegetables), ishikari nabe (a stewed dish consisting of salmon and vegetables in a miso based broth), ruibe (an Ainu dish of sliced, frozen raw salmon served with soy sauce and water peppers), sanpei jiru (a winter miso soup made with salmon, daikon radish, carrots, potatoes and onions), chanchan yaki (a miso grilled salmon with beansprouts and other vegetables, a specialty in fishing villages), Hokkaido ramen (especially Sapporo ramen) and ika somen (squid sliced into very thin noodle-like strips and eaten with dipping sauce).

Of course, these are the more common regional dishes associated with Hokkaido. Hokkaido has 14 sub-prefectures (支庁/ shicho) and, as a result, you can probably delve deeper into the region's specific cuisine by visiting each individual shicho.

Hokkaido is connected to Honshu via the Seikan Tunnel Underwater Railway, part of the Kaikyo Line portion of the Hokkaido Railway Company's (JR Hokkaido) Tsugaru-Kaikyo Line.

The New Chitose Airport (http://www.new-chitose-airport.jp/en/) is the largest airport in Hokkaido serving the Sapporo metropolitan area. Opened in 1991, it is one of the busiest airports in Japan and serves the world's most traveled air route between Tokyo and Sapporo.

Web Page: http://www.pref.hokkaido.lg.jp/foreign/english.
htm (Hokkaido Prefectural Web Page)

11

Akan Kokuritsu Koen (阿寒国立公園): Akan National Park

Akan National Park, located in eastern Hokkaido, was established on December 4, 1934. Along with Daisetsuzan National Park they comprise the oldest national parks in Hokkaido. Consisting of 90,481 hectares (22,3583 acres), Akan is primarily made up of volcanic craters and forests. It has two separate parts: the smaller, western portion contains Lake Akan with the lakeside hot spring resort of Akankohan Onsen; the larger, eastern part contains Lake Mashu, Lake Kussharo, Iozan (Sulfur Mountain) and the Kawayu Onsen. Although the lakes are often covered by fog, their waters are some of the clearest in the world. Akan is also known for the large marimo that forms there. Marimo literally means seaweed ball. It is a species of filamentous green algae that grow into large green balls with a velvet like appearance.

Iozan is an active volcano near Kawayu Onsen. Its yellow, sulfurous vents can be viewed in close proximity as visitors are permitted to walk around without any restrictions. Eggs cooked by the natural heat of the volcano (onsen tamago) are usually available for sale near the vents.

The park's vast forests are the perfect habitat for the wildlife of eastern Hokkaido. Twenty-four species of mammals inhabit the area including brown bears, Ezo Deer, mice, and squirrels. A number of rare and endangered birds such as the Black Woodpecker, Blakiston's Fish Owl, Steller's Sea Eagle, and White-tailed Eagle can also be found in the confines of the park. The Ainu, the indigenous people of Hokkaido, specialize in wood carvings of the wildlife living in this region.

The Lake Akan area is home to the largest remaining settlement of Ainu. Visitors to Akan National Park can see traditional Ainu dances performed at their kotan (village) and enjoy outdoor activities such as canoeing, mountain bike tours, and camping.

Akan National Park is easily accessible by train via the JR Senmo Line which runs north-south across the park on its way from Abashiri to Kushiro, stopping at Kawayu and Teshikaga (Mashu Station). There are four trains daily to Abashiri and six to Kushiro.

Location(s):   2-2-6 Kawayuonsen, Kawakami-gun,
                Teshikaga-cho, Hokkaido

Web Page: http://www.env.go.jp/en/nature/nps/park/aka
                n/index.html

Biei-cho (美瑛町)： Town of Biei

Shikisai no Oka (色彩の丘)：Hills of Seasonal Colors

The town of Biei or Biei-cho as it is known in Japan is located in central Hokkaido in the hilly Kamikawa District at the foot of the Tokachidake mountain range. This small town, surrounded by a picturesque landscape of gently rolling hills and vast fields, attracts as many as 1.2 million visitors each year. Why? You might ask. It is because of the spectacular views of flowers that can be found in such places as Road of Patchwork, Shikisai no Oka, and Hills of Zerubu. Biei was recognized as one of the premium sightseeing spots in Hokkaido in the 1970s thanks to the work of the world-renowned landscape photographer, Shinzo Maeda. Mesmerized by the town's beautiful scenery, Maeda visited Biei over a ten-year period photographing the stunning landscapes that were subsequently featured in photo collections, postcards, posters, films, and TV commercials.

Located in the southern part of Biei is the seven-hectare (17 acre) (three times bigger than Tokyo Dome) field of flowers known as Shikisai no Oka, which translates to Hills of Seasonal Colors. From April through October, an astonishing number of flowers including tulips, lupine, lavender, salvia, sunflower, dahlias, and Japanese anemones bloom on these hills. The garden has a mascot named Roll-kun. He and his female counterpart, Roll-chan, can be found at the entrance to the flower fields. Visitors to the area will be pleasantly surprised to learn that there are more than just beautiful flowers at Shikisai no Oka. The gardens also feature a produce shop, a souvenir shop, and a restaurant.

Guests can travel around the facility on the Shikisai no Rokko, a tractor bus tour, or rent buggies and four passenger carts to explore the fields on their own.

Shikisai no Oka is open from 9:00 AM to 5:00 PM (April to May and October), 8:30 AM to 6:00 PM (June to September), 9:00 AM to 4:30 PM (November), 9:00 AM to 4:00 PM (December to February), 9:00 AM to 4:30 PM (March). Admission is free however, vehicles are subject to a minimal parking fee.

With its extensive hills and fields covered with fragrant and beautiful flowers, the Hills of Seasonal Colors is truly a masterpiece of color worth visiting.

Location(s):   No.3 Aza Shinsei, Biei-cho, Kamikawa-gun, Hokkaido

Web Page: http://www.jnto.go.jp/eng/location/spot/natu scen/shikisai-no-oka.html

Sapporo-shi (札幌市)：Sapporo City

Sapporo White Illumination Festival and Christmas Market

A winter illumination event that began with merely 1,000 bulbs in 1981 has since grown into an annual event hosted in Sapporo's Odori Park, which utilizes over 400,000 bulbs to help herald the arrival of the snow season. It is a well-recognized fact that Hokkaido, Japan's northernmost island, does get a lot of snow. The average annual snowfall in Sapporo is 235 inches (596 cm).

The festival begins in late November and runs through mid-February. Odori Park, located in the center of town, is Sapporo's most famous park. While it is quite narrow, it stretches over fifteen blocks. In addition to Odori Park, which is thematically decorated with lights and lighted sculptures, Sapporo's main street is also transformed into a kaleidoscope of lights, where trees are decorated with millions of tiny light bulbs, providing a romantic backdrop for strolling couples. In Japan, Christmas is considered to be a romantic time. Snuggling up in the cold and enjoying the beautiful lights of the Sapporo White Illumination Festival is just one way for couples to enjoy the season.

All of the lights used during the White Illumination Festival are powered with renewable energy, including recycled cooking oil and solar panels especially designed to produce power even during the heaviest snow season. In these times of global warming and concerns about nuclear power, the festival is a showcase of ways energy can be produced while taking better care of the planet.

Taking place at the same time as the White Illumination Festival, the German Christmas Market celebrates the sister city relationship between Sapporo and Munich. The market was established in 2002 to commemorate the 30th anniversary of the sister city affiliation and has been an annual event ever since. During the event, various shops fill one section of Odori Park offering everything from traditional Christmas ornaments and dolls to food such as German sausage and mulled hot wine. The German Market begins in late November and runs through December 25.

The market features an outdoor stage where you can enjoy performances by dancers, jugglers and a choir singing gospel and Christmas songs. There is an indoor pavilion which showcases numerous events and workshops where you can experience making Christmas decorations and mulled wine. You can even participate in a class offering German language lessons.

The Sapporo White Illumination Festival is an awe-inspiring collaboration of nature and light to be enjoyed after the sun goes down in Japan's cold and snowy northern region. It is an event worth witnessing at least once if you happen to be in the area.

Location(s):   Sapporo Ekimae Dori (Sapporo Station Street)
                Minami 1-jyo Dori (South 1-jyo Street)

Web Page: http://white-illumination.jp/en-us/

Sapporo-shi (札幌市): Sapporo City

Shiroi Koibito Park (白い恋人パーク）

Ishiya Co., Ltd. in Sapporo, Hokkaido is a Japanese confectioner best known for its European style Shiroi Koibito (White Lover) cookies, which it began selling in December of 1976. Today, the cookies rank as Hokkaido's top selling souvenir. Just 25 minutes by car from Sapporo's downtown area, you will find the Shiroi Koibito Park, where the company's factory is located.

The park is comprised of two areas: a free area consisting of a shop, café and restaurant, and a paid area with various exhibits and a miniature six-car steam train called the Shiroi Koibito Railway. There is also a soccer field that serves as the practice ground for Consadole Sapporo, the local J-League soccer team.

The park is open year-round. Visitors have the option of touring the Tudor house free of charge where they can enjoy the display of classical toys from the Meiji, Taisho, and Showa periods, and the rose garden. Located on the first floor of the Tudor house is the Shop Piccadilly, which sells all of Ishiya's confectionaries. Also on the first floor is the Candy Labo offering unique candy designs that can only be found at the Shiroi Koibito Park. Visitors are permitted to watch the candy artisans at work, crafting these beautiful, edible pieces of art. On the second floor of the Tudor house, you will find the Gramophone Gallery displaying various gramophones from days gone by as well as related materials. Please note that there is a fee to tour the Gramophone Gallery.

The Sapporo Mechanical Clock Tower located outside in the courtyard features a troupe of dancing mechanical dolls that perform in The Chocolate Carnival at the top of each hour. Stop off at the nearby Soft Ice Cream House, pick up some Shiroi Koibito ice cream, and settle in to watch the clock tower spectacle.

From there, visit Entrepot Hall, where you will find the Aurora Fountain on the second floor. The fountain dates back to 1870 and was produced by England's famous Royal Doulton Company. In the same building, you will also find an elaborate display of chocolate cups. Chocolate was a popular drink among the aristocrats up until the 18th century and this particular collection exhibits some of the most prized cups for serving chocolate.

Finally, stop off at the Chocolate Factory, which houses a viewing gallery on the third floor, enabling visitors to observe how the Shiroi Koibito cookies are made from start to finish. Located on the fourth floor of the Chocolate Factory is the Chocolate Lounge, decorated with antique furniture from England. Here, surrounded by opulence, patrons can enjoy chocolate drinks and Shiroi Koibito parfaits. Also on the 4th floor, children and adults can gain firsthand experience in the art of cookie making at the Cookiecraft Studio. For a fee of ¥1,080, amateur confectioners can try their hand at creating their own cookies. The entire experience takes 80 minutes and there is a limit of one cookie per person.

A visit to the park is an excellent opportunity to learn more about Hokkaido's famous omiyage (souvenir) and to sample Ishiya's other confectionaries.

Location(s):	Miyanosawa 2-jo 2-chome, Nishi-ku, Sapporo-shi, Hokkaido
Web Page:	http://www.shiroikoibitopark.jp/english/

Sapporo-shi (札幌市)：Sapporo City

Yuki Matsuri: Snow Festival

Every year approximately two million people brave the snow and frigid temperatures of Sapporo to enjoy one of the most popular snow festivals in Japan known as the Sapporo Yuki Matsuri (the Sapporo Snow Festival).

The festival, which takes place over the course of seven days in early February, began in 1950 when a group of high school students constructed a few snow sculptures in Odori Park. Since then, it has developed into a large, commercialized event featuring spectacular snow and ice sculptures, some measuring more than 82 feet wide and 49 feet high (27m x 15m) and spread out across three sites: Odori, Susukino, and Tsu Dome.

The main site is Odori where, along with the large scale sculptures, there are more than 100 smaller creations on display. There are also several concerts and events that take place here, many of which utilize the sculptures as their stage and background.

The Susukino site is located in what is known as Sapporo's largest entertainment district. Here you will find approximately one hundred ice sculptures. The site is only one subway stop south of Odori Park and easily accessible.

The family-oriented Tsu Dome site is less centrally located and features three types of snow slides, snow rafting, and more snow sculptures. Inside the dome, there are numerous food stands and a performance stage.

The subject of the sculptures varies and often features an event, famous building or person from the previous year. Visitors can also enjoy a bird's eye view of Odori Park from the observation deck of the Sapporo TV Tower. Access to the observation deck costs ¥700.

Odori Park is accessible via the Odori Subway Station, using the Tozai Line, the Nanboku Line or the Toho Line.

Often, tourists plan their travel to Japan during the spring to glimpse a view of the country's famous blooming cherry trees or during the fall when the Japanese maple leaves change color. The Snow Festival is just one of many reasons to visit Japan and Sapporo during the winter months.

Location(s):   Odori Park

                      Main Street in Susukino

                      Community Dome Tsudome

Web Page: http://www.snowfes.com/english/

Shiretoko Peninsula (知床半島)

Shiretoko Goko (知床五湖) and Oshinkoshin Falls (オシンコシンの滝)

Shiretoko Goko or the Shiretoko Five Lakes are hidden in the native forests of the Shiretoko Peninsula situated in the northeastern corner of Hokkaido. Formed by the eruption of nearby Mount Io, the lakes are part of the Shiretoko National Park. The area is renowned for its beautiful views of Shiretoko's unspoiled wilderness.

There is a 2,600 foot (800 m) long, elevated wooden boardwalk from the parking lot to the first lake, which allows visitors to enjoy views of the lake, the Sea of Okhotsk, and the surrounding mountains without damaging the fragile ecosystem. The boardwalk is free to use, wheelchair accessible, and open for the entire season (late April to late November). Aside from the elevated boardwalk, there are 1.85 miles (2.6 km) of regular nature trails that lead around the picturesque five lakes and take approximately 90 minutes to traverse.

Bears are very common in the area and are most active between May and July. For safety reasons, visitors are obliged to join a guided tour, which costs ¥5,000. The guided tour lasts 2-3 hours and guests are required to watch a short video, which provides the essentials of what to do in the event of a bear encounter.

Not far from Shiretoko Goko you will find the Oshinkoshin Falls. Designated as one of Japan's best 100 waterfalls, its name originated from the Ainu language meaning the beautifully forked waterfalls.

A staircase enables visitors to get closer to the rushing waters. There is an observatory at the top of the waterfalls, from which you can glimpse views of the Sea of Okhotsk and the Shiretoko mountain range. Parking is free at the site and public toilets and a souvenir shop are available.

The Oshinkoshin Falls are easily accessible by the Shari bus from the Shiretoko-shari bus terminal, next to Hotel Grantia Shiretoko-Shari Ekimae. However, due to the low frequency of buses, driving would be advisable.

If you happen to be visiting the Shiretoko Peninsula, why not travel to the Oshinkoshin Falls and see why it was selected as one of the eight beautiful sites of Shiretoko?

Location(s):   Shari-gun, Shari-cho, Hokkaido

Web Page: http://www.visitshiretoko.com/en/sightseeing
.html

Yoichi-cho (余市町)： Town of Yoichi

<u>Nikka Whisky Distillery (ニッカウヰスキー株式会社)</u>

Yoichi-cho is a small coastal town located 30 miles (50 km) west of Sapporo with a particularly nice beach that is popular with surfers. It is a well-liked tourist destination for the Japanese between July and August when the temperatures in the areas south of Hokkaido become almost unbearable. Aside from its beach and cooler temperatures, another attraction has contributed to a steady influx of visitors to this sleepy town: the Nikka Whisky Distillery, which was featured on the NHK drama Massan.

Massan was a Japanese morning TV drama that premiered on September 29, 2014. It was based on the lives of Masataka Taketsuru and his wife, Jessie Roberta "Rita" Cowan and their attempts to begin the Nikka Whisky Distillery in 1934.

Today Nikka Whisky is one of Japan's top whisky makers and Masataka Taketsuru is known as the father of Japanese whisky. Taketsuru studied whisky making techniques for several years in Scotland before bringing the trade to Japan. He was instrumental in establishing the country's first whisky distillery, the Yamazaki Distillery near Kyoto, before he set out on his own.

Nikka whiskies have been recognized among the world's best single malt whiskies and have won numerous awards. In 2010, Yamazaki Whisky was awarded the title of Supreme Champion Spirit at the 15th International Spirits Challenge 2010 while Suntory Liquors (originally known as Kotobukiya), the producer of the whisky, was named Distiller of the Year. Both achievements were firsts for any Japanese company.

Nikka Whisky was originally called Dai Nippon Kaju (Great Japanese Juice Company) as it started out producing apple juice, apple brandy, and other apple-based products from Yoichi's famed apples. The name was later changed to Nikka Whisky in 1952 to reflect its new (and originally intended) focus on making whisky. The first bottles of Nikka Whisky went on sale in 1940.

Today, there are two distilleries in Japan including the Yoichi Distillery in Hokkaido and the Miyagikyo Distillery in Aoba-ku, Sendai in Miyagi Prefecture. The company also owns the Ben Nevis Distillery (acquired in 1989) in Scotland. Since 2001 Nikka Whisky has been owned by Asahi Breweries.

The original distillery in Yoichi is still fully functional, although parts of it have been converted into a working museum. The museum focuses on the history of the company and the life of its founder. In the museum you will find a tasting room that offers samples of select Nikka whiskies.

Other buildings on the grounds house hundreds of barrels in which whisky rests and ages. There is also a restaurant and a souvenir shop where you can purchase various whiskies and apple brandy produced there.

Whether you are a fan of the NHK drama or you simply appreciate the quality of Japanese whisky, touring the original distillery is a must.

The distillery is located just west of Yoichi Station on the JR Hakodate Line. Alternatively, you can take the local trains from Otaru or Sapporo to Yoichi Station.

Location(s):   7-6 Kurokawa-cho, Yoichi-machi, Yoichi-gun,
                 Hokkaido

Web Page: http://www.nikka.com/eng/distilleries/yoichi/i
                 ndex.html

Points of Interest: Hokkaido Region

Akan Kokuritsu Koen: Akan National Park

Shikisai no Oka: Hills of Seasonal Colors

Shiretoko Goko

Shiretoko Goko

Oshinkoshin Falls

Sapporo TV Tower

Sapporo Yuki Matsuri :Sapporo Snow Festival

Tohoku Region

Introduction to Tohoku (東北地方)

The Tohoku region, sometimes referred to as the Ou region, comprises the northeastern portion of the island of Honshu. The region consists of six prefectures: Akita, Aomori, Fukushima, Iwate, Miyagi, and Yamagata.

It is a large, mountainous, and sparsely populated area originally inhabited by the aboriginal people known as Ezo or Emishi. Not until the Kamakura period (1192-1333) did it come under the control of the central government.

Tohoku remains remote and economically underdeveloped, known primarily as an agricultural region renowned for its rice crop, with the region producing 20 percent of the national yield.

On March 11, 2011, a catastrophic 9.0-magnitude earthquake and tsunami inflicted massive damage along the east coast of this region, killing 20,000 people. It was considered the costliest natural disaster ever that, along with the radioactive fallout from the Fukushima Daiichi Nuclear Plant, left 500,000 people homeless.

Today, most areas of Tohoku are considered safe and have begun welcoming tourists to explore its many castles and samurai residences and to sample their kyodo ryori (regional cuisine).

Tohoku kyodo ryori (regional cuisine) features: ichigo-ni (a clear soup with sea urchin and abalone associated with Aomori), jappa jiru (a fish gut and vegetable soup associated with Aomori and Akita), senbei jiru (a soy based soup with baked rice crackers and vegetables), wanko soba (soba noodles served in small bowls which are refilled repeatedly and associated with Iwate), morioka reimen (a variation of the North Korean cold noodle soup), harako meshi (rice cooked in a salmon and soy stock and topped with ikura/ salmon roe), kiritanpo (pounded rice wrapped around a skewer and grilled), and gyutan (beef tongue typically grilled but can also be served sashimi style).

Additionally, since the cherry trees blossom a few weeks later in Tohoku than they do in Tokyo and Kyoto, the region serves as a good backup plan for cherry blossom viewing.

Unfortunately, there are no major airports in Tohoku and most travelers arrive via Tokyo. The Sendai and Akita airports do receive some international flights, but mostly to/from China and South Korea.

The Tohoku Shinkansen is a good alternative connecting Tokyo, Sendai, Morioka, and Aomori. The journey from Tokyo to Sendai is an hour and 40 minutes.

Web Page: http://en.tohokukanko.jp/ (Tohoku Tourism
                             Promotion Organization)

Akita Prefecture (秋田県)

Akita-shi (秋田市)： Akita City

Akarenga-kan Museum (秋田市立赤れんが郷土館)： Red Brick Museum

Japan is a country filled with wonderful and unique museums. One worth visiting when in Akita is the Akarenga-kan Museum, which hosts various art exhibitions in addition to exhibiting a number of crafts and historical materials.

What makes this museum unique is that it was once the opulent headquarters of Akita Bank. The building was constructed in 1912 by local architect Naoaki Yamaguchi and served as a functioning bank until 1969. In 1981, on the 100th anniversary of Akita Bank, the building was donated to Akita City, which renovated it and reopened it as a museum in 1985.

The building's exterior is in the Renaissance style and the interior, with its colored tiles, white marble staircases, and plaster ceilings and archways is in the Baroque style. The huge metal bank vault doors still remain and viewing the building details is just as entertaining as seeing the artwork!

There are specific rooms dedicated to the works of Katsuhira Tokushi and Sekiya Shiro.

Katsuhira Tokushi (1907-1971) was a distinguished wood block artist who worked in bold colors depicting scenes of local Akita life and customs. Katsuhira's studio is also recreated at the museum, displaying his original tools.

Sekiya Shiro (1907-1994) was a metalwork artist who specialized in a fusion technique called hagiawase. The second floor of the building is dedicated to the artist's masterpieces and a selection of his tools are on display in the Sekiya Shiro Memorial Room.

If you would like to learn more about life in Akita, are interested in architecture, or are simply devoted to appreciating the work of artists from Japan, visiting the Akarenga-kan Museum will satisfy all of these interests. The museum is open from 9:30 AM to 4:30 PM and admission is ¥200, which makes visiting all the more enticing.

Location(s):   3-3-21 Omachi, Akita-shi, Akita

Web Page: http://www.city.akita.akita.jp/city/ed/ak/

Kakunodate-machi (角館): Town of Kakunodate

Kakunodate was a small town located in the Senboku District of Akita Prefecture in Japan. Although it was merged with the town of Tazawako and Nishiki to create the city of Senboku in 2005, the area has been remarkably unchanged since its founding in 1620.

The town originated as a castle town with two distinct areas, the samurai district and the merchant district. Although Kakunodate Castle no longer exists, the city still has some of the best examples of samurai architecture in Japan. The samurai houses are located along Bukeyashiki Street (Samurai House Street) and some are open to the public for viewing, including the Aoyagi House, the Ishiguro House, the Odano House, the Kawarada House, the Iwahashi House, and the Matsumoto House. These houses are free to tour with the exception of the Aoyagi House and the Ishiguro House, which charge a nominal entrance fee. Touring these homes is interesting as it gives the visitor a fascinating insight into the life of the samurai.

Kakunodate is also famous for the hundreds of weeping shidarezakura (cherry trees) that attract significant crowds to the city around late April and early May. These trees were imported from Kyoto and as a result the town was sometimes referred to as the little Kyoto of Tohoku.

The town plays host to several festivals as well. In February, there is the Kamifuusen Age (the Paper Balloon Festival). Dating back more than a century, the festival features large decorated paper balloons that are lit and allowed to float off into the evening sky. Also in February, the Fire and Snow Festival takes place during the course of two days. It is a type of purification ritual where people twirl flaming pieces of straw on a string above their heads.

If you yearn for a glimpse of feudal Japan, do make an effort to visit Kakunodate. It is relatively easy to reach using the Akita Shinkansen Komachi from Tokyo. The journey takes roughly four hours but please note that seats on the Komachi trains are all reserved and must be booked in advance.

Web Page: http://www.city.semboku.akita.jp/en/sightseeing/spot/07.html

Yokote-shi (横手市)： Yokote City

Yokote Kamakura Matsuri (横手かまくら祭り)：Yokote Igloo Festival

Each year on February 15th and 16th, the Doro Koen Park located in front of the City Hall in Yokote City plays host to a 400-year-old festival that is really worth seeing. Known as the Yokote Kamakura Festival, the event features countless snow houses called kamakura, a room made by carving out a mound of snow.

Although the park is the primary location for the festival, a fantastic world also emerges each evening extending east of Yokote Station down to Yokote Castle. There are kamakura built beside houses throughout the neighborhood and hundreds of small kamakura, the size of lanterns, can be seen along the Yokote River. Within the larger kamakura there is a snow altar dedicated to the water deity to whom people pray for ample water. There is a charcoal grill on which rice cakes are grilled and the grill also provides warmth. Children invite visitors into their kamakura and offer them warm rice cakes and warm amazake (sweet rice wine) in return for an offering to the deity.

Yokote Castle, which is normally closed to visitors from December through March, is opened during the festival from 10:00 AM to 9:00 PM, giving visitors an opportunity to view the city below from its observation deck.

As with any festival in Japan, there are food stalls set up throughout, offering all kinds of local festival delicacies.

If you do not get an opportunity to see the snow houses during the festival, the Kamakurakan Hall displays a few kamakura year-round in a -10°C (12°F) room. If you are fortunate enough to visit Akita during the Yokote Kamakura Matsuri, take advantage of the children's hospitality in the kamakura and enjoy the breathtaking nighttime views of Yokote City illuminated with hundreds of lights radiating from the snow houses.

To reach Yokote City, take the Akita Shinkansen from Tokyo to Omagari Station (3.5 hours). From there, local trains run hourly to Yokote Station and the journey is 20 minutes to your final destination.

Location(s):   269 Maego Aza, Shimosanmaibashi, Yokote-
                      shi (Yokote City Hall)

Web Page: http://www.city.yokote.lg.jp/

Aomori Prefecture (青森県)

Aomori-shi (青森市)： Aomori City

Nebuta Matsuri (ねぶた祭) (Festival)

The Aomori Nebuta Matsuri is counted among the three largest festivals in the Tohoku region and it was designated as an Important Intangible Folk Cultural Property in 1980. Nebuta refers to the colorful floats shaped in the forms of famous historical and mythological Japanese characters.

The festival takes place annually from August 2-7. Local residents devote an entire year to constructing the floats, which typically measure 15 to 30 feet (4.5 m-9 m) tall and are made of fragile washi paper placed over a wire and bamboo frame. Hundreds of light bulbs are placed throughout the floats enhancing the stunning colors of the nebuta at night.

There are three types of nebuta floats: the children's nebuta, the local organization's nebuta, which are smaller in size, and the regional nebuta, which are immense. The smaller nebuta, often pulled by children, are paraded throughout the city during the first two days of the festival, August 2-3. The larger nebuta require excessive strength to move and therefore are only displayed from August 4 to 7. The floats are carried through the city on a designated route after nightfall from August 2 to 6 and only during the daytime on August 7. A fireworks show is held on the evening of the final day as the top three floats are transported to ships in Aomori Harbor to cruise along the bay.

Festival participants dressed in traditional haneto outfits dance around the hand-pulled floats to music provided by taiko drummers and other musicians. Onlookers are encouraged to participate, provided that they wear the haneto. Costumes are sold in supermarkets and department stores all across the prefecture and a full set (excluding the flower hat) can be purchased for around ¥10,000. Costumes can also be rented at places along the processional route for ¥4,000.

The festival draws an estimated 3 million people annually from all walks of life. If you have an opportunity to visit Aomori in August, be sure to take advantage of this awe-inspiring spectacle.

Web Page: http://www.atca.info/atca_language/culture_e n.html

Aomori-shi (青森市): Aomori City

Sannai Maruyama Ruins (三内丸山遺跡)

Many tourists who travel to Japan are in love with the country's rich history and they often visit the countless castles and historic sites associated with Japan's feudal period. But did you ever stop to consider what Japan was like 5,000 years ago, during what is known as the Jomon period? Fortunately, now you can get a glimpse of what life was like during that period when you visit Aomori City, the capital of Aomori Prefecture. I am referring to the Sannai Maruyama Ruins, a vast archeological site spanning 350,000 square meters (86.5 acres).

The site was discovered in 1992 when Aomori Prefecture was surveying the land for a planned baseball stadium. There were earlier excavations led by teams from Keio University and the Board of Education of Aomori City, which began in 1953 and continued through 1967. There were additional excavations conducted by the Board of Education and Aomori City in the southern part of the site in 1976 and 1987. It wasn't until 1992 that a major breakthrough was made.

It was determined that the site was initially inhabited by a group of hunter-gatherers who utilized the land as a seasonal camp. Between 3900 BC and 2900 BC the site became a settled village. To date, the excavations have unearthed 500 residences, 30 buildings with post holes and 60 graves. In 2000, the Sannai Maruyama Ruins were registered as a National Special Historic Site.

One of Sannai Maruyama's most famous structures is a large, pillared building built around 2600 BC. This structure consisted of six large pillars that are believed to have held up platforms.

Each one of these pillars measured around one meter (39 in) in diameter and they were placed exactly 4.2 m (14 ft) apart. Due to its large size, it is believed that this structure functioned as a monument or watchtower. Remains of other six-pillared buildings from different time periods have also been found throughout the site.

In the exhibition room, you will find displays of various flat clay figures, earthenware, personal ornaments and small knitted baskets called Jomon Pochette. There are dioramas which recreate life during that period along with commentary from digital photo frames and videos.

If you are so inclined, try your hand at one of the interactive workshops offered. You have the option of making items such as Jomon Pochettes and amber pendants utilizing the techniques employed by the Jomon people. The experience will be both educational and entertaining.

Sannai Maruyama is located about 3 hours from Tokyo Station via the JR Tohoku Shinkansen Line. The attraction will enable you to have a broader understanding of Japan's overall history and is a worthwhile stopover during your visit to Aomori City.

Location(s):   305, Aza Maruyama, Oaza Sannai, Aomori-shi, Aomori

Web Page: http://sannaimaruyama.pref.aomori.jp/english /index.html

Fukushima Prefecture (福島県)

Higashiyama Hot Spring Town (東山温泉)

Located just east of downtown Aizu Wakamatsu in Fukushima is the small hot spring town of Higashiyama. The area is well known for its beautiful scenery year-round and over the years many famous artists have stayed there. Inspired by the beauty surrounding them, they donated numerous paintings, poems, and other works of art to the ryokans (traditional Japanese inns) where they stayed.

In fact, Higashiyama has twenty-eight different hotels to satisfy every taste and budget. Whether you want a modern hotel or a traditional ryokan, you will find them here. If you do not want to stay in town, you can visit the hot springs on a day trip. Many of the hotels and ryokans allow visitors to use their facilities during the day at a set time period for a small fee.

If you simply want to wander around town and enjoy the scenery, you will be rewarded by the beautiful pink cherry blossoms in the spring and the fiery reds, oranges and yellows of the turning leaves in the fall. Further up the valley is the Higashiyama Dam. The area around the dam is a popular spot for relaxation and picnics.

From August 13 to 18, the town hosts a bon dance festival. During the festival, a large yagura (bandstand tower) is constructed in the center of town and hundreds of chochin (lanterns) illuminate the streets. Ladies wearing their yukatas (cotton summer kimonos) and men in traditional dress dance around the yagura until late at night. The high energy atmosphere attracts both tourists and locals alike.

Whether you want to relax in the town's hot springs, marvel at the beauty of the cherry blossoms, enjoy the changing leaves of autumn, or soak up the high energy atmosphere of the bon dance festival, Higashiyama is the place to be.

The town is accessible during the morning and late afternoon hours by the Aizu Loop bus. The journey takes 35 minutes from Aizu Wakamatsu Station. However, between the hours of 10:00 AM and 1:00 PM the bus only runs as far as Aizu Bukeyashiki. Higashiyama is only a 10 to 15-minute journey on foot from that point.

Location(s):   Ekimae-cho, Aizuwakamatsu, Fukushima

             (Aizu Wakamatsu Station)

Web Page: http://aizu-higashiyama.com/

Iwaki-shi (いわき市)： Iwaki City

Fukushima Aquamarine (ふくしま海洋科学館)

If you are interested in marine life, there is an attraction located in Iwaki City that you should not miss while visiting Fukushima Prefecture. Officially called the Marine Science Museum, the facility opened in July of 2000. The museum's nickname, Fukushima Aquamarine, was selected in 1998 from a total of 4,722 entries.

The highlight of the museum is the main tank, which holds 540,000 gallons (2,044,122 L) of water. There is a unique triangular walkway that gives visitors the sensation of actually being in the tank, surrounded by the water and the creatures swimming in it.

On the first floor, visitors will be provided with a look at the evolution of life in the seas. It contains living fossils such as the Nautilus, the White Sturgeon, the Giant Salamander, and the Spotted Ratfish. The main tank can be found on the second floor while the third floor is dedicated to the marine mammals and sea birds from the Northern Pacific. There is a botanical garden on the fourth floor that showcases plant life in Fukushima and from where visitors can glimpse the top of the main tank.

During the earthquake and ensuing tsunami of 2011, power was cut off to the aquarium and a majority of the fish perished. Some of the marine mammals and sea birds were transferred to Kamogawa Sea World located 62 miles south of the aquarium as well as Ueno Zoo in Tokyo, Tokyo Sea Life Park, Mito Sea Paradise, and New Enoshima Aquarium. The main building sustained only minor damage but the outside pools were washed away. Fortunately, restoration work began soon after and the aquarium re-opened to the public on July 15, 2011.

If you are hungry, the Oishii Aquarium Aqua Cross restaurant on the premises serves seafood. There are also three gift shops where you can select a memento from your visit or an omiyage (souvenir) to bring home to your family and friends.

A trip to the aquarium is an experience the entire family can enjoy. From Yumoto Station, take the bus bound for Onahama. The aquarium is 15-20 minutes on foot from the Onahama stop.

Location(s):   Onahama Pier 2, 50, Tatsumi-cho, Onahama, Iwaki

Web Page: http://www.marine.fks.ed.jp/index.htm

Ouchijuku (大内宿)

Nestled in the mountains of southwestern Fukushima Prefecture is the small, isolated thatch-roofed village of Ouchijuku. The village was a former post town along the Aizu-Nishi Kaido trade route during the Edo period. Travelers at the time were restricted to journeying on foot, prompting post towns to develop along various routes. They provided food and accommodations to the weary voyagers.

Today, Ouchijuku has been restored to look as it did in the Edo period. Its telephone and electric wires have been buried out of sight so as not to disrupt the period look. The unpaved main street is lined with thatched-roofed buildings that house a variety of shops, restaurants, and minshuku (small traditional Japanese inns). Restaurants serve up soba (buckwheat) noodles and locally caught iwana (char fish) roasted on sticks to the 1.2 million visitors who travel to this village each year.

The former Honjin, the inn reserved for high ranked government officials, is also located along the main street and open to the public as a museum. Inside, visitors can see the elegant interior of a traditional house from the Edo period as well as a collection of dishes, clothing, and other artifacts.

At the end of the main street, you will find a temple at the end of a steep set of stairs, which offers magnificent views of the street and the thatched-roofed houses below. Within a five-minute walk from the main street is a shrine with a unique purification fountain worth visiting.

Tourists often make a day trip to the village while they are visiting some of the esteemed Aizu onsens (hot springs) nearby. The village is served by Yunokami Onsen Station on the Aizu

Line. Yunokami Onsen Station is the only railway station in Japan with a thatched-roof.

If you are not planning on staying at one of the onsens overnight, you can combine a trip to Ouchijuku with a visit to the castle town of Aizuwakamatsu (会津若松市), located just one hour away from Ouchijuku. The town has a long samurai tradition that it proudly displays for visitors and what better way to observe that tradition than to visit Aizuwakamatsu Castle also known as Tsuruga Castle. The castle is a concrete replica of the original constructed by Ashina Naomori in 1384. It was the military and administrative center of the Aizu region until 1868.

During the Battle of Aizu in 1868, the newly-formed Imperial Army laid siege to the castle causing significant damage to the castle walls with artillery fire. Deemed structurally unstable, the castle was demolished by the new government in 1874. The tenshu, the largest tower of the castle, was reconstructed in 1965 in concrete and currently houses a museum and an observation gallery on top with panoramic views of the city.

A journey to Ouchijuku is a step back in time and a wonderful way to observe what life may have been like for travelers during the Edo period. To reach Ouchijuku, take the Aizu Railway Aizu Line from Tokyo Station and exit at Yunokami Onsen Station. From there, your destination is just ten minutes away.

Location(s):   Shimogo-machi, Minami-Aizu-gun, Fukushima

Web Page: http://www.jnto.go.jp/eng/location/spot/histt own/ouchi-juku.html

Iwate Prefecture (岩手県)

Hiraizumi-cho (平泉町): Town of Hiraizumi

Takkoku no Iwaya (達谷窟毘沙門堂)

Located in the southwestern part of Iwate Prefecture, Hiraizumi-cho once thrived as the second largest city after Heian-kyo (Kyoto). Today, Hiraizumi-cho is a popular destination for visitors who come to see one of the more unusual temples in Japan.

Constructed partially into the rock face of a cliff, Takkoku no Iwaya was founded during the 9th century by General Sakanoue no Tamuramaro. The temple's founding was in commemoration of the general's victory over a local warlord during his bid to expand into the northeastern territory. According to legend, the warlord, Akuro, was hiding out in this cave when he was defeated by Tamuramaro; hence, this location was chosen for the temple site. Fittingly, the temple is dedicated to Bishamon, the god of war.

Bishamon Hall is built below an overhanging cliff and has been rebuilt several times following destructive fires. It was built in the style of Kyoto's Kiyomizudera and there used to be 108 statues of Bishamon enshrined within its walls. The current hall is the reconstructed version completed in 1961. There was also a Ganmen Daibutsu (giant carving of Buddha) on the side of the cave. Unfortunately, an earthquake in 1896 destroyed the body and today only the head remains intact.

Although Bishamon Hall is the main attraction of Takkoku no Iwaya, there are other halls worth exploring such as Benten Hall, Fudo Hall, and Kondo (Golden Hall). There is a pond surrounding Benten Hall called Gama no Ike (Toad Pond).

Touring Takkoku no Iwaya takes approximately 30 minutes; therefore, it may be a good idea to combine this trip with tours of Hiraizumi-cho's other famous temples, Chusonji and Motsuji. Takkoku no Iwaya is open to the public between 8:00 AM and 5:00 PM (April 1 – November 23) and from 8:00 AM to 4:30 PM (November 24 – March 31). There is a nominal admission fee of ¥300.

Access is relatively easy via local bus from JR Hiraizumi Station. The journey will take you approximately ten minutes.

Location(s):   16 Hiraizumi Kitazawa, Nishiiwai-gun, Hiraizumi-cho

Web Page: http://hiraizumi.or.jp/en/index.html

Kitakami-shi (北上市): Kitakami City

Tensochi Park

With over 10,000 cherry trees planted alongside the Kitakami River in Tenshochi Park, Kitakami City is one of Tohoku's best three cherry blossom viewing spots.

The trees are in bloom for only 1-2 weeks during late April, but visitors flock to the area in droves to stroll under the canopy of white blossoms that cover the 1.25-mile (2 km) path that runs through the park. Additionally, there are sightseeing boats that depart from the rest house located at the south end of the park allowing visitors to view the cherry blossoms from the river. The boat ride lasts approximately 20 minutes and costs ¥1,000.

The park hosts the Kitakami Tenshochi Sakura Festival from mid-April to early May. The path and the park are illuminated in the evenings between 6:00 PM and 9:00 PM enabling festivalgoers to view the blossoms in the evening. In addition to the beautiful cherry blossoms, there are scheduled performances and numerous food vendors to enhance the festival experience.

Next to the park, you will find Michinoku Folklore Village, comprised of thirty preserved farmhouses and other structures from different historical periods. A majority of the buildings are open to the public and display various household items and tools that give visitors a perspective into what traditional life was like in Tohoku. Located near the village's entrance gate, the Kitakami City Museum displays an assortment of cultural and historical artifacts, as well as various examples of Buddhist art. Entry to the museum is included in the admission fee to the village.

It is not necessary to plan your visit to Tensochi Park during the festival since there are many things to do and see throughout the year.

Kitakami City is accessible via the Tohoku Shinkansen from Tokyo, exit Kitakami Station. The one-way journey takes approximately three hours and is covered by the Japan Rail Pass. From the station, the park is approximately 20 minutes on foot.

Location(s):   Tachibana, Kitakami, Iwate

Web Page: http://www.city.kitakami.iwate.jp.e.ny.hp.tran
                 ser.com/

Tono-shi (遠野市): Tono City (The Legend of the Kappa)

Located just under four hours from Tokyo Station via the JR Tohoku Shinkansen Line is the city of Tono. Known as The City of Folklore, Tono was made famous through a collection of folktales known as Tono Monogatari, penned by Kunio Yanagita in 1910.

There are a number of sightseeing spots worth visiting in Tono including the beautiful Fukusenji Temple and Tono Furusato Village, where several L-shaped houses, known as magariya, from the 18th and 19th centuries have been preserved. But the place that draws most visitors is known as Kappabuchi, a pool where mythical creatures called Kappa are said to reside. While the Kappa are found throughout Japan, Tono is widely considered their hometown.

The Kappa are believed to be creatures who reside in rivers, lakes, ponds, and other watery realms. It is said that they were created as warnings to keep children from drowning. They are often portrayed with the body of a tortoise, an ape-like head, scaly limbs, webbed feet and hands, and about the size of a 6-10-year-old child. They are said to attack horses, cattle, and humans, dragging them into the water and draining their life force. The defining characteristic of the Kappa is the hollow cavity atop their heads. This saucer-like depression holds a strength-giving fluid. It is advised that if you chance upon a quarrelsome Kappa, remember to bow deeply. If the courteous Kappa bows in return, it will spill its strength-giving water, rendering it feeble and forcing it to return to its watery kingdom.

Throughout the town, you will see statues of Kappa including the one in front of Tono Station and another in the pond at the square near the railway station. Tono's mascots are a modern mangaesque Kappa named Karin, a green male, and his wife, Kururin, who is pink.

In early February, the town holds the Tono Folktales Festival, during which time local storytellers recite tales from the Tono Monogatari, pretty much in the same manner these folk legends were passed down from generation to generation. In August, the Tono Tanabata Festival is held featuring a parade of dancers and in mid-September, there is the Tono Festival, which includes a parade and Yabusame Archers (archers on horseback).

The town is also famous for Genghis Khan, a spicy grilled lamb dish and hittsumi (wheat dumplings). The Miyamori section of town is known for its wasabi production and there is a local brewery that manufactures a wasabi beer.

If you are curious about these mythical creatures and want to familiarize yourself with the famous folktales, a visit to Tono City is highly recommended. While there, be sure to sample some of the delicious dishes that are characteristic to the area and cap off the day with a nice cold glass of wasabi beer. When you return home, perhaps you can recite some of the tales from the Tono Monogatari to your family and friends.

Web Page: http://www.tonojikan.jp/Several_languages/en glish/english.html

Miyagi Prefecture (宮城県)

Naruko-cho (鳴子町) : Town of Naruko

Naruko Gorge ((鳴子峡)

Japan is a beautiful country to visit all year-round, but particularly striking during spring when the cherry blossoms are in full bloom and autumn when the momiji (Japanese maple) leaves change color. There are countless settings throughout the country to see these breathtaking events, but one place that is very special during autumn is the Naruko Gorge in Tohoku. Located just 43 miles from Sendai, the capital of Miyagi Prefecture, the gorge transforms into one of the region's most popular spots for observing the brilliant autumn colors from late October to early November.

The best spot for viewing the fiery colors is an area that stretches approximately one and a quarter mile (2 km) east-west near the Naruko-kyo Rest House. There is an observation deck located next to the rest house from where you can see the Ofukazawa Bridge, the most photographed location in the area. The more adventurous can elect to follow the Ofukazawa Walking Trail starting from the bridge and ending at the rest house. The path will take you through the forested side of the valley and will require approximately 45 minutes to traverse.

The town of Naruko is also known for its kokeshi dolls. Located at the eastern end of the gorge, you will find the Japan Kokeshi Museum, exhibiting numerous dolls from the various prefectures in the Tohoku Region. For a small fee, visitors can try their hand at painting their own kokeshi doll, which makes a nice souvenir to bring home from your visit to Naruko.

56

After your tour, you may consider soaking in one of the many affordable and high quality onsens (hot springs) that dot the area. Most are open to the public until 10:00 PM.

You can easily access Naruko Gorge from Tokyo via the Tohoku Shinkansen, exiting at Furukawa Station and changing to a local train on the JR Rikuu-to Line to Naruko Onsen.

Location(s):   Narukonsen Shitomae, Osaki, Miyagi

Web Page: http://en.naruko.gr.jp/

Sendai-shi (仙台市): Sendai City

Sendai is the capital city of Miyagi Prefecture and the largest city in the Tohoku Region. The city is best known for the Sendai Tanabata Festival, the largest Tanabata festival in Japan, and the Pageant of Starlight which takes place in the winter where the trees are decorated with thousands of lights.

The Tanabata Festival celebrates the meeting of the deities Orihime and Hikoboshi (represented by the stars Vega and Altair) who, according to legend, are allowed to meet only once a year on the seventh day of the seventh lunar month. The festival attracts more than two million visitors each year and is relatively quiet compared to other traditional Japanese festivals because its main attractions are intricate Tanabata decorations.

By contrast, the Pageant of Starlight (http://www.sendaihikape.jp/), which takes place during the entire month of December, finds the Zelkova trees that line Jozenji-dori (a ten-minute walk from Sendai Station) and Aoba-dori illuminated with about 600,000 brilliant lights creating a tunnel of illumination. The event, which began in 1986, draws millions of visitors to Sendai.

Sendai is also home to various historical sites related to the Date family. The Date clan was a Japanese samurai family that took its name from the Date District of Mutsu Province (now Fukushima Prefecture). The Zuihoden is one of these historical sites and houses the tomb of Date Masamune. Many artifacts related to the Date family can also be found there. The Zuihoden is located on a hill called Kyogamine, the traditional resting place for members of the Date family.

You can easily combine a visit to Sendai with a trip to another tourist destination in the Miyagi Prefecture, the town of Matsushima. Located only 30 minutes from Sendai and easily accessible by train, Matsushima's seaside attractions are within walking distance of the train station and pier. The town is famous for its bay, which is dotted with some 260 tiny islands covered with matsu (pine trees). The islands can be viewed up close from various cruise boats.

Matsushima was hit by the 2011 earthquake and tsunami, but escaped major damage thanks to its protected location. Most tourist attractions, shops, and hotels reopened within a few weeks or months of the earthquake.

Whether you are drawn to the Tanabata celebrations or you just want to relax and enjoy the seascape of Matsushima, a visit to Sendai will allow you to experience Tohoku's omotenashi (the spirit of Japanese hospitality) first hand.

Web Page: http://www.sentabi.jp/en/tohoku/matsushima.
             html

Tashirojima (田代島) (Cat Island)

Traditionally, cats have been highly regarded in Japan and they have often been epitomized by the maneki neko. The maneki neko is a good luck talisman in the shape of a cat that is typically found in shops, restaurants, pachinko parlors, and other businesses. The figurine is always depicted with one paw up in the air. It is a common belief that if the left paw is raised, the maneki neko will beckon customers and if the right paw is raised, it will bring good luck and wealth.

Hence, it is quite easy to understand why a large population of cats in any given location can draw a steady stream of tourists throughout the year. One such place is located in Miyagi Prefecture, not far from Ishinomaki City. The tiny island of Tashirojima, known as Cat Island, is a place where the cat population literally outnumbers the human population and dogs are strictly prohibited. The island measures approximately seven miles in circumference and is home to about 100 citizens, most over the age of 70. The island's main industry used to be silkworm farming and the cats were kept to ward off the mice, the natural predators of silkworms. The silkworm industry has since given way to fishing and the island is now famed for its oysters and abalone. However, the cats have remained on the island and their population has increased over the years. There is even a cat shrine near the center of the island where locals pray for prosperity and good fishing.

The island consists of two villages: Odomari and Nitoda. These villages have been designated as Genkai-shuraku/限界集落, meaning that the survival of the villages is threatened with a large majority of the population being over 65 years of age. The cat island campaign was conceived as a way in which to draw people to the island to visit and eventually live there, thus ensuring the survival of the villages.

Tashirojima is also referred to as Manga Island. Shotaro Ishinomori, a Japanese manga artist, known for creating several popular manga series including Kamen Rider, built several manga related buildings on the island in the shape of cats. The buildings comprise a camping resort which is open daily from April through October (with the exception of Tuesdays). Reservations are required and generally must be made at least two weeks in advance.

The island suffered substantial damage during the 2011 earthquake and tsunami. Both villages were flooded and several buildings close to the coast were destroyed. Fortunately, the debris was cleared away within a year and the tourists have returned to the island to photograph, play with, and feed the cats. The cats roam freely mostly around Nitoda on the southeastern part of the island.

There are a small number of minshukus (Japanese style bed and breakfasts) around Nitoda. There are no restaurants on the island and very few shops or public toilets available so plan accordingly. Further, visitors are asked to carry home all the garbage they produce on the island.

So whether you are a cat lover, appreciate the manga created by Shotaro Ishinomori, or you simply want to escape to a place where the pace is more relaxed, a day trip to Cat Island may be the right choice.

Tashirojima can be accessed via the Ajishima Line Ferry which departs from Ishinomaki City. The journey lasts one hour each way and costs around ¥1,200. There are three departures per day and tickets can be purchased on the ship.

Web Page: http://www.miyagi-
             kankou.or.jp/tourist_infomation/en/index.htm

Yamagata Prefecture (山形県)

Obanazawa-shi (尾花沢市): Obanazawa City

Ginzan Onsen (銀山温泉)

One of the many alluring traits of Japan is its abundance of onsens (hot springs). Japan sits on the Ring of Fire and is home to 108 active volcanoes, which makes it a prime location for hot spring water. Here you will find a hot spring to suit just about everyone's taste ranging from the ultra-luxurious spa to the do-it-yourself type where you bring a shovel and dig your own bath. There are many towns scattered throughout Japan that are known for their onsens and draw large numbers of visitors both locally and from abroad.

One such place is Ginzan Onsen (Silver Mountain Hot Spring) nestled in the mountains of Yamagata Prefecture. This picturesque area along the Ginzan River is a part of Obanazawa City, which is known to have an average snowfall of over 6.5 feet (2 m) during any given winter season.

Originally developed around a silver mine, Ginzan Onsen's attraction is its physical beauty. Secluded between the hills, it has a number of quaint bridges spaced every 65 feet (20 m) connecting houses, shops, and ryokans (traditional Japanese inns) on either side of the river. The ryokans are three and four story wooden buildings that evoke nostalgic feelings of a bygone era. There is one exception, however: the Fujiya Ryokan (http://www.fujiya-ginzan.com/english/index.php), a reconstructed 300-year-old inn. Fujiya was rebuilt by the famous architect Kuma Kengo, whose unique modern design incorporates the traditional design elements of the surrounding structures.

The center of Ginzan Onsen is designated as a pedestrian-only zone. It is particularly scenic in the evenings when the various buildings are all lit up and the streets and bridges are illuminated by gas lamps. The scenery is further enhanced during the winter by heavy snow that clings to the rooftops and walkways. This is the area where you can find two public baths and an ashiyu (Japanese foot bath), which you can take advantage of rather inexpensively. Further, many of the inns allow non-staying guests to utilize their baths during the day for a nominal cost.

Behind Ginzan Onsen you will find the Shirogane-koen (park). The park offers many interesting attractions such as the 72-foot (23 m) high Shirogane-no-taki (waterfall). At the base of the waterfall, you will find an entrance to the historic silver mine. Visitors can enter the lit-up tunnel and wander into the mine for 65 feet (21m). There is also a nature trail located 10-15 minutes away from the waterfall where you will find another entrance into the mine. Please note that the nature trail is inaccessible during the winter months.

Visiting a Japanese onsen is an experience like no other and highly recommended to all visitors exploring Japan. Whether you are drawn to the historic silver mine or you want the experience of an overnight stay at a traditional hot spring, Ginzan is the ideal choice. Ginzan Onsen is accessible from Tokyo via the JR Yamagata Shinkansen to Oishida Station. From there it is another 40-minute bus ride to your destination.

Location(s):   Ginzan Shinbata, Obanazawa, Yamagata

Web Page: http://www.ginzanonsen.jp/

Yamagata-shi (山形市): Yamagata City

<u>Yamadera (山寺)</u>

Located in the mountains northeast of Yamagata City is a scenic temple known as Yamadera (Mountain Temple). Founded in 860, the temple grounds extend up a steep mountainside offering spectacular views of the valley below.

At the base of the mountain, there are several temple buildings including Konponchudo Hall, the temple's main hall, as well as dozens of shops and restaurants. The main hall stores various Buddhist statues and a flame that is purported to have been burning since the temple's founding. To reach the upper temple grounds, one must hike up a trail that begins after the Sanmon Gate. The journey takes approximately 30 minutes and there is a small admission fee. The path contains about 1,000 steps and there are stone lanterns and small statues in the surrounding forest along the way.

The upper temple grounds begin past the Niomon Gate where the Kaisando Hall and the Nokyodo Building are situated. Kaisando Hall is dedicated to the temple's founder, Jikaku Daishi, and the Nokyodo Building was used primarily for copying sutra texts. Beyond this point, there are more stairs leading to Godaido Hall which dates back to the 1700s and extends out over the cliff. There is an observation deck that affords the best views of the valley below and makes the climb definitely worthwhile.

The famous poet, Matsuo Basho visited Yamadera in the late 1600s and composed his most enduring haiku there:

"Ah this silence

Sinking into the rocks

Voice of cicada"

There is a statue of Basho and an inscription of his haiku in the lower area of the temple grounds. There is also a museum dedicated to the poet called the Yamadera Basho Memorial Museum, which is a short walk up the hill on the opposite side of the valley.

If you would like to see the sites that inspired poetry, the temple is easily accessible via the JR Senzan Line, exit Yamadera Station. Your destination is approximately five minutes on foot from the station.

Location(s):   4456-1 Yamadera, Yamagata

Web Page: http://www.yamaderakankou.com/

Yamagata-shi (山形市): Yamagata City

Zao Onsen (蔵王温泉)

Situated on the border between Yamagata and Miyagi Prefectures is the Mount Zao volcanic mountain range. On the Yamagata side of the range, you will find the popular hot spring resort village of Zao Onsen. The area is known for having the most sulfuric hot springs in Japan, with a pH value close to 1. In addition to the onsens available at the various hotels and ryokans (traditional Japanese inns) that dot the village, there are three public bathhouses and three open-air hot springs facilities.

One of these open-air baths is Dai Rotenburo, built into the mountain ravine. For a fee of ¥450, visitors can enjoy its soothing waters and the remarkable scenery between 6:00 AM and 7:00 PM. Please note that this onsen is closed from late November to late April.

The village also features several ashiyus (foot baths), where you sit while immersing your feet in the onsen water. The ashiyus are free of charge and attract many who are looking for a spot to simply rest and congregate after exploring the resort area.

People from all over the country and abroad come to Zao Onsen not only for its therapeutic waters but also for the Juhyo (ice monsters). The ice monsters are evergreen conifer trees located at the top of the mountain, which have frozen over. This natural phenomenon takes place during the coldest months, usually from late December to the middle of March. During the peak tourist season (New Year, weekends in January and all of February), the Juhyo are illuminated at night creating a unique scenery.

For skiers and snowboarders, the resort has fifteen different slopes and twelve courses with varying degrees of difficulty from beginners to experts including children and seniors. The slopes are accessible via three ropeways and 35 chair lifts.

The resort is popular year-round. From spring until fall, visitors can take advantage of the countless trekking and sightseeing paths. Mountain guides are available to guide hikers to different vantage points and various areas of interest. The signage is in English, Korean, and Chinese as well as Japanese and makes navigating the resort relatively easy.

Zao Onsen is just 40 minutes by bus from Yamagata train station (approximately 2 ½ hours from Tokyo).

Location(s):   Zao Onsen, Yamagata, Yamagata

Web Page: http://www.zao-spa.or.jp/english/index.html

Mount Zao (蔵王山)

<u>Okama Crater Lake (御釜)</u>

Reaching a height of 6,040 feet (1,900 m), Mount Zao is one of the most prominent mountains in the Tohoku Region. This active volcano features a beautiful crater lake known as Okama Crater Lake.

Okama Crater Lake is considered to be one of the world's most beautiful crater lakes. Situated in the caldera of Mount Zao, it is surrounded by 155 square miles (250 km) of protected landscape which forms the Zao Quasi-National Park. The lake is referred to as Goshiki Numa meaning five-color pond. The highly acidic and mineral-laden lake changes colors in conjunction with prevailing weather conditions. The lake has a 8 hectare (20-acre) surface area and is reported to be 28 meters (90 feet) deep. The colors are best observed during the summer months as the lake tends to freeze during the winter.

A caldera is a cauldron-like volcanic feature that is formed when a magma chamber is emptied. Mount Zao's caldera was created in the 1720s when the volcano erupted. Although currently dormant, Mount Zao is the most active volcano in northern Honshu. However, this does not stop the droves of visitors that visit the area annually.

The Zao Quasi-National Park is a very popular hiking destination split into three areas: North, Middle, and South. The main hiking area, the ski area, and Okama Crater Lake are located in the Middle section. Although the lake is not directly accessible due to the active fumaroles that emit noxious gasses, many visitors do hike to the rim of the crater. There is a designated viewing point that affords ample photo opportunities as well as a ski lift allowing visitors to observe the lake from above.

The lake is accessible via the Yamagata Shinkansen exit at Kaminoyama Onsen Station. From that point there are two buses that operate twice a day and are free of charge! The one-way trip requires approximately one hour.

Location(s):   Inside Zao National Park, Zao-machi, Miyagi

Web Page: http://www.jnto.go.jp/eng/location/spot/nat
                 uscen/okama.html

Points of Interest: Tohoku Region

Downtown Aomori City

Okama Crater Lake

71

Yamadera

Kakunodate

Tashirojima (Cat Island)

Kanto and Chubu Regions

Introduction to Kanto (カントー地方) & Chubu (中部地方)

The Kanto region, which translates as "east of the border", is situated on the island of Honshu. It was the heartland of feudal power during the Kamakura era and the center of modern development during the Edo period.

The region includes the Greater Tokyo Area and encompasses seven prefectures: Gunma, Tochigi, Ibaraki, Saitama, Tokyo, Chiba, and Kanagawa. It is the most densely populated area of the country, home to one third of Japan's population.

The area is subdivided into North and South. The North is comprised of Ibaraki, Tochigi, and Gunma Prefectures, while the South includes Saitama, Chiba, Kanagawa Prefectures, and Tokyo Metropolis. Often, the South is regarded as the Greater Tokyo Area.

Kanto houses not only Japan's seat of government but also the nation's largest group of universities and cultural institutions. Its major cities, Tokyo and Yokohama, form a single industrial complex with a concentration of light and heavy industries along Tokyo Bay. Other prominent cities include Kawasaki, Saitama, and Chiba.

It is said that Kanto sets the pace that the rest of Japan attempts to follow.

The Chubu Region, next door, is comprised of nine prefectures including: Fukui, Ishikawa, Toyama, Shizuoka, Aichi, Gifu, Yamanashi, Nagano, and Niigata.

Known for its beautiful mountains, Mount Fuji and the Japanese

Alps, Chubu is divided into three distinct sub-regions: Tokai, Koshinetsu, and Hokuriku. Three sub-regions mean three different dialects and the food culture is different for each region as well.

For instance, in rural communities in Nagano and Gunma, you will find something called inago no tsukudani. Inago is a type of grasshopper that is stewed in sweetened soy sauce. In many souvenir shops within the area, you will find this delicacy packaged to bring home to your loved ones and friends as omiyage (souvenirs).

Other regional fares popular in Nagano (Shinshu) are oyaki and soba. Oyaki is a flour dumpling stuffed with vegetables seasoned with miso and soy sauce. The type of vegetables used vary with specific areas within Nagano.

Nagano is synonymous with soba noodles. Anywhere you go in Japan, the locals will tell you that you haven't sampled soba until you have had Shinshu soba! The area's highlands are perfectly suited for growing buckwheat, which is then ground and mixed with fresh, clean water flowing from Nagano's mountains. The taste is quite remarkable!

But getting away from some of the more "exotic" kyodo ryori, other regional food items associated with the Kanto and Chubu regions include hoto (udon noodles stewed in a miso-based soup with vegetables such as kabocha, potatoes, mushrooms, and meat) and monja yaki (a savory pancake similar to okonomiyaki but much runnier). It is eaten directly off the grill using a special metal spatula. Masuzushi (associated with Toyama) is sushi rice steamed in bamboo leaves with trout placed on top. Sauce katsudon (pork cutlet, breaded and fried, placed on top of rice with Worcestershire sauce) and tekonezushi (cuts of red-meat fish, such as skipjack tuna or bluefin, placed in a soy flavored marinade then arranged on top of vinegared rice) is garnished to taste with slivers of green shiso leaf, ginger root, or nori seaweed.

This list is by no means an all-inclusive list of kyodo ryori associated with these two regions, but an introduction and a mere starting point for discovering all the wonderful delicacies the Kanto and Chubu Regions have to offer.

Most visitors arrive in the Kanto region via Tokyo using Narita Airport, Japan's main international gateway.

The major gateway into the Chubu Region is the Chubu Centrair International Airport, Japan's third major international airport located on an artificial island 30 minutes south from Nagoya. Alternatively, you can take the shinkansen (bullet train) from Tokyo. The Hokuriku Shinkansen (北陸新幹線) connects Tokyo with Kanazawa. When the shinkansen line originally opened in 1997, it only went as far as Nagano and was known as the Nagano Shinkansen. In 2015, the line was extended to Kanazawa and today it is called the Hokuriku Shinkansen.

| Web Page: | http://www.jcci.or.jp/kanko/kanko-eng.htm#kanto (Japan Chamber of Commerce and Industry/ Kanto Region Tourism) |
| | http://en.go-centraljapan.jp/ (Central Japan Tourism Promotion Association/ Chubu Region Tourism) |

Kanto Region

Chiba Prefecture (千葉県)

Chiba-shi (千葉市): Chiba City

QVC Marine Field (QVCマリンフィールド)

QVC Marine Field is one of Chiba's famous landmarks and home to the Chiba Lotte Marines baseball team. The stadium, which holds 30,000, officially opened in April of 1990 when Madonna performed there during her Blonde Ambition Tour. It was called the Chiba Marine Stadium until 2011 when the name was changed to QVC Marine Field.

The Chiba Lotte Marines are a professional baseball team in Japan's Pacific League and are owned by the Lotte conglomerate, a multinational food and shopping company with headquarters in South Korea and Japan. The franchise began in 1950 as the Mainichi Orions and went through a merger and several name changes in 1958, 1964, and 1969. The team played in central Tokyo until 1972 and moved to Sendai in 1973. They returned to Tokyo in 1978 and remained until 1992 when the team was relocated to Chiba City, taking on the name Chiba Lotte Marines. The Chiba Lotte Marines won the Pacific League Championship six times in 1950, 1960, 1970, 1974, 2005, and 2010. They also won the Japan Series (日本シリーズ, Nippon Shiriizu) in 1950, 1974, 2005 and 2010. (The Japan Series is a seven-game series between the winning clubs of the league's two circuits, the Central League and the Pacific League.)

The stadium is situated along Makuhari Beach and you can easily glimpse a view of Tokyo Bay from the infield upper deck seats on a clear day. The right field bleacher seats are almost always sold out. The fans congregate in that area sporting their Marines white jerseys and chanting throughout the game, adding to the already charged atmosphere!

In addition to hosting the Chiba Lotte Marines, the stadium hosts the rugby union and the annual Summer Sonic Festival.

Founded in 2000, the Summer Sonic Festival is a 2 to 3-day festival held simultaneously in both Osaka and Chiba. The festival hosts both major national and international acts and the lineup has included such performers as Coldplay, Arrested Development, Oblivion Dust, Green Day, Beck, Marilyn Manson, Guns 'n Roses, Blondie, Cheap Trick, Perfume, Lady Gaga, XJapan, and Vamps.

If you happen to be in Chiba during baseball season, make a point of seeing a Japanese baseball game at the QVC Marine Field. You will find the experience truly rewarding.

The stadium is just ten minutes on foot from JR Kaihin Makuhari Station. Alternatively, you can catch the free shuttle bus from the JR station.

Location(s):	1 Mihama, Mihama-ku, Chiba-shi, Chiba
Web Page:	http://www.marines.co.jp/stadium/

Chiba-shi (千葉市): Chiba City

Chiba Port Tower (千葉ポートタワー)

Since their construction, Tokyo Tower and Tokyo Skytree have been drawing crowds, both locals and tourists, for their magnificent bird's eye views of Tokyo. But did you know that there is another tower where you can glimpse very unique views of Tokyo Bay and even Mount Fuji on a clear day?

Chiba Port Tower, constructed in 1986, stands approximately 410 feet (130 m) tall and offers 360° panoramic views of the area. Located in Chiba Port Park and close to the Chiba Prefectural Museum of Art, the tower was constructed to commemorate Chiba Prefecture's population exceeding the five million mark. The exterior of the tower is covered with mirrored glass, which reflects the sun and makes the tower appear blue during the day.

The tower has four stories. The middle portion of the tower is hollow, which provides an interesting perspective during the elevator ride. When you enter through the first floor, you will find a souvenir shop selling items unique to Chiba, along with an exhibition room, theater, and a children's room. Visitors take the elevator from the first floor to the fourth floor observation deck. The third and second floor can be accessed from the fourth floor via a stairway. There is an elevator located on the second floor that takes visitors back to the first floor.

The second floor contains a special wall painting called Aqua Fantasy, painted with special luminous paint. After the sun sets, the painting is illuminated by black light and the objects in the painting appear to be three-dimensional. There is also an area called Lover's Sanctuary, with seats set together in close pairs near the windows. Couples can purchase a heart-shaped lock and after writing their names on it, fasten it onto a window grate permanently. In a way, it is reminiscent of the lover's bridge in Paris, the Pont des Arts, where couples toss the keys into the River Seine after attaching their locks to the bridge.

The third floor houses a coffee shop called Café La Plage. The shop can accommodate 50 people and it can be reserved for weddings and parties.

The main observation deck is located on the fourth floor. From here, visitors can see the Chiba Marine Stadium, Mount Tsukuba, and the Chiba Zoo to the North, the Tokyo Electric Power Company and the Tokyo Bay Aqua Line to the South, Narita Airport, Chiba Prefectural Museum of Art, and Chiba Port Square to the East, and finally, Haneda Airport, Rainbow Bridge, Tokyo Disney Resort, Mount Fuji, and Tokyo Tower to the West.

From the middle of November to the end of December the exterior of Chiba Port Tower is decorated with 3,000 Christmas lights that form a large Christmas tree.

The tower is somewhat underrated; hence, it is less expensive to access its observatory than its more formidable neighbors, Tokyo Tower and Tokyo Skytree. The views are quite nice if you overlook the Keiyo Industrial Zone.

You can access Chiba Port Tower via the JR Keiyo Line, exit Chiba Minato Station. From that point, your destination is merely 15 minutes on foot.

Location(s):   Chuoko, Chuo-ku, Chiba-shi, Chiba

Web Page: http://chiba-porttower.com/

Chiba-shi (千葉市): Chiba City

Chiba Prefectural Museum of Art (千葉県立美術館)

Chiba Prefecture is home to Narita International Airport and adjacent to Japan's capital, Tokyo. Consequently, it is visited by countless tourists and has many sightseeing spots to enjoy. Among these are Chiba Port Tower and the nearby Chiba Prefectural Museum of Art.

The museum opened on October 23, 1974 and displays works by artists who have an association with Chiba Prefecture. The 2,400-piece collection includes both domestic and international works and focuses primarily on modern and contemporary pieces. Included among the displays are works by Chu Asai, an artist born into a former samurai household, who established the Meiji Bijutsukai (Meiji Art Society), the first group of western-style painters in Japan. Also featured are works by Hotsuma Katori, a Meiji period metalsmith known for his artwork, who was born in Chiba in 1874.

There are various exhibitions of alternating themes held throughout the year that feature both the museum's own collection and works borrowed from other sources. The Chiba Prefectural Museum of Art also lends its collection to traveling exhibitions, enabling those outside the area to enjoy and appreciate its various works of art. There is a reference room and a video library open to the public and the museum hosts numerous lectures and workshops to help deepen the public's appreciation for the arts.

The museum studios offer courses on Japanese style and western-style painting, sculpture, and calligraphy throughout the year. There is also a museum gift shop offering various art-related items for sale. If you are hungry after touring the open gallery spaces, you can always stop at the museum café for a quick bite to eat.

If you happen to be visiting Chiba Port Tower, why not combine your visit with a stop at the Chiba Prefectural Museum of Art? Museum hours are 9:00 AM to 4:30 PM. Admission fees are ¥300 for adults and ¥150 for students.

The Chiba Prefectural Museum of Art is a ten-minute walk from Chiba-Minato Station on the JR Keiyo-Line or the Chiba-Toshi Monorail system.

Location(s):   1-10-1 Chuokou Chuo-ku Chiba-shi, Chiba

Web Page: http://www.chiba-muse.or.jp/ART/english/index.html

Tateyama-shi (館山市): Tateyama City

Situated on the southern part of the Boso Peninsula in Chiba Prefecture is Tateyama, a small, unhurried city that is virtually unknown to foreigners. Located just two hours from Tokyo, with average temperatures hovering around 60°F (14°C) and a coastline stretching nearly 20 miles (32 km), the city is a renowned mecca for marine sports and a popular beach destination for Tokyoites. Compared to the beaches of Kanagawa, Tateyama's brown sand beaches are less crowded and cleaner. Its underwater world is just as amazing with its precious resources of coral and abundance of umihotaru (sea fireflies), which emit a mysterious blue light at night.

The economy of Tateyama is based on commercial fishing, horticulture, and summer tourism. Consequently, the city is one of the best spots for fresh and delicious seafood. Also due to its warm climate, don't be surprised to see flower fields alive with color during the month of January!

There are several festivals worth seeing in Tateyama. The Tateyama Fireworks Festival held every August is the premier summer event. During the festival, the night skies over Hojo Beach are lit up with 10,000 fireworks for nearly two hours and there is simultaneous salsa dancing put on by local community groups along the beach. In September, the two-day Yawata Matsuri brings together neighborhoods as they compete with one another in taiko drumming and costume design. The mikoshi (portable shrine) and floats travel up and down between Tateyama Station and the Hachiman Shrine under the hot summer sun during the day and at night they are illuminated by lantern light. On the third Sunday of October, Tateyama stages the Nanso Satomi Matsuri, a festival that recreates the battle that took place during Japan's Sengoku (Warring States) period. The battle follows a procession of warriors representing the Satomi clan marching from Tateyama Station to Shiroyama Park.

Located at the top of Shiroyama Park is Tateyama Castle, which offers magnificent views of the bay and surrounding areas from its upper balcony. On a clear day, you can glimpse Mount Fuji.

Tateyama Castle is one of four castles in Chiba Prefecture. It was originally constructed in 1580 by Yoshitomo Satomi and underwent restoration in 1982. The castle currently houses the Hakkenden Museum. The exhibits are all dedicated to the 106-volume novel by Kyokutei Bakin, called Nanso Satomi Hakkenden (Legend of the Eight Dog Warriors). The story is very popular and has been widely adapted into movies, television shows, video games, manga, and anime series. Please note that taking photos inside the museum is strictly prohibited.

Also within Shiroyama Park, you will find the Tateyama Municipal Museum, Peacock Aviary, and a Japanese Garden/Teahouse.

The Sunosaki Lighthouse is another area with great views. Commissioned in 1919, the lighthouse still assists vessels entering the Uraga Channel and Tokyo Bay. The locals have planted nano hana (rapeseed) plants around the lighthouse and the scenery is particularly beautiful when the bright yellow plants are in full bloom.

For those of you who are avid World War II buffs, a visit to Cape Taibusa Misaki Park is a must. During the war this area served as a Japanese Army base with bunkers and pillboxes constructed to protect the bay in the event of an Allied assault. Although most defense fortifications were dismantled during the postwar occupation of Japan, this site survived and several emplacements are still there.

From Cape Taibusa Misaki Park, travel to the Akayama Underground Tunnels and see the largest surviving air raid shelters in Japan. The tunnels, which stretch approximately one mile (1.6 km) were used by Tateyama's Naval Air Force as shelters during the end of the Pacific War when the U.S. air raids were intensifying. The tunnels were officially opened to the public in 2004.

Tateyama is full of charm and a great place to catch your breath from the hustle and bustle of Tokyo.

The city is accessible from Tokyo via the Keiyo Expressway. There are also 3-4 limited express trains that run between Tokyo Station and Tateyama Station daily.

Web Page: http://www.city.tateyama.chiba.jp/en/index.ht
             ml

Gunma Prefecture (群馬県)

Ikaho-machi (伊香保): Town of Ikaho

Omocha to Ningyo Jidousha Hakubutsukan (伊香保おもちゃと人形 自動車博物館): Toy, Doll, and Car Museum

Gunma Prefecture, located on the northwest corner of the Kanto Region, is a rural area known for its hot springs and safari park. The last thing one would expect to find here is an omocha (toy), ningyo (doll), and classic car museum!

The Omocha to Ningyo Jidousha Hakubutsukan is a private museum hidden in the hills of Gunma. It was the brainchild of Masahiro Yokota, a former carpenter who amassed a large quantity of discarded toys and memorabilia from demolished houses. The museum opened in 1994 and has been luring visitors down the post-war Japanese nostalgia lane ever since.

The first floor of the museum houses countless Showa era toys and posters. Here you will find movie posters, memorabilia, and publicity stills for idols from the 1950s through the 1980s. There is also a sizeable teddy bear collection displaying adorable stuffed bears gathered from all over the world. If you are feeling creative, visit the Kewpie Factory where you can make your own original Kewpie doll. For the big kids there is the World of Wine & Beer. As the name indicates, it is a collection of rare and unique bottles of beer and wine from around the world.

The second and third floors comprise the classic car museum. Here you will find such rare vehicles as the 1963 Daihatsu Midget three-wheeler, the 1972 Honda Vamos, the 1938 Datsun 17, the 1972 Skyline 1500, and the 1967 Toyota 2000GT, just to name a few. Many of the cars are from Yokota-san's private collection as he used to race cars back in the day and collected quite a few vehicles he was fond of.

As you exit the museum, you will encounter Candy Shop Alley where you can find unique candies for sale. The final stop at the Omocha to Ningyo Jidousha Hakubutsukan is Squirrel Garden. It is an area out in the back where you will encounter dozens of chipmunks and red squirrels.

The museum is open daily from 8:30 AM to 6:00 PM (4/25-10/31) and 8:30 AM to 5:00 PM (11/1 – 4/24). Admission is ¥1,080 for adults and ¥860 for junior high and high school students. Children aged four years and up (elementary school students) are admitted for ¥430. If your birthday falls on the day of your visit, you will be admitted for free.

The museum offers the ideal atmosphere for those that want to relive the memories of the past or simply want to share their childhood memories with their own children. Regardless of your country of origin, you will certainly find something to identify with or relate to at the Omocha to Ningyo Jidousha Hakubutsukan.

Location(s):	2145 Kaminoda, Kitagunma-gun, Yoshioka-machi, Gunma
Web Page:	http://www.ikaho-omocha.jp/

Kusatsu-machi (草津町): Town of Kusatsu

<u>Kusatsu Onsen (草津温泉)</u>

One of the things Gunma Prefecture is renowned for is its high quality onsens (hot springs). Among them, Kusatsu Onsen, situated three quarters of a mile above sea level, is considered to be one of Japan's top three hot spring resorts along with Gero Onsen in Gifu and Arima Onsen in Hyogo.

Kusatsu has the greatest natural flow of hot spring water in all of Japan, much of which surfaces at the Yubatake (hot water field) in the center of town. For many centuries, the sulfurous, highly acidic waters have been credited with curing just about every illness. In terms of the quality and quantity of onsen water, Kusatsu remains unrivaled.

Walking toward the center of town, you will notice the characteristic smell of sulfur and see the vapors rising from the drains. The Yubatake itself resembles an emerald green waterfall. Beneath the water's surface you can catch a glimpse of the white mineral deposits (yunohana) that have formed. The yunohana are prized souvenirs among visitors to Kusatsu, who use the clusters to prepare an onsen bath at home.

Kusatsu's healing waters can also be enjoyed at the various public sentos (bath houses) and ryokans (inns). The most prominent bath houses are the Sainokawara Rotenburo, the Otakinoyu with its unique Awaseyu baths (multiple wooden baths with different water temperatures), and the Gozanoyu. The onsen water in Kusatsu is around 52°C (126°F) and requires cooling before people are able to enter the baths. This is done using a method called yumomi, which involves stirring the water with large wooden paddles. The water is cooled in such a stylized, rhythmic manner that visitors often flock to the Netsunoyu Bath House directly across from the Yubatake to see the Yumomi Performance (湯もみ). There are 3-6 performances per day given by women in traditional dress singing folk songs while cooling the onsen waters. There is a small charge of ¥500 for adults and ¥250 for children to see the performance.

Of course, visitors do not need to go to a bath house or ryokan to enjoy the onsen water. There are ashiyus (foot baths) found in town that can be used free of charge by tourists. One of the foot baths is located next to the Yubatake, while another is just outside the bus terminal building.

If you get hungry, try the onsen tamago, a poached egg cooked with the hot onsen water. It has a unique texture and is definitely worth trying. Kusatsu is also famous for its onsen tamago flavored soft-serve ice cream. For those preferring a sit down meal, there are various restaurants and izakayas (an informal Japanese drinking establishment that serves food) throughout town as well.

The most convenient way to reach Kusatsu Onsen from Tokyo is via the limited express train from Ueno Station. The train travels as far as Naganohara-Kusatsuguchi Station from which point you will need to take one of the JR buses to Kusatsu Onsen.

Location(s):	3-9 Kusatsu, Agatsuma-gun, Nakanojo-machi, Gunma
Web Page:	http://kusatsuonsen-international.jp/en/

Naganohara-machi (長野原町): Town of Naganohara

Karuizawa Toy Kingdom (軽井沢おもちゃ王国)

Naganohara-machi is a town located in the Agatsuma District of western Gunma Prefecture. It is just 94 miles (155 km) from Tokyo and only an hour via the shinkansen, so it is a popular destination during the sweltering summer months. The area is renowned for its rich natural surroundings and prized onsens (hot springs), including the Kusatsu Onsen which was named one of "Japan's Best 100 Onsens" for ten years in a row.

Aside from its natural beauty, Nagaonohara-machi is also a dream destination for the little ones. It is home to the Karuizawa Toy Kingdom. Despite its name, it is not located in Karuizawa, a popular mountain resort town located next door in Nagano Prefecture.

With one look around the amusement park, you will realize that the Kingdom of Toys pulls out all the stops to capture childhood dreams. There are ten air-conditioned indoor playrooms filled with all sorts of toys both old and new school, including dolls, trains, cars, and Legos, all designed to engage a child's imagination and encourage interaction with parents, siblings, and other little ones visiting the park that day.

There are also many outdoor activities to tire out the little adventurers. Taking advantage of the surrounding wilderness, the park has created a tree house, rope bridges, a climbing wall, and up to 20 different activities to get the kids moving. There is an additional fee of ¥500 per person to take advantage of this area and children under the age of two are not permitted. When the kids get tired out, they can relax in one of the hammocks that are stretched out in between the trees or try their hand at one of the wood crafting classes. The crafting classes will teach them how to make a piggy bank or a photo frame. They will also be afforded the opportunity to fish for rainbow trout, make sand castles in the sandlot and splash around in a specially designed water park area.

The amusement park area includes a large ferris wheel, a Thomas the Tank train ride, racing go carts, a carousel, a dragon coaster, a trampoline area, a five-story castle jungle gym, and many other rides that will excite and delight the kiddies and their parents. There is an additional charge ranging from ¥200 to ¥500 for these rides.

Like all amusement parks, you will find a gift/souvenir shop and restaurants at the Karuizawa Toy Kingdom. There are a variety of themed items including bento boxes, towels, key rings, snacks, and toys. The restaurants are more like stalls serving up all sorts of goodies such as curry, donuts, fries, udon dishes, ramen, fried rice, omelets, soft-serve ice cream, caramel corn, and Dippin' Dots! The stalls do offer kid's menus with items like children's curry, omelets and lunch sets, decently priced from ¥300 to ¥1,000. There is a large, covered food court area where you can enjoy your meals.

After lunch, you can sit down and enjoy one of the stage shows featuring various characters such as Anpanman. There are two performances, one at 11:00 AM and another at 2:00 PM. Check the web page for detailed information regarding the stage shows as staging changes frequently.

The park is open from 10:00 AM to 5:00 PM on weekdays and from 9:30 AM to 5:00 PM on weekends and holidays. During Golden Week which runs from late April to early May, the park hours are 9:00 AM to 5:00 PM. Please note that, due to the severe winters in Gunma, the park does close from mid-November to mid-April.

Admission is ¥1,100 for adults and ¥800 for children. Discount tickets to the park can be purchased in advance at convenience stores such as 7-Eleven, Lawson, FamilyMart, Circle K Sunkus, and Ministop. Discounted package deals are also available for hotel guests at the nearby Hotel Green Plaza Karuizawa.

Karuizawa Toy Kingdom is a great destination for families trying to escape the hot Tokyo summers and attempting to find activities that everyone can enjoy. With the convenience of the shinkansen, there is no reason why this destination should not be included on your travel itinerary.

Location(s):   2277, Omaehosohara, Agatsuma-gun,
                 Naganohara-machi

Web Page: http://www.omochaoukoku.com/karuizawa/

Numata-shi (沼田市): Numata City

Tambara Lavender Park (たんばらラベンダーパーク)

Numata City is a city located in northern Gunma Prefecture. The kanji for Numata (沼田) loosely translates as boggy field, but that is not what you will find there. From mid-July until mid-August a brilliant carpet of purple lavender covers the slopes of Tambara, which is reputed to have the largest lavender park in the Kanto Region. This being Gunma, the highlands of Tambara are famous for skiing during the winter months but the summer months are punctuated by over 50,000 flowering lavender bushes and various types of Alpine and other multi-colored plants that form the Irodori no oka, the six-colored flower carpet fields.

The view is particularly spectacular from above and visitors to the park can board the ski lift to view the magnificent murasaki (purple) carpet from this vantage point. Just be aware that the ski lift stops operating a half hour before the park is scheduled to close. There is a fee to ride the ski lift, ¥800 for adults (roundtrip) and ¥600 for elementary school students. A one-way trip costs ¥500 for adults and ¥350 for elementary school students.

Stop at the gift shop and you will find everything from lavender scented soaps to dried lavender bouquets. Near the entrance area, there is an herb shop and lavender museum. Lavender seedlings, potted flowers and herbs can be purchased here.

There are two restaurants on-site if you get hungry. The ハイランドガーデン (Highland Garden) serves pizza, burgers, and the popular lavender-flavored soft-serve ice cream. If you are really daring or truly hungry, try the towering Tambara King

Burger. The レストハウス (Rest House) is a western-style restaurant offering a variety of family style dishes including steaks and katsu sandwiches. There is also a soba and udon restaurant within the Rest House serving the traditional Japanese noodle bowls. If you do not have the time to stop off at the restaurants, you can still enjoy the lavender flavored ice cream, which can be purchased from a stand located near the entrance.

A visit to Tambara's fragrant lavender fields is a soothing way to cool down during Tokyo's scorching summers. The park is open from late June to late August, 8:30 AM and 5:00 PM. Parking is free and can accommodate 1,500 cars. There is an admission charge of ¥1,000 (elementary school students and younger children are admitted free).

The best way to access the park is via the JR Joetsu Line and exit at Numata Station. From there you can board a bus or hire a taxi.

Location(s):   Tambara Kogen, Numata-shi, Gunma

Web Page: http://www.tambara.co.jp/lavenderpark/
                   (Tambara Park)

                   http://www.city.numata.gunma.jp/
                   (Numata City)

Takasaki-shi (高崎市): Takasaki City (The Daruma Capital)

Approximately 62 miles (100 km) north of Tokyo is the city of Takasaki. It is easily accessible within an hour from Tokyo Station via the Joetsu Shinkansen. The city is home to Shorinzan Darumaji, the temple where the daruma doll originated. It is said that the daruma doll is modeled after the famous Buddhist priest who sat meditating for so long that his legs atrophied and fell off. Hence, the daruma doll maintains an egg-like shape.

The daruma dolls are typically red, range in size from about 2.5 inches to 30 inches (6.35 to 76 cm) and serve as a talisman for good luck. They are a symbol of perseverance and often a popular gift of encouragement. They are traditionally purchased at the beginning of each New Year without the pupils painted on. One pupil (left) is painted on when a wish is made and if the wish comes true, the second pupil (right) is added. This ritual is called kaigen or the opening of Daruma's eyes. At the end of the year, regardless of the outcome, the doll is returned to the temple where it is burned.

The city holds its annual Daruma-Ichi (Daruma Fair) on January 6-7, attracting over 400,000 people. During this event, there are countless booths set up on the temple grounds selling new Fuku-Daruma dolls produced by local families. It is here where many Japanese families purchase their dolls for the New Year and have them blessed.

Next to the temple there is a small, one-room museum dedicated to the daruma doll. It is filled with daruma dolls of all types including some rare antique ones. You will also find packets of daruma instant ramen noodles here!

If you do not want to visit the temple, you can purchase your daruma doll at the omiyage (souvenir) shop at Takasaki JR Station. They are available in many different colors. The station also sells daruma eki-bento (train station lunch boxes). These make rather cute keepsakes and some of the bento containers even come in likenesses of the popular Hello Kitty character.

Location(s):   296 Hanadakamachi, Takasaki, Gunma

Web Page: http://www.city.takasaki.gunma.jp/
                   (Takasaki City)

                   http://www.daruma.or.jp/eng/index.html
                   (Shorinzan Darumaji)

Tatebayashi-shi (館林市): Tatebayashi City

Kenritsu Tsutsujigoaka Koen (つつじが岡公園) : Kenritsu Azalea Hill Park

Just 37 miles (60 km) north of Tokyo you will find the city of Tatebayashi. The city is famous for its Morin-ji temple, which was the setting for the famous Japanese folktale about a shape-shifting tanuki (raccoon). The story, "Bunbuku Chagama", tells the tale of a magical tanuki that changes its form to a tea kettle to help reward his rescuer for his kindness.

From mid-April through mid-May, however, tourists flock to the city for another reason: to view the 10,000 tsutsuji bushes (azaleas) in Kenritsu Tsutsujigaoka Koen (Azalea Hill Park), the largest azalea park in Japan. The park is approximately 12.6 hectares (31 acres) and records show that it dates back to 1556. It is said that the azalea bushes were first planted during the 17th century at this location by the lords of Tatebayashi Castle. As a matter of fact, today you can still see some of these 800-year-old tsutsuji bushes which tower over 16 feet (5 m) high.

The park was converted to a prefectural park in 1923 and has been maintained by Gunma Prefecture ever since. The azaleas reach full bloom in mid-April and the blooms last through early May. During this prime time, the park increases its admission fee from ¥310 to ¥620. The Azalea Festival takes place during this time at the park. There are 50 different types of azaleas that bloom in the park, covering the grounds in a carpet of red, purple, and white.

If you venture to the north, you will see the Jonuma Pond. During the months of July and August, wild lotus flowers bloom here. A lotus flower festival takes place at the park during this time showcasing 200 different kinds of lotus flowers. Also, since the renkon (lotus root) is a common item on the Japanese dinner table, visitors will be afforded the opportunity to purchase lotus root bento (lunch boxes) and pasta at the Tsutsujigaoka Park Inn during the festival.

Kenritsu Tsutsujigaoka Koen draws over 200,000 visitors during the height of the azalea season. Access to the park is easy via the Tobu Railway Isesaki Line. Exit at Tatebayashi Station and you will reach your destination in 25 minutes on foot or five minutes by local taxi.

Whether you want to learn more about the famous Japanese folktale or you simply want to enjoy the beauty of the flowers at Kenritsu Tsutsujigaoka Koen, Tatebayashi City can easily fit into your itinerary when you are traveling in the Tokyo area.

Location(s):   3278 Hanayama-cho, Tatebayashi-shi, Gunma

Web Page: http://www.city.tatebayashi.gunma.jp/tsutsuji/

Tomioka-shi (富岡市): Tomioka City

<u>Tomioka Silk Mill (富岡製糸場)</u>

UNESCO, the United Nations Educational, Scientific, and Cultural Organization, has been maintaining a list of World Heritage Sites since 1972. To be considered a UNESCO World Heritage Site, a place (such as a forest, mountain, lake, island, desert, monument, building, complex, or city) must represent an "outstanding universal value", and must also meet at least one of ten criteria such as "representing a masterpiece of human creative genius", "containing exceptional natural beauty", or "being an outstanding example of a traditional human settlement." To date, there are more than 1,000 sites all over the world that are included on the UNESCO list.

Japan has 18 sites included on the World Heritage List with the addition of the Tomioka Silk Mill and Related Sites being the most recent.

Located in the city of Tomioka in Gunma Prefecture, the Tomioka Silk Mill is Japan's oldest modern model silk reeling factory. Built by the Meiji government in 1872, the factory represents the country's efforts to update its methods of traditional silk production and move it into the modern industrialized world.

Raw silk was the most important export and sustained the growth of Japan's economy during the Meiji restoration. However, during this boom the Japanese silk industry began to sacrifice the quality of its silk for quantity, which affected the country's reputation as a raw silk manufacturer. Consequently, the national government decided to establish the Tomioka Silk Mill as a model facility equipped with the most sophisticated machinery, in an effort to improve the quality of raw silk.

When the factory began operations, there were 150 silk reeling machines and 400 female workers who operated the machines in the mill. Although Tomioka Silk Mill produced high-quality raw silk which was valued overseas, the business was always operating in the red. Even after reducing costs, they continued to suffer chronic deficits. As a result, the government decided to privatize Tomioka Silk Mill and in 1893 transferred its business to companies beginning with the Mitsui Finance Group. It continued this way until March 1987, when the Tomioka Silk Mill was finally closed.

On June 21, 2014, UNESCO's World Heritage Committee registered the Tomioka Silk Mill and Related Sites on its list stating that the sites in Gunma Prefecture "marked Japan's entry into the modern, industrialized era."

The number of visitors to the mill went up substantially after the government decided to recommend the site to the World Heritage list in 2012 and those numbers will probably continue to grow given the site's designation. But due to conservation concerns, the complex can receive only about 5,000 visitors per day so do plan in advance.

If UNESCO Heritage sites spark your curiosity, Tomioka City is just over two hours by train from Tokyo. You can catch the Joetsu Shinkansen from Tokyo Station to Takasaki Station, where you can transfer to the Joshin Dentetsu to Joshutomioka Station.

Location(s):   1-1 Tomioka, Tomioka, Gunma

Web Page: http://www.tomioka-silk.jp/hp/en/index.html

Ibaraki Prefecture (茨城県)

Hitachinaka-shi (ひたちなか市): Hitachinaka City

Hitachi Seaside Park (国営ひたち海浜公園)

Located less than two hours from Tokyo, the 190-hectare (470 acre) Hitachi Seaside Park is an ever changing palette of colors and a year-round destination for both locals and tourists. The park is located in the city of Hitachinaka in Ibaraki Prefecture next to the Ajigaura Beach. Each season, the hill known as Miharashi No Oka is covered with different varieties of flowers, the most popular being the powder blue nemophilas. These annuals, 4.5 million in total, bloom during spring (April to mid-May) and they make the park seem as if it were awash in a sea of blue.

In addition to the nemophilas, the park has 170 varieties of tulips and other flowers, a small amusement area, bicycle trails, a family golf area, a barbeque area, and various restaurants serving delicious treats.

The 328-foot ferris wheel, known as the Giant Flower Ring ferris wheel, is the symbol of the park. A complete revolution takes 12 minutes and offers amazing panoramic views of the park and ocean below. The spacious gondolas can accommodate up to six people and when it comes to having fun, the more the merrier!

After taking a spin on the ferris wheel, hop on the Family Banana Coaster or try your hand at shooting ray guns at the Salamander Legend Shooting Ride. The Water Plaza is popular during the hot summer months, where kids can splash around in the Jabu Ponds, the Tunnel of Water, or the Fountain Plaza.

If you get hungry, the park has various options to choose from. You can have a nice, sit-down meal at the 200-seat resort-style restaurant called the Garden Restaurant. The Glass House is a glass enclosed café that serves organic coffee, pasta, and snacks and offers breathtaking views of the ocean. You can also elect to grill your own food in the designated barbeque area among the shady pine trees. Grilling equipment can be secured free of charge; however, please note that reservations are required three months in advance. There are also a number of food stands serving fast food, crepes, and snacks. Be sure not to miss the Kuma-san no Castella stand which offers bear-shaped bite size castella cakes. You can also find the famous kakigori (shaved ice) Japan is famous for here.

Before you depart the park, stop at one of the gift shops to pick up a nice souvenir. The shops offer a wide range of items, including traditional Kasama ceramic art, local products, original park souvenirs, and children's clothing.

The park is generally closed on Mondays, with a few exceptions. (Check the link provided for hours). Park hours are 9:30 AM to 5:00 PM (March 1-July 20, September 1-October 31), 9:30 AM to 6:00 PM (July 21-August 31), and 9:30 AM to 4:30 PM (November 1-end of February).

You can easily access the park from Tokyo via Ueno Station, the JR Joban Line to Katsuta Station. From there catch the Hitachinaka Seaside train on the Minato Line to Ajigaura Station. The park is a 20-minute walk from that point.

Location(s):   605-4 Onuma, Mawatari, Hitachinaka, Ibaraki

Web Page: http://en.hitachikaihin.jp/

Tsukuba-shi (つくば市): Tsukuba City

Tsukuba Space Center

If you grew up in the United States, you are probably familiar with NASA (National Aeronautics and Space Administration) established in 1958, which oversees the civilian space program. But have you ever been curious about the Japanese counterpart of NASA, known as JAXA (the Japan Aerospace Exploration Agency)?

JAXA was founded on October 1, 2003 through the merger of three, previously independent organizations. It owns and runs about a dozen space, research, and testing centers across Japan with the Tsukuba Space Center (TKSC) serving as the operations facility and headquarters. Located in Tsukuba Science City in Ibaraki Prefecture, the facility opened in 1972 and serves as the primary location for Japan's space operations and research programs. Japanese astronauts involved in the International Space Station are trained here in addition to the training they receive at the Lyndon B. Johnson Space Center in Houston, Texas.

The 530,000 square-meter (5,704,873 ft²) facility is surrounded by nature and houses state-of-the-art equipment and testing facilities. The TKSC offers both self-guided and guided tours of the facility. Given that the guided tours are free to the public and offer a much greater understanding of the work that goes on here, why not opt for the guided tour? Tours are offered in English but need to be scheduled in advance as they are less frequent than tours offered in Japanese.

The tour begins with a rocket launch simulation, which allows visitors to hear what a launch sounds like from various distances. From there you can access the Space Dome Exhibition Hall, which offers insight into the current status of JAXA's space development programs. There are various interactive displays in the Space Dome but do pay attention to the signs as not everything is interactive. For your convenience, each display is accompanied by a detailed English description.

Do make a point of visiting the Planet Cube Lounge, which runs various events and exhibitions, and don't forget to stop off at the Space Shop where assorted space-related items including freeze-dried foods are available for sale. Outside in Rocket Square, you will find a genuine 50-meter-long (155 ft) H-II Launch Vehicle, which makes an interesting backdrop for your photos.

The facility draws visitors of all ages and backgrounds, all sharing one thing in common, a child-like enthusiasm for the mysteries of space!

Admission is free and passports are required during the weekdays but not on the weekends. The tour will not require an entire day so combine your visit with other things to do and enjoy around Tsukuba.

Location(s):   2-1-1 Sengen, Tsukuba, Ibaraki

Web Page: http://global.jaxa.jp/about/centers/tksc/files/t raffic_e.pdf

Kanagawa Prefecture (神奈川県)

Hakone-machi (箱根): Town of Hakone

Hakone-en Aquarium (箱根園 水族館)

Ashi no Ko or Lake Ashi is a scenic lake in the Hakone area of Kanagawa Prefecture. The area is known for its splendid views of Mount Fuji, numerous hot springs, historical sites, and ryokans (inns).

Located at the edge of Ashi no Ko, you will find Hakone-en, a 4,924 m² (53,000 square-foot) recreation complex operated by Prince Hotels & Resorts, consisting of an aquarium, shops, restaurant, barbequing area, theater, and much more.

Opened in 1999, the Hakone-en Aquarium is home to 450 species of fish, approximately 32,000 in total, collected from the lakes, rivers, and oceans all over the world. The facility features both salt water and fresh water aquariums. The fresh water section displays over 2,000 rare fresh-water fish from 150 species, including the African Lungfish. The salt water section houses a massive tank that is 17 m (56 feet) wide and 11 m (36 feet) long. This tank is home to over 20,000 salt water fish. The Hakone-en Aquarium is known as the highest aquarium located above sea level in Japan. Consequently, seawater is transported by tanker from Numazu City in Shizuoka twice daily to meet the aquarium's requirement of 20 tons of sea water per day.

The salt water fish are fed once every weekday and twice on Saturdays and holidays. Visitors flock to view the divers swimming together with the fish underwater during feeding time.

Aside from the massive collection of fish, perhaps the biggest attraction at the aquarium is the Baikal Seal Square where the seals are famous for a routine involving so-called drinking in the hot spring pose. The seals are floating in the water holding a cypress bucket with a sake bottle placed within and a small hand towel placed on their heads. The scene is just beyond description and really merits being seen to be believed. The seal show takes place twice on weekdays and three times per day on Saturdays and holidays.

You can easily incorporate the aquarium into a day trip from Tokyo as it is only an hour and 43 minutes by train from Tokyo Station via the Tokaido-Sanyo Shinkansen. Exit the shinkansen at Odawara Station and switch to the Romancer (Hakone 83) to Hakoneyumoto Station.

The aquarium's hours of operation are from 9:00 AM to 5:00 PM. Admission is ¥1,500 for adults and ¥750 for children aged four through elementary school level.

Location(s):   139, Motohakone-cho, Ashigarashimo-gun

Web Page: http://www.princehotels.co.jp/amuse/hakone-en/suizokukan/index.html

Yokohama-shi (横浜市): Yokohama City

Yokohama Chukagai (横浜中華街): Yokohama Chinatown

Chinatown: Just about every major city around the world has one including Johannesburg, South Africa, Buenos Aires, Argentina, Liverpool, United Kingdom, Calcutta, India, Bangkok, Thailand, Vancouver, and Toronto, Canada just to name a few. In the United States alone there are nine including Boston, New York, Chicago, Los Angeles, San Francisco, Philadelphia, Seattle, Washington D.C., and Honolulu. However, for many the Chinatown located in Yokohama, Japan stands head and shoulders above the rest.

Yokohama has been the entry point for foreign cultures ever since Japan opened its doors to the world. Consequently, a large influx of Chinese immigrants (traders) migrated to Japan after 1859, bringing their own culture with them. At the time, foreign residents were restricted to living in designated areas and therefore formed a very tight community within the area they were allowed to inhabit. Today, with its over 150-year history, Chinatown has over 500 businesses and roughly 150 restaurants which draw 20 million visitors annually to the 20-hectare (50-acre) district!

Located within the Naka Ward, Chinatown is easy to recognize by its main, Eastern Chinese-style gate called paifang. The gate was constructed in 1955 as a gesture of goodwill following the 1937 full-scale war between China and Japan. It was also the year when Chinatown was officially recognized by the Japanese and called Yokohama Chukagai (Yokohama Chinatown). There are nine other paifangs at major points within the district.

The main attraction in Chinatown is not so much the

107

architecture and historic sites but its cuisine. The style of cuisine ranges from Peking to Cantonese.

Peking cuisine originated in China's political, economic, and cultural center, Beijing. Great cooks and superb ingredients were gathered here to influence and develop today's Peking (Beijing) cuisine. Because of its cold climate, many dishes are hot and sizzling.

Shanghai cuisine originated in Shanghai located in the Yangtze Delta. With its status as a top world trade port, the cuisine consists of plentiful fresh-water and salt-water fish, a variety of grains, fresh vegetables, and choice teas.

Szechwan cuisine originated near the Yangtze River in Szechwan Province. Because it is far from the ocean, chefs developed a variety of seasonings for their dishes and in the process became master creators of complex tastes delicately blended with herbs and spices.

Cantonese cuisine originated in China's southern costal Canton Province. Many ingredients and cooking styles were imported from foreign countries to create complex dishes, which use generous portions of sea food, pork, poultry, vegetables, and dry food.

After sampling the cuisine, wander around Chinatown in a rickshaw. A ride through the city will cost anywhere from ¥3,000 – ¥5,000.

Stop off at the Guan Di Miao Temple, which was founded in 1862 when a Chinese immigrant brought a sculpture of Guan Gong and enshrined it in a modest temple. The small temple attracted fellow migrants to worship and soon became the central focus in the local community. By 1871, Guan Di Miao Temple had become a major landmark in Yokohama Chinatown.

The temple was destroyed in 1923 by the Great Kanto Earthquake and sustained damage during the 1945 Allied air attack. In 1981, it was struck by lighting and caught fire. In 1986, another fire engulfed the temple. Every time disaster struck, the local community came together and rebuilt the temple. Each rebuilding project produced a more elaborate temple. The current temple was completed in April of 2000.

When all is said and done, pop into one of the countless classic Chinese gift shops with its rows and rows of omiyage (souvenir) gifts. It is easy to see that the shops are typical tourist traps but nonetheless are unavoidable.

There are various events and festivals that are held in Chinatown, such as the Chinese New Year celebrations, which take place around the beginning of February. If you are fortunate enough to witness one of these events while you are there, you will find that they offer a colorful and wondrous glimpse into Chinese culture.

Chinatown is the top sightseeing spot in Yokohama and definitely worth exploring. The closest stations to Yokohama Chinatown are Motomachi-Chukagai Station along the Minato Mirai Line and Ishikawacho Station along the JR Negishi Line.

Location(s):   118-2 Yamashitacho, Naka-ku, Yokohama, Kanagawa

Web Page: http://www.chinatown.or.jp/e

Yokohama-shi (横浜市): Yokohama City

Yokohama Doll Museum

The city of Yokohama is the capital of Kanagawa Prefecture and the second largest city in Japan after Tokyo. Located less than half an hour south of Tokyo by train, it is a great destination for those looking for a great day trip away from Tokyo. The city has numerous gardens, parks, museums, and amusement parks to choose from; therefore, you will certainly find something to please even the most finicky among your travel group. The Yokohama Doll Museum, for instance, is a wonderful sightseeing spot and a timeless place that brings together people of all ages.

The Museum is one of the largest doll museums in Japan with 1,300 rare dolls from 140 countries on display. It introduces visitors to the doll making method and offers them the opportunity to actually see and touch the various tools and materials used in the process. Not only are visitors introduced to the craftsmanship of Japanese doll making but the craftsmanship of western doll making is also compared and contrasted, offering an interesting perspective into the various regional techniques.

The dolls come in all shapes, sizes, and materials. You will find dolls on display representing various celebrities, sportsmen, and politicians as well as traditional Japanese dolls and dolls from countries like New Zealand, Peru, Russia, Spain, and many more. The Japanese dolls are categorized into dolls used for prayer, play, and for display. There is a nice collection of Ichimatsu Ningyo, Japanese antique dolls dressed in spectacular kimonos that became significant pieces presented as wedding gifts during the early 20th century. In 1927, fifty-eight of these dolls were sent to the United States as gestures of good will during the Friendship Doll Exchange campaign.

Each year with the coming of spring, the museum brings out its China dolls in celebration of Hinamatsuri. Hinamatsuri otherwise known as Doll's Day or Girl's Day is celebrated on March 3rd and involves an elaborate display of dolls representing the Emperor, Empress, attendants, and musicians in traditional court dress of the Heian period, all arranged on tiered platforms.

The museum is constantly updating its doll collection and organizes various temporary exhibits throughout the year; therefore, there is something new and different to see with each visit. When you are done viewing the various dolls on display, make your way to the puppet show theater or grab a bite to eat at the café.

The museum is open daily between 10:00 AM and 4:30 PM. (Closed on Mondays, year end and New Year holidays.) The entrance fee for adults is ¥400 and ¥200 for children.

Location(s):   18 Yamashita-cho, Naka-ku, Yokohama-shi

Web Page: http://www.doll-museum.jp/

Yokohama-shi (横浜市): Yokohama City

<u>Yokohama Silk Museum</u>

Many people have heard about the Silk Road, an ancient trade route between Rome and China, but few realize that the port of Yokohama in Japan also played an important role in the silk trade.

After closing its doors to foreigners for nearly three centuries (with the exception of the Chinese and the Dutch), Japan once again welcomed foreign trade in the mid 1800s. The port of Yokohama opened in 1859 as a modern trading town engaged in exporting Japanese silk, tea, rice, and seafood with raw silk comprising 25-40 percent of total Japanese exports. Today, the city is recognized as the birthplace of Japan's modern culture.

Raw silk was produced primarily in the northern Kanto region and sent to Hachioji, which is part of the Greater Tokyo Area. From there it was transported to Yokohama on horseback and later by railway. Today, Japan is ranked fifth in the world after China, India, Brazil, and Uzbekistan in the production of raw silk.

Hence, it doesn't come as a surprise that there is a museum dedicated to the silk industry in Naka-ku, Yokohama. It opened in March of 1959 in commemoration of the centennial anniversary of the opening of the port of Yokohama. The two-story museum housed in the Silk Center International Trade and Sightseeing Building illustrates the history of silk, displays silk garments from Japan and around the world, and introduces visitors to silk producing technologies, which include live silkworms.

The first floor of the museum is divided into several zones

consisting of the Wonder Farm (which illustrates the life cycle of the silkworm), Hall, and Library. The library contains over 5,000 books on the subject of raw silk, weaving, and dyeing, designs, colors, accessories, manners and customs of people, and statistics. (The books are in Japanese only.) There is a gift shop that offers numerous silk related products for purchase including silk scarves and other silk products, books, and foods containing silk. The gift shop is located near the entrance of the building; therefore, visitors can shop there without having to pay for admission to the museum.

The second floor of the museum is devoted to the history of silk in Japan and displays several garments that were reproduced to represent the use of silk during various points in history. You will also find a range of modern kimonos and displays on how silk is woven and dyed.

The museum is open daily (except Mondays) from 9:30 AM to 4:30 PM. It is closed on national holidays and between December 28 and January 4. Admission is ¥500 for adults, ¥200 for students, and ¥100 for young children.

The Yokohama Silk Museum is relatively close to the Yokohama Doll Museum (ten minutes on foot) making it easy to combine a visit to both locations during a day visit to Yokohama. To access the Silk Museum, use the Minato Mirai Line (exit Nihon-odori Station). From that point, your destination is a five-minute walk.

Location(s):   Silk Center, 1, Yamashita-cho, Naka-ku, Yokohama

Web Page: http://www.silkmuseum.or.jp/english_main/information/

Kawagoe-shi (川越市): Kawagoe City

If you think that in this day and age you would be hard pressed to find a place in Japan that still retains the ambiance of an old Edo period town, you would be mistaken. Located only 30 minutes by train from Tokyo is the city of Kawagoe, often referred to as Little Edo or Koedo. Its old wooden houses, along with the elegant examples of early twentieth century brick, cement, and stone architecture inspired by Taisho Romanticism still draw tourists searching for a taste of old Japan.

Kawagoe prospered during the Edo period due to the over 200 two-storied kurazukuri warehouses that were used to store goods on their way into Edo via the Kawagoe-Kaido highway. Today, approximately 30 of these ornate, earthen walled storehouses still survive. These historic buildings are conveniently grouped in an area about half a mile north of Kawagoe Station along Chuo-dori, the town's main north-south street. Some of the kurazukuri were converted into small museums, such as the Kurazukuri Shiryokan, an old tobacco warehouse rebuilt after a devastating fire in 1893. Others serve as shops and restaurants.

Just 15 minutes away from the kurazukuri area are the ruins of Kawagoe Castle. Only one building, the Honmaru Goten, where the feudal lord dwelt, still remains and is open to visitors. The structure dates back to 1848 and contains amazing tatami rooms and a Chinese-style tiled roof.

Other famous landmarks include the Toki no Kane (Tower of Time), a 54-foot (16 m) bell tower dating back to the 1890s, which was used to warn residents of a fire, and the 1,200-year-old Kita-in Temple. The temple contains the only surviving structures from the original Edo Castle, which were moved to

Kawagoe along the Shingashi River. On the temple grounds you will find 540 statues of the disciples of Buddha and the Toshogu Shrine, dedicated to Ieyasu Tokugawa, founder and first shogun of the Tokugawa Shogunate of Japan. In January, the temple hosts a Daruma Matsuri, during which time visitors purchase their daruma for good luck. Additionally, there is a Setsubun Matsuri (Bean Throwing Festival) and a Sakura Matsuri (Cherry Blossom Festival).

The Kawagoe Matsuri Kaikan or festival museum houses several ornate floats, some reaching as high as three stories, used in Kawagoe's annual festival. Behind the museum you will find Kashiya Yokocho, a charming street with 14 candy stores and children's gift shops dating back to the early Showa era.

If you happen to work up an appetite after touring Kawagoe, try to sample some of the cuisine the city is famous for including sweet potatoes, unagi (eel), and various Japanese confections.

You can access Kawagoe from Tokyo via the Tobu Line from Ikebukuro Station to Kawagoe Station. Alternatively, you can take the Seibu Shinjuku Line Koedo Limited Express train from Shinjuku to Hon-Kawagoe.

Web Page: http://www.city.kawagoe.saitama.jp/

Saitama-shi (さいたま市): Saitama City

Tetsudo Hakubutsukan (鉄道博物館): The Railway Museum

Saitama City is home to the largest railway museum in the country. Opened to the public in October of 2007, the three-story, 28,200 square meter (303,542 ft²) museum is Japan's leading railway historical museum run by the East Japan Railway Culture Foundation. The museum exhibits, researches, and studies the materials relating to the rail system in Japan and abroad. Visitors can learn the history and the structure of railways through interactive exhibits, view previously used train cars, and learn about operating trains via the use of simulators. The museum features approximately 30 railway cars, numerous train cab simulators, mini trains, video booths, two restaurants, a museum shop, and a research room.

When you enter the museum, you will find the world's only steam locomotive simulator (additional charge of ¥500 and reservations are required) just to the left of the entrance. The first floor of the museum consists of the Teppaku Library, a Park Zone with miniature operational trains for the kids, the main museum shop, the NRE Restaurant, the Simulator Hall, and the Teppaku Playground. The highlight of the first floor is the History Zone, which contains several historic carriages and engines, including old imperial carriages, Meiji-era steam trains, the reconstructed Shinbashi Station when it first opened in the 19th century, an early series shinkansen, freight trains, and historic electric and diesel locomotives.

The second level includes the Learning Zone, the Collection Zone featuring another library, and a collection of Japan railway memorabilia including station signs, uniforms and photographs,

116

a Kid's Space, another museum shop, and restaurant. The main feature of the second level is the Railway Model Diorama, the largest in Japan.

The third floor has a viewing deck and the rooftop features a panorama deck with amazing views of the surrounding area.

Whether you are a train enthusiast or you simply want to learn more about the history of Japan through its railway system, the train museum provides a fun and informative atmosphere for the entire family.

The museum is open daily except Tuesdays from 10:00 AM to 6:00 PM. Admission is ¥1,000 for adults and ¥500 for junior high school students. Children ages 3 years and up are admitted for ¥200.

Location(s):   3-47 Onari-cho, Omiya-ku, Saitama-shi, Saitama

Web Page: http://www.railway-museum.jp/en/index.html

Tochigi Prefecture (栃木県)

Nikko-shi (日光市): Nikko City

Edo Wonderland Nikko Edomura (江戸ワンダーランド 日光江戸村)

While visiting Nikko City, you may want to set some time aside to tour a unique theme park that reproduces the culture and lifestyle of the Edo period (1603-1868). Edo Wonderland or Nikko Edomura as it is known in Japanese, is a 500,000-square-meter (5,381,955 ft²) park featuring six theaters, a traditional Edo village, a samurai residential area, and a ninja village. Visitors can stroll the park in Edo period costumes available for rent at the costume store and enjoy mingling with the townspeople, including merchants, courtesans, and old world policemen.

You can witness an oiran parade much like the ones that were the feature of Yoshiwara, Edo era's red light district made familiar in such films as *Memoirs of a Geisha* and *Sakuran*. There are museums, ninja training houses, and interactive amusements such as the Edo Work Experience, where children can run around acting out different roles. There are various shops that sell souvenirs such as teapots, woodblock prints, and toy weapons. Other shops, such as the Blacksmith and Armor Repair Shop, are replica storefronts that demonstrate how period craftsmen once worked. There are two wax museums, the Kodenmacho Jail House and the Kira-Kozukenosuke Residence, where visitors can witness the grisly scenes of prison life, torture, battle, and vengeance.

Edo Wonderland has five restaurants on site. If you are in the mood for chicken noodles, stop in at Tori-soba. Tenjiku to

Miyako offers a selection of Japanese sake, shochu and ume-shu (plum wine) as well as mizore-cha soba (chilled tea-flavored soba noodles topped with chicken and grated daikon radish). Yama Kujira specializes in the beef rice bowl and also serves motsu-nabe stew and Kushi-yaki skewers. Yabu's main menu features Kaki-age soba noodles, and Café Dejima serves delicious desserts with coffee or fresh-squeezed mikan citrus juice. Do not be surprised when you enter one of these establishments and encounter Edo townspeople relishing a meal!

Visit the haunted temple filled with Japanese spirits and demons or the House of Illusion where the walls seem to bend and balls roll uphill. A favorite with most visitors seems to be the Ninja Trick Maze, a human-sized labyrinth that definitely presents a challenge to escape from. You can also engage in some hands-on experiences such as indigo dyeing at Konya Dyer's Shop or learn how to throw ninja stars at Ninja Star Knives.

Finally, take advantage of the performances taking place in the various theaters around Edo Wonderland. You can choose from comic shows and traditional water magic to live action, including the popular Grand Ninja Theater, where sword battles, magic, and martial arts are part of the show. The shows are held daily with multiple performances each day.

Admission is ¥4,500 for adults and ¥2,300 for children aged 7-12. The theme park has been the setting of several period TV shows and is definitely worth checking out.

Location(s):   470-2 Karakura, Nikko, Tochigi

Web Page: http://edowonderland.net/en/

Nikko-shi (日光市): Nikko City

Tobu World Square (東武ワールドスクウェア)

Only 35 minutes on foot from Edo Wonderland is another great place to visit called Tobu World Square.

Tobu World Square is a theme park featuring 1/25th replicas of famous buildings and structures from around the world. Opened on April 24, 1993, the park took five years to complete. There are 102 models that include ancient monuments, cultural treasures, and UNESCO World Heritage Sites, reproduced with great detail all the way down to the cars, trains, and miniature people. There are even gardens that change with the seasons.

The park is divided into zones based on the various regions of the world. Beginning with the Japan Zone, visitors can view scenes of Japan along with culturally significant sights from across the country, including Himeji Castle, Nara's Horyu-ji Temple, and Todai-ji Daibutsuden. Next is the Asia Zone which takes visitors to Korea, China, and India and includes such things as the Great Wall of China and the Taj Mahal. The Egypt Zone is characterized by the Great Pyramids of Khufu, the Sphinx, and the Temple of Abu Simbel. The Europe Zone comprises the park's largest and most diverse area. Here, ancient wonders such as the Parthenon and the Coliseum sit side by side with more recent structures like the Eiffel Tower. Moving on, is the America Zone, home to the White House, the Statue of Liberty and a section of downtown New York City, complete with the World Trade Center Twin Towers destroyed during the 9/11 terrorist attack. Finally, Tobu World Square closes with a Modern Japan Zone with more contemporary structures such as the Diet Building, the Tokyo Dome, Tokyo Tower, and Tokyo

Skytree. As a matter of fact, the scale model of Tokyo Skytree was unveiled on April 24, 2010, far ahead of the actual opening of the structure on February 29, 2012. The Modern Japan Zone also features a partial replica of busy Narita Airport.

Aside from the models, visitors to the park can enjoy countless other facilities including restaurants and shops selling food and items from all around the world. Free guided tours through Modern Japan, Europe, and America Zones are conducted once a day in Japanese. English pamphlets are available and all the signage around the park is in both Japanese and English.

This is a unique way to spend your day touring Japan and the rest of the world in just a few hours!

The park is open all year and park hours are 9:00 AM to 5:00 PM (mid-March through November), 9:30 AM to 4:00 PM (December through mid-March).

Location(s):   209-1 Kinugawa Onsen Ohara, Nikko, Tochigi

Web Page: http://www.tobuws.co.jp/default_en.html

Utsunomiya-shi (宇都宮市): Utsunomiya City

Are you interested in seeing Japanese festivals? If so, Utsunomiya, the capital of Tochigi Prefecture, is your spot!

The city hosts a festival just about every month of the year celebrating everything from the blooming of the cherry blossoms to gyoza (pot stickers as they are known in the West). Utsunomiya in fact is renowned for being the city of festivals.

Certainly there are other attractions aside from the festivals that draw tourists to the city. Perhaps the most visited is the Utsunomiya Castle Ruins Park located near City Hall. The castle's walls, turrets, and moat were reconstructed and the park opened to the public in 2007. The park is most beautiful when the plum and early blooming cherry trees are in season. Hachimanyama is the largest park located in downtown Utsunomiya and hosts a cherry blossom festival in April. In May, visitors can enjoy the beauty of the azaleas and if you visit in November, the park is ablaze in autumn colors. Chuo Koen (Central Park) is spectacular in June with the roses and irises in full bloom at opposite ends of the park. A cobblestone walkway known as Kamugawa Promenade with its cherry trees in full bloom is a romantic spot for strolling. It crosses over a covered shopping arcade called Orion-dori, where you will find countless clothing stores and bars that are open in the evening hours.

As you explore further you will see a number of warehouses known as kura, some of which have been converted into restaurants. The stones used to build them and the garden walls throughout the city come from Ohya, where visitors can explore the underground quarry that was used to manufacture planes during World War II. There is also a temple set into a cave known as Ohya-ji. Here, you will find ancient Buddhist figures carved on the walls. Another great tourist spot is the towering Heiwa Kannon statue (the Peaceful Goddess of Mercy). The statue, completed in 1954, is equivalent in height to a nine-story building. There is a set of stairs just behind the statue enabling visitors to view the statue from a different vantage point.

Another beautiful building constructed using the Ohya stone is the Matsugamine Church. Built in 1932 by Swiss architect Max Hinder, it is a complete Romanesque cathedral, something that you may have thought you would never see in Japan.

If you work up an appetite from all the exploring, try the gyoza the city is famous for. There are dozens of shops that serve this delicious dish but you may want to try Kirasse located near PARCO. The restaurant offers twenty-six varieties of gyoza to choose among!

After your meal, you may want to visit the Shinohara Family Residence. The former home of a wealthy merchant is just three minutes on foot from JR Utsunomiya Station.

As you can see, there are plenty of things to see and do in Utsunomiya. The city is a major train hub served by the Tohoku Shinkansen Line, the JR Tohoku Main Line, the Tobu Nikko Line, and the JR Utsunomiya Line. From Narita Airport, the fastest way to reach Utsunomiya is to take the Narita Express train to Tokyo Station and transfer to the Tohoku Shinkansen.

Web Page: http://www.utsunomiya-cvb.org/en/

Tokyo-to (東京都): Tokyo Metropolis

Multiple Wards: Adachi, Arakawa, Chuo, Kita, Koto, Sumida, Taito

Sumida-gawa (隅田川) : Sumida River

The Sumida River flows through Tokyo, running 17 miles (27 km) around the city and passing under 26 bridges. It branches from the Arakawa River at Iwabuchi and flows into Tokyo Bay. The river is a great place to go on a boat cruise, passing under the colorful bridges and viewing Tokyo Skytree, Tokyo Tower, and Shinto shrines. The Sumida River shows Tokyo's river-born heritage where the vibrant river systems served as the arteries through which its commerce has flowed from the Edo period to the present day.

You can take advantage of the river cruises while visiting Asakusa where you can sail down the river to Hamarikyu Gardens. Alternatively, you can cruise across Tokyo Bay, traveling from old-fashioned Asakusa to the modern amusements of the man-made island of Odaiba. The Tokyo Cruise Ship Company offers various types of cruises to choose from: http://www.suijobus.co.jp/en/.

Among Sumida's 26 bridges, the major ones include:

The Ryogoku Bridge: The present bridge dates back to 1932, having replaced the bridge built in 1659. This bridge was immortalized many times by Utagawa Hiroshige, a well-known Japanese Ukiyoe artist.

The Eitai Bridge: Dates back to 1924 when it replaced a bridge that was constructed in 1696.

The Senju Bridge: Dates back to 1921 and replaced a bridge constructed in 1594, which had served as the only bridge across the river for a long period of time.

The Sakura Bridge: One of the newer bridges dating back to 1985.

The Kototoi Bridge: Dates back to 1928 and was reconstructed at the location of the bridge that originally linked two nearby temples, the Mimeguri-Jinja and the Matsuchiyama-shoden.

The Azuma Bridge: Dates back to 1931 and replaced the bridge in that location since 1774. This bridge is closest to Asakusa Station and the Kaminari Gate.

The Komagata Bridge: Dates back to 1927 and takes its name from the Matsugata Temple dedicated to the patron goddess of horses.

The Umaya Bridge: Dates back to 1929 and replaced the bridge that was built in 1875.

The Kuramae Bridge: Dates back to 1927 and is 570 ft. (196 m) long and 70 ft. (20 m) wide. It includes six traffic lanes and wide sidewalks. Large stone piers support the arches and the bridge decks.

The Shin Ohashi Bridge: Dates back to 1976 and replaced the bridge that was originally built in 1693.

The Kiyosu Bridge: Built in 1928, it was modeled after the Deutz Suspension Bridge in Cologne, Germany.

The Chuo Bridge: Was constructed in 1994 and is the newest of all of the bridges that cross the Sumida River.

The Tsukuda Bridge: Built in 1964, it was the first bridge constructed after World War II, crossing the river from the Tsukiji to Tsukishima.

The Kachidoki Bridge: Dates back to 1940 and was constructed to commemorate the victory of the Japanese Army at Lushun during the Russo-Japanese War. This bridge is the only drawbridge on the Sumida River but it has not been raised since 1970.

As you are cruising the river and passing under the various bridges, see if you can identify the ones listed above.

Each year on the last Saturday in July, The Sumidagawa Fireworks Festival takes place. The festival is a revival of the celebrations that were held during the Edo period. Similar events take place at the same time of year at other locations throughout Japan. The great summer festival atmosphere that accompanies the fireworks draws close to a million celebrants, many of whom are dressed in yukatas (casual summer kimonos). Folks strolling around in Asakusa, especially around Sensoji Temple, patronize the food vendors and game stalls lining the streets. In addition, many of restaurants in the area provide outdoor seating where you can enjoy delicious food while watching the fireworks.

The best places to view the fireworks display are right along the Sumida River itself. One area stretches from the Sakura Bridge to the Kototoi Bridge while another is located downstream of the Komagata Bridge stretching down to the Umaya Bridge. It is advisable to get there early as these prime spots are taken up rather quickly.

Sumida-gawa (隅田川)：Sumida River

Yakatabune Pleasure Boats

Sailing on the Sumida River on a hot and humid summer day in Tokyo is a pleasure that is hard to resist. There are many tour boats offering excursions on the Sumida River but the more traditional way is on a yakatabune, which literally means roof-shaped boat. These wooden tour boats (although today many are made from light weight fiberglass) were popular among the well-to-do in Japan during the Edo era. With lanterns under their roofs, tatami floors and tables inside, these unique boats are in reality moving restaurants. Some boats even come with kotatsu tables covered by a futon with a heat source underneath that helps take the chill out of a cool evening cruise on the river. Often, the yakatabune are rented for special occasions such as year-end parties and weddings.

The typical menu consists of appetizers such as handmade tofu, salmon, tuna, shrimp, and scallop sashimi. This is followed by a course of fish and vegetable tempura. You can expect to be served noodles and a final course of fruit or Japanese pickles. Of course there is also plenty to drink.

Some boats feature entertainers/musicians while others offer the do-it-yourself type of entertainment with a Karaoke machine.

Tokyo has more than fifty companies that operate yakatabune. The tours typically last anywhere from two to three hours. Although there are some boats that operate during the daytime (i.e., cherry blossom viewing cruises), the weekend evening cruises are the most popular.

128

The yakatabune represent the Japanese spirit of hospitality. Many of the boat operators have been in business for several generations; therefore, it is not uncommon to encounter a fifth or sixth generation owner.

An excursion on a yakatabune offers an experience of Tokyo unlike any other. You can enjoy a different experience each season. You may enjoy viewing the sakura (cherry) trees that run alongside the Sumida River during spring, the hanabi (fireworks) in the summer, and the beautiful fall foliage in autumn. So, there is something for everyone throughout the year.

Further, not only can you enjoy a yakatabune cruise in Tokyo but you can also take part in excursions offered in Osaka, Kobe, Kochi, and Fukuoka.

Bunkyo-ku (文京区): Bunkyo Ward

Tokyo Dome City (東京ドーム)

As a tourist in Tokyo, you may have visited Harajuku, Asakusa, Tokyo Tower, Tokyo Skytree, the Imperial Palace, Roppongi Hills, Ginza, and Odaiba and you may be wondering what else is left. How about a trip to Tokyo Dome City, an amusement park in the center of Tokyo, which is open 365 days a year and does not charge an admission fee?

Tokyo Dome City is a leisure complex in central Tokyo consisting of the 55,000 seat Tokyo Dome baseball stadium, the 43-story Tokyo Dome Hotel, an amusement park, the LaQua Spa, numerous shops, and over fifty restaurants, cafés and bars serving Japanese, Western, and Asian fusion cuisine.

The Tokyo Dome is the home of the Yomiuri Giants baseball team and has hosted numerous concerts, festivals, and other events since its opening in 1985. Mick Jagger was the first international act to play in the Tokyo Dome in 1988. Other well-known acts like L'Arc~en~Ciel, XJapan, Bon Jovi, Michael Jackson, Paul McCartney, Guns N' Roses, Britney Spears, and Luna Sea have all performed to sold-out audiences at the stadium once referred to as the "Big Egg" due to its dome-shaped roof.

The amusement park area known as the Tokyo Dome City Attractions opened in May of 1988 and is comprised of a variety of rides and entertainment facilities including roller coasters, a ferris wheel, a merry-go-round, and a parachute tower that drops riders from a height of 262 feet (85 m)! The park is open 365 days a year from 11:00 AM to 9:00 PM and there is no admission charged to enter.

The large, western-style Tokyo Dome Hotel (http://www.tokyodome-hotels.co.jp/e/) opened in June of 2000 and has 1,006 guest rooms, eleven restaurants serving both Western and Asian dishes, bars, and several banquet rooms.

LaQua Spa opened in 2003 and features true hot spring pools, saunas, relaxation spaces, and various massage and beauty services. The onsen (hot spring) water is pumped to the surface from a depth of more than 3,280 feet (1,000 m). The spa charges an admission fee of ¥2,634 and there is an extra charge during weekends, holidays, and after midnight.

Beginning in early November and ending in mid-February (right after Valentine's Day), Tokyo Dome City hosts a winter illumination event known as the Tokyo Dome City Winter Festival. It is considered to be the top illumination event in terms of scale and duration and boasts over two million lights. The Tokyo Dome and the surrounding areas are lit up from 5:00 PM until 11:00 PM and draw visitors from all over Japan.

No matter what time of year you choose to visit Tokyo Dome City, you will be certain to find something that will capture your interest. From Tokyo Station, Tokyo Dome City is eight minutes away on the Marunouchi Subway Line. If you choose to drive, there are three parking areas that accommodate up to 700 vehicles. The cost to park is ¥400 for 30 minutes.

Location(s):   1-3-61 Koraku, Bunkyo-ku, Tokyo

Web Page: https://www.tokyo-dome.co.jp/e/

Chiyoda-ku (千代田区): Chiyoda Ward

Kokyo (皇居): Imperial Palace

The Imperial Palace (Kokyo, meaning Imperial Residence) was completed in 1888 and stands on the former site of Edo Castle. Located in the Chiyoda area of Tokyo, the palace is within walking distance from Tokyo Station.

The palace compound is comprised of several buildings including the main palace, the private residences of the Imperial Family, an archive, a museum, and several administrative offices. The total palace area including the gardens is 1.32 square miles (3.42 km²).

After the defeat of the Shogunate, who ruled Japan from 1603 to 1867, the inhabitants of Edo Castle, including the Shogun Tokugawa Yoshinobu, were forced to vacate the premises. In 1868, the emperor relocated from Kyoto to Edo Castle and renamed it Tokei Castle. On May 5, 1873, a fire destroyed the Nishinomaru Palace (formerly the shogun's residence) and the new Imperial Palace Castle was constructed on the site in 1888.

From 1888 to 1948, the compound was called Palace Castle. On the evening of May 25, 1945 a majority of the structures of Palace Castle were destroyed by the Allied fire-bombing raid. It was from the basement of the concrete library that Emperor Hirohito declared the surrender of Japan on August 15, 1945, ending World War II. Due to the large-scale destruction of the palace, a new main palace hall and residences were constructed on the western portion of the site in the 1960s. The area was renamed Kokyo in 1948 while the eastern part was renamed Higashi-Gyoen (East Garden), which became a public park in 1968.

Except for the Imperial Household Agency and the East Gardens, the palace is generally closed to the public. On each New Year (January 2) and during the Emperor's birthday (December 23), the public is permitted to enter through the Nakamon (inner gate) and gather in the Kyuden Totei Plaza in front of the Chowaden Hall. The Imperial Family appears on the balcony before the gathered crowd and the emperor delivers a short speech greeting and thanking the visitors.

From Kokyo Gaien, the large plaza in front of the Imperial Palace, visitors can view the Nijubashi, two bridges that form an entrance to the inner palace grounds. The stone bridge in front is called Meganebashi (Eyeglass Bridge) for it resembles a pair of eye glasses. The bridge in the back was formerly a wooden bridge with two levels, from which the name Nijubashi was derived.

Although many are not in existence today, the inner citadels of Edo Castle were protected by multiple large and small wooden gates, constructed in between the gaps of the stone wall surrounding it. From south to southwest to north, the main gates are Nijubashi, Sakuradamon, Sakashitamon, Kikyomon, Hanzomon, Inuimon, Otemon, Hirakawamon, and Kitahanebashimon. The Otemon gate was once guarded by 120 men, while the smaller gates were guarded by 30 to 70 armed men.

The Sakuradamon Gate is well known for an assassination that occurred there. Known as the Sakuradamon Incident, it involved Ii Naosuke, the Japanese Chief Minister and a proponent of the reopening of Japan after more than 200 years of seclusion. It is said that Naosuke had also made strong enemies in the dispute for the succession of Shogun Tokugawa Iesada.

The assassination took place just as Ii Naosuke was reaching the castle. He had been warned about his safety and many encouraged him to retire from office, but he refused, replying that "My own safety is nothing when I see the danger threatening the future of the country."

Ii Naosuke was ambushed by 17 men and a samurai named Arimura Jisaemon. Arimura cut Ii Naosuke's neck and then committed seppuku (a form of Japanese ritual suicide by disembowelment).

Although tourists can see very little of the palace, it does not affect the numbers visiting the compound on a daily basis. Tours offered by various agencies such as Hato Bus Tours are common and would probably serve as the best means to see the Imperial Palace, combined with other historic sites such as The Diet Building and Tokyo Station.

Location(s):   1-1 Chiyoda, Chiyoda-ku, Tokyo

Web Page: http://sankan.kunaicho.go.jp/english/guide/k
oukyo.html

Chiyoda-ku (千代田区): Chiyoda Ward

<u>Tokyo Station (東京駅) and National Diet Building (国会議事堂)</u>

Tokyo is a scenic city whose architecture has been largely shaped by its history. The metropolis was destroyed twice in recent history, first during the Great Kanto Earthquake of 1923 and second in the extensive fire-bombing of World War II. Consequently, Tokyo's current urban landscape consists mainly of modern and contemporary buildings; older buildings are very scarce.

Of these scarce structures, two that are definitely worth seeing while visiting Tokyo are the National Diet Building and Tokyo Station.

Built in 1936, the National Diet Building is an imposing granite structure that sits on land that was once inhabited by feudal lords. For 46 years prior to the building's completion, the National Diet, comprised of two chambers, the House of Representatives (the Upper House) and the House of Councilors (the Lower House), assembled in temporary quarters, with the first meeting taking place in 1890. When the Diet is not in session, visitors can enjoy free, 60-minute tours of the House of Councilors chamber, the public gallery, the Emperor's room, the central hall, and the front courtyard.

Tokyo Station, which opened on December 20, 1914, was first conceived in 1896 by the Imperial Diet, which wanted to open up a new station on the line connecting the Shinbashi and Ueno terminals. They wanted to name it Central Station. Unfortunately, construction was delayed until 1908 due to the First Sino-Japanese War and the Russo-Japanese War. When the station was finally completed, it consisted of four platforms, two of which were dedicated to electric trains while the other two served non-electric trains. In the early days, the station had gates only on the Marunouchi side, with the north side serving as an exit and the south side serving as an entrance. Today, this brick-faceted side is the one that is most easily recognized when referring to Tokyo Station.

Unfortunately, much of the station was destroyed in the fire-bombing that occurred on May 25, 1945. The bombing shattered the impressive rooftop domes and when the station was rebuilt within the year, simple angular roofs were used in place of the domes and the restored building was only two stories tall rather than three.

The Marunouchi side underwent an extensive five-year renovation, which was completed in October of 2012, and it was restored to its pre-war condition. The modern day Tokyo Station (main station) consists of ten island platforms serving 20 tracks, raised above street level running in a north-south direction. The main concourse runs east-west below the platforms. It is the main intercity rail terminal in Tokyo and the busiest station in Japan in terms of number of trains per day (over 3,000). Inside the station, you will find a large shopping area including the multi-story Daimaru department store, event halls, coffee shops, restaurants, an art gallery, and a hotel.

The Tokyo Station Hotel opened its doors on November 2, 1915. The hotel has 150 guest rooms and suites designed in a classic European decor. It features a variety of fine and casual dining restaurants as well as several bars and lounges. The Atrium Lounge designed by the British firm, Richmond International Ltd., features a 9-meter (28 ft) high ceiling with a massive skylight.

Chances are, you are going to utilize Tokyo Station when traveling in Japan. Why not linger a little and tour the station and enjoy all it has to offer before boarding your train to your destination?

Location(s):   1-chome, Nagatacho, Chiyoda-ku, Tokyo (National Diet Building)

1-9-1 Marunouchi, Chiyoda-ku, Tokyo (Tokyo Station)

Web Page: http://www.sangiin.go.jp/eng/guide/national/index.htm (National Diet Building)

http://www.thetokyostationhotel.jp/ (Tokyo Station Hotel)

Chuo-ku (中央区): Chuo Ward

<u>Ginza District (銀座)</u>

Today, many people know that the Ginza district in Tokyo is home to numerous upscale shopping, dining, and entertainment venues. But before one square meter of land in the district's center became valued at well over ten million yen, Ginza was a swamp, which was filled in during the 16th century. Its name was derived from the silver coin mint established there in 1612 during the Edo period. (Ginza means silver mint in Japanese.)

A fire destroyed most of the area in 1872, from which point the Meiji government designated Ginza as an area for modernization. The government planned the construction of fireproof, European-style brick buildings and larger, improved streets connecting Shinbashi Station to Tsukiji and important government buildings. In 1873, a western-style shopping promenade on the street from the Shinbashi Bridge to the Kyobashi Bridge was completed. It wasn't until after the 1923 Great Kanto Earthquake when Ginza developed into the upscale shopping district for which it is known today.

Most of the European-style buildings have disappeared over the years, but some of the older buildings still remain. The most famous structure is the Wako building with its iconic Hattori Clock Tower. The building and clock tower were originally built by Kintaro Hattori, the founder of Seiko.

Having evolved into a prominent outpost of western luxury shops in recent years, Ginza is a popular destination on weekends, when the central Chuo-dori Street is closed to traffic. The traffic ban began in the 1960s under Governor Ryokichi

Minobe. The closure takes place from 2:00 PM to 5:00 PM on Saturdays and from 12:00 PM to 5:00 PM on Sundays (until 6:00 PM from April to September). Ginza is where shoppers and tourists can find the infamous $10 cup of coffee and virtually every leading brand name in fashion and cosmetics.

Aside from the shopping and dining, another popular destination in Ginza is the Kabuki-za, the premier theater in Tokyo for the traditional Kabuki drama.

The original Kabuki-za was a wooden structure constructed in 1889. It was destroyed and rebuilt several times due to fires, earthquakes, and World War II raids. The current Kabuki-za underwent a transformation beginning April 30, 2010, where the facade was retained but a 29-story modern building was added to house the theater and commercial office space. The theater was reopened to the public on April 2, 2013.

Shopping may not be your primary goal when visiting Japan, but the Ginza district is definitely worth browsing when you are there. If you have time, try and catch a performance at the Kabuki-za if one is available. Your travels in Ginza will definitely provide you with experiences that you cannot find anywhere else.

Web Page: http://www.ginza.jp/en/

Chuo-ku (中央区): Chuo Ward

Ginza District (銀座): Kabuki-za (歌舞伎座)

First performed in the early 17th century, Kabuki, a classical Japanese dance drama known for its elaborate costumes and makeup, has become a symbol of Japanese culture in modern times. Kabuki is written "歌舞伎" in Kanji and from left to right, the individual characters mean sing (歌), dance (舞), and skill (伎). The principal theater for this traditional Japanese art form is located in Tokyo's trendy Ginza district and is known as the Kabuki-za.

The theater first opened in 1889 and was managed by a Meiji era journalist, dramatist, and educator, Fukuchi Genichiro. He retired in 1903 and the theater was taken over by the Shochiku Corporation in 1914, which has been the theater's exclusive management company since.

Unfortunately, the Kabuki-za was destroyed by fire in October 1921. Rebuilding began in June of 1922; however, the unfinished building was damaged by the Great Kanto Earthquake in September of 1923. In December of 1924, the Kabuki-za reconstruction was finally completed. Plays continued to be performed at the theater during the war years until the building was totally gutted during the massive Tokyo air raid of May 1945. When the building was restored in 1950, it was designed in the same architectural style as the 1924 building.

The Kabuki-za continued to operate until concerns over the theater's ability to survive earthquakes as well as accessibility issues compelled the city to demolish the structure in the spring of 2010. A series of farewell performances, entitled Kabuki-za Sayonara Koen (Kabuki-za Farewell Performances), were held from January through April of 2010, after which Kabuki performances took place at the nearby Shinbashi Enbujo and elsewhere until the opening of the new theatre complex in the spring of 2013.

The 2013 version of the Kabuki-za features an extensively renovated facade in front of a twenty-nine-story modern building, which houses the new theater and commercial office space.

The inside of the theater is opulent and the stage is enormous. There is a walkway leading down one aisle from the back of the theater, which enables actors to enter the stage from different directions. Performances are offered nearly every day and tickets are sold for individual acts as well as for each play in its entirety. Programs are organized monthly. Each month, there is a given set of plays and dances that make up the afternoon performance and a different set comprising the evening show. Headsets are available for rental with English narration to explain what is going on during the play.

Matinee performances are offered between 11:00 AM and 3:45 PM, while evening shows take place from 4:30 PM to 9:00 PM.

If you happen to be touring the Ginza district, try and take in one of the Kabuki performances offered at the Kabuki-za and discover for yourself why this art form has endured since the 17th century or merely go and witness the opulence of the theater itself. Either way, you will come away with an enriching experience.

Location(s):   4-12-15 Ginza, Chuo-ku, Tokyo

Web Page: http://www.kabuki-za.co.jp/

Chuo-ku (中央区): Chuo Ward

<u>Hamarikyu Gardens (浜離宮恩賜庭園)</u>

Hamarikyu Gardens are a large group of traditionally styled gardens at the mouth of the Sumida River, which stands in stark contrast to the skyscrapers of the adjacent Shiodome District. Opened to the public on April 1, 1946, the gardens have had several functions over the centuries. They were originally constructed as part of a feudal lord's Tokyo residence and duck hunting grounds during the Edo period (1603-1867). The gardens later served as the strolling gardens of a detached Imperial Palace before being opened to the public in its current form. Remnants from the past are still visible throughout the gardens including several reconstructed duck hunting blinds and the remains of an old moat and reconstructed rock wall.

The gardens are divided in two major sections. The southern garden once included the residence of the feudal lord. The northern garden was added later. The park features a seawater pond (Shioiri Pond), which changes levels with the tides. Actually, Hamarikyu itself is surrounded by a seawater moat that is filled from Tokyo Bay.

There is a teahouse (Nakajima no Ochaya) on an island where visitors can rest, enjoy the scenery, and partake in the various refreshments available, including maccha (Japanese green tea) and Japanese sweets served in a tea ceremony style.

Hamarikyu is attractive in any season. Late February brings ume (plum) blossoms, while the spring cherry blossom season starts in late March and continues to early April. Several varieties of flowers bloom in spring including fields of peony, cosmos, and canola blossoms. Japanese falconry and aikido are demonstrated during the New Year. The gardens are not as famous for fall foliage as some of the other gardens around Tokyo, but they do offer plenty of maple, ginkgo, and other trees that display their beautiful autumn colors between late November and early December.

If you schedule a cruise down the Sumida River, combine it with a stop at Hamarikyu Gardens. The cruise boats will drop you off at the gardens and the journey from Asakusa to Hamarikyu takes approximately 35 minutes.

Location(s):   1-1 Hamarikyu Teien, Chuo-ku, Tokyo

Web Page: http://www.tokyo-park.or.jp/english/park/detail_04.html

Koto-ku (江東区): Koto Ward

Kameido Tenjin Shrine Wisteria Festival

The Kameido Tenjin Shrine, constructed in 1662, is home to one of Japan's few remaining red drum bridges, which was immortalized in Utagawa Hiroshige's "One Hundred Famous Views of Edo." It is also one of the few places in Tokyo, and the most popular one in fact, where you can see beautiful wisteria flowers in late April and early May. During this time, the shrine hosts its annual Fuji Matsuri or Wisteria Festival where over 100 wisteria roots appear in full bloom. The blooms are illuminated from sunset until midnight and are a site to see with the lit up Tokyo Skytree in the background.

Wisteria is a flowering plant that is native to the Eastern United States as well as China, Korea, and Japan. Replicas of these flowers dangling from hair pins have been used to decorate the hair of maiko (apprentice geisha) during the month of May. These hair pins are known as hana kanzashi and the flower ornaments change to reflect the season.

At the shrine, these lovely lavender-colored flowers that are comprised of several bunches dangle from overhead trellises and reflect off of the pond under the famous drum bridge. They were planted during the Edo period and are legendary in Japan due to the numerous ukiyoe prints and other works of art that featured them.

During the matsuri, several food stalls line the grounds of the shrine and various traditional Japanese musical performances are offered lending to the true festival atmosphere.

The Kameido Tenjin Shrine is a 15-minute walk from either the north exit of Kameido Station or Kinshicho Station on the Sobu Line. You can also take the Tokyo Metropolitan bus to the Kameido Tenjin-mae stop.

As the season moves from the pink sakura (cherry blossoms) to the lavender fuji (wisteria), both locals and tourists cram into the relatively small space that comprises the shrine hoping to get a glimpse of these beautiful flowers. The weekends are particularly busy; therefore, it is advisable to visit during the week if you can.

Location(s):   3-6-1 Kameido, Koto-ku, Tokyo

Web Page: http://www.kameidotenjin.or.jp/english/index
              .html

Meguro-ku (目黒区): Meguro Ward

Meguro River Winter Sakura Illumination

The Meguro River (Meguro-gawa) is almost five miles (8 km) long and flows through Tokyo passing through the Setagaya, Meguro, and Shinagawa wards, finally flowing into Tokyo Bay. Its beautifully landscaped banks are very popular for the hanami (cherry blossom viewing) ritual each spring.

The neighborhood of Nakameguro through which the Meguro River flows has over 500 cherry trees lining both sides of the river. Visitors arrive early from all over Tokyo to reserve spots along the river to picnic and to simply enjoy the beauty of the sakura (cherry blossoms). In the evenings, the trees are lit up and afford a romantic atmosphere where one can enjoy the beautiful pink blooms.

Since 2010, in the winter months Nakameguro has been transforming into the Winter Sakura Illumination. Starting from Nakameguro Station all the way to Ikejiri-Ohashi Station, the cherry blossom trees are brilliantly illuminated with pink LED lights mimicking the sakura blooms. The pink bulbs are powered by biodiesel fuel produced from used cooking oil collected from homes and restaurants in the area. So not only is the display visually pleasing, it is also ecologically beneficial. It is estimated that 400,000 LED bulbs light up the walkways along the river from late November to Christmas day.

After viewing the lights display, you can dine at one of the many trendy cafés, traditional Japanese restaurants, or izakayas located nearby. The neighborhood also has numerous art galleries, fashion boutiques, specialty shops, and design stores where you can browse.

146

Nakameguro is bordered by Ebisu and Shibuya, and served by the Tokyo Metro Hibiya Line and the Tokyo Kyuko Electric Railway Toyoko Line.

Minato-ku (港区)： Minato Ward

<u>Tokyo Tower (東京タワー)</u>

Standing at 333 meters (1,093 ft), Tokyo Tower is the second tallest structure in Japan. Inspired by the Eiffel Tower in Paris, Tokyo Tower is approximately 13 meters (43 ft) taller and painted white and orange in compliance with air safety regulations.

Construction on the tower began in June of 1957 and it was officially opened to the public on December 23, 1958. The cost to complete the tower was ¥2.8 billion (US$8.4 million in 1958). The tower serves as a TV and radio broadcast antenna as well as a tourist attraction.

Japan experienced a communications boom in the 1950s with the inception of NHK in 1953 followed by several private broadcasting companies that began operating in the following months. The government realized that this boom would eventually lead to the construction of transmission towers all over Tokyo, eventually overrunning the city. They proposed constructing one large tower capable of transmitting to the entire region. Further, due to the country's postwar boom in the 1950s, Japan was searching for a monument to symbolize its growth as a global economic powerhouse.

Tokyo Tower was constructed of steel, a third of which was scrap metal taken from US tanks damaged in the Korean War. When the 9-meter (30 ft) antenna was bolted into place on October 14, 1958, Tokyo Tower became the tallest freestanding tower in the world, overtaking the Eiffel Tower. Despite being taller than the Eiffel Tower, Tokyo Tower weighs about 4,000 tons, 3,300 tons less than the Eiffel Tower. While other towers have since surpassed Tokyo Tower's height, the structure is still the tallest self-supporting steel structure in the world and was the tallest artificial structure in Japan until April 2010, when the new Tokyo Skytree became the tallest building in Japan.

Foot Town, a four-story building, located directly under the tower, houses souvenir shops, restaurants, the Tokyo Tower Aquarium, and a gallery. On the structure's roof, one can find an amusement park/ roof garden and a playground for kids. With elevators departing from Foot Town, guests can visit two observation decks. The Main Observatory is located at 150 meters (490 ft), while the Special Observatory reaches a height of 250 meters (820 ft). There are guides throughout the attraction to point guests in the right direction and answer any questions.

Over 150 million people have visited the tower since its opening in 1958. Current estimates indicate that Tokyo Tower attracts approximately three million visitors per year! It is recommended to combine a visit to Tokyo Tower with a visit to Zojoji Temple, one of Tokyo's major temples, just next to the tower.

Naturally, Zojoji Temple can be seen from Tokyo Tower. Six of the 15 Tokugawa shoguns are buried in the temple cemetery. The graves of Hidetada, Ienobu, and Ietsugu had been designated National Treasures of Japan, but were burned in World War II. At present, parts of two of their graves have the distinction of being Important Cultural Properties of Japan. Additional graves are located in the cemetery behind the Great Hall. Sections of the temple grounds are currently occupied by a golf practice range and a hotel.

In one particular garden at the cemetery, called the Unborn

Children Garden, there are rows of stone statues known as Jizo dedicated to the unborn children of Japan, including miscarried, aborted, and stillborn children. Parents can choose a Jizo (a statue said to be the guardian of unborn children) in the garden and decorate it with small clothing and toys. Usually, parents also place a small gift next to the statue to ensure that the spirits of the children are brought to the afterlife safely. Occasionally stones are piled by the statue in an effort to help shorten the amount of suffering a child has to go through on the way to the afterlife.

You can access Tokyo Tower via various modes of public transportation. The Metropolitan Subway Odeo Line, exiting at Akabanebashi Station is the closest, with the tower located five minutes on foot from the exit. Alternatively, you can take the Metropolitan Subway Mita Line and exit at Onarimon Station. Your destination from this point is only six minutes on foot.

Location(s):   4-2-8 Shiba-Koen, Minato-ku, Tokyo

Web Page: http://www.tokyotower.co.jp/eng/

Minato-ku (港区): Minato Ward

Toranomon Hills (虎ノ門ヒル

When Tokyo Skytree opened to the public on May 22, 2012, the landmark was the talk of the town, drawing thousands of visitors from all over the world who waited in long lines to get a peek at this marvelous new structure. Now with the Tokyo Summer Olympics of 2020 imminent, Tokyo has added yet another landmark that is generating quite a bit of excitement. Standing at 810 ft. (247 m), Toranomon (Tiger's Gate) Hills is the newest skyscraper. Designed by Nihon Sekkei and built by Mori Building, it was unveiled in the Minato district of Tokyo on June 11, 2014. Toranomon Hills is the second tallest building in Tokyo after the Midtown Tower, which stands at 814 ft (248 m).

The skyscraper complex is built around the new Loop Road No. 2, a trunk road running from Shinbashi to Toranomon and is at the heart of the revitalization efforts in the Minato district.

The main tower of the complex is called Mori Tower. The different levels of the building are utilized as follows:

B3F – B1F: Parking for 544 cars

1F – 4F: Retail space

4F – 5F: Conference space

6F – 35F: Offices

37F – 46F: Private residences (172 units)

47F – 52F: Andaz Tokyo Toranomon Hills Hotel *

(*A boutique hotel in the Hyatt chain with 164 guest rooms.)

Plans to build an arterial road between Shinbashi and Toranomon districts have been in the works since 1946, but the plan remained unrealized for decades due to the government's inability to annex the necessary prime real estate in central Tokyo. A solution was finally reached in 1989, which involved building a new skyscraper above the road and offering to relocate displaced residents into the skyscraper. Construction for Toranomon Hills began in April 2011 and took three years to complete.

The logo for Toranomon Hills consists of four black vertical bars forming the letter "M" (and resembling "門," kanji of the Toranomon name). The complex's mascot, Toranomon (トラのもん) inspired by the Japanese manga character, Doraemon, is popular and its image can be found throughout the complex.

The Toranomon Hills venture has been the largest project pursued by Mori Building since the Roppongi Hills development in the early 2000s. If your travels in Japan take you to the Minato Ward, spend a few minutes exploring this brand new skyscraper and maybe even enjoy a meal or a cocktail at one of its many bars and restaurants.

Location(s):   23 Toranomon 1 cho-me, Minato-ku, Tokyo

Web Page: http://toranomonhills.com/en/#/Index

Nakano-ku (中野区): Nakano Ward

Nakano Broadway (中野ブロードウェイ)

The Akihabara district in Tokyo's Chiyoda Ward draws millions of visitors from all over the world for its vast array of electronics/appliance shops, anime/manga shops, and maid cafés. But did you know that there is another, lesser known neighborhood just northwest of Shinjuku called Nakano City, which has just as much to offer in the way of Japanese pop culture merchandise and is less frequented by non-Japanese?

The main draw in Nakano City is Nakano Broadway, a multi-level shopping mall famous for its many stores offering anime and idol-related goods as well as game consoles, toys, video games, souvenirs, clothes, shoes, second hand goods, and even groceries. Just a five-minute train ride from Shinjuku via the JR Chuo Line, this four-level shopping mall is an otaku (Japanese term for people with obsessive interests, commonly the anime and manga fandom) heaven.

The second and third levels are primarily dedicated to the anime and idol-related shops while the ground level houses stores selling clothing, shoes, and second-hand merchandise. Mandarake, a popular Japanese manga, anime, and doujinshi (amateur manga publications) shop, occupies much of the real estate here. The basement level has a marketplace offering everything from fruits and vegetables to meat and seafood. You will also find numerous restaurants offering cheap and tasty yakitori (grilled chicken skewers), okonomiyaki (a Japanese savory pancake containing a variety of ingredients including pork), and ramen (noodle soup dish), all for around ¥1,000. If you happen to leave room for dessert, try the eight layer/ flavor softo cream (soft serve ice cream) at Daily Chiko. Here, you will find unusual flavors like murasaki imo (purple potato) and various soda flavors. Aside from the soft serve ice cream, they also sell an udon (a type of thick wheat flour noodle) dish for only ¥180!

If you miss the maid cafés of Akihabara, don't fret. Kuroneko, a maid café where the girls wear cat ears, is just the thing. You will find one Kuroneko café on the first floor and another on the second floor of Nakano Broadway. Patrons can enjoy all you can drink beverages for ¥1,000 for 30 minutes.

Leading up to the mall, you will come across a 740-foot (226 m) long covered shopping arcade with a variety of shops including restaurants, cafés, jewelers, pharmacies, and boutiques. It is a great place where one can switch gears from an adventure in shopping to an adventure in gastronomy. There are also many little food alleys lined with restaurants and izakayas (a type of Japanese drinking establishment that serves food) surrounding the mall and arcade that offer a variety of different dishes to sample. You can practically spend an entire day exploring the area!

While Akihabara is more or less a tourist attraction, Nakano is a place where you can find those very rare pop culture items not available anywhere else and get an opportunity to shop at the places where the locals shop for such items.

Location(s):   5-52-15 Nakano, Nakano-ku, Tokyo

Web Page: http://nbw.jp/index_e.html

Shibuya-ku (渋谷区): Shibuya Ward

<u>Harajuku (渋谷区) District: Takeshita-dori (竹下通り)</u>

Located within the Harajuku district in Tokyo, Takeshita-dori is a narrow, 0.2-mile (.32 km) pedestrian-only street lined with a wide variety of trendy shops, crepe stands, fast food outlets, used clothing stores, and fashion boutiques featuring the latest visual kei, gothic, and lolita fashions. It is also home to Daiso Harajuku, one of the largest ¥100 shops in Tokyo!

Situated directly across from JR East's Harajuku Station, Takeshita Street is very popular with teenagers visiting Tokyo during school excursions and local young people shopping for small kawaii (cute) goods. Harajuku itself is the center of Japan's most extreme teenage cultures and fashion styles. Therefore, it does not come as a surprise to see many of the fashion and trend-conscious teens wandering the street dressed up in eccentric costumes to resemble anime characters and punk musicians.

Shops along Takeshita-dori tend to stay open daily from 11:00 AM to 8:00 PM and it isn't uncommon to find aggressive store clerks who call out to lure customers into their shops. The area is also famous for what is known as nama shashin (unofficial or paparazzi photos) of popular idols such as AKB48 and Arashi.

Takeshita-dori also draws many tourists who view it as a fun place to look around the many reasonably priced, one-of-a-kind shops.

Just south of Takeshita-dori is Omotesando, a broad, tree lined avenue sometimes referred to as Tokyo's Champs-Elysees. Here you can find famous brand name shops, cafés, and restaurants catering to the fashion conscious urbanites in their 30s and 40s. Not too far away is the Ota Memorial Museum of Art (http://www.ukiyoe-ota-muse.jp/eng) featuring amazing ukiyo-e paintings from Seizo Ota's personal collection. To the west of the railway tracks lies Meiji Jingu, one of Tokyo's major shrines.

Centrally located and easy to access, Harajuku provides many options to help plan your day and immerse yourself in the local culture.

Location(s):   Jingumae 1 chome, Shibuya-ku, Tokyo

Web Page: http://www.takeshita-street.com/

Shibuya-ku (渋谷区): Shibuya Ward

Meiji Shrine (明治神宮)

Tokyo is a city full of many wonders, but perhaps the most mystifying is the Meiji Jingu (Meiji Shrine), situated within a forest covering 69 hectares (170 acres) right in the middle of a concrete urban jungle. This evergreen forest has 120,000 trees of 365 different species, all donated by people from various parts of Japan when the shrine was first established.

Meiji Jingu is dedicated to the deified spirits of Emperor Meiji, the 122nd Emperor of Japan, and his wife, Empress Shoken (born Masako Ichijo). The Emperor reigned from February 3, 1867 until his death on July 30, 1912. When the Emperor passed away, the Japanese Diet passed a resolution to commemorate his role in the Meiji Restoration. It was decided that a shrine would be built in his honor and an iris garden in Tokyo, which the Emperor and Empress used to visit, was chosen as the building's location.

Construction of the shrine began in 1915 and it was completed in 1921. The shrine grounds were officially finished in 1926. Unfortunately, the original building was destroyed during the World War II air raids and the current building was completed in 1958 through a public fund-raising effort.

The shrine grounds are made up of two areas: Naien and Gaien. The Naien area comprises the inner precinct/garden and includes the shrine buildings and the Meiji Jingu Homotsuden (Treasure House), which houses articles belonging to the Emperor and Empress. The Gaien area is made up of the outer precinct/garden and includes the Meiji Memorial Picture Gallery, which houses a collection of 80 large murals illustrating the various events that took place in the Emperor's and Empress' lives. The Meiji Memorial Hall and a variety of sports facilities including the National Stadium can also be found within the Gaien.

The Meiji Shrine is popular and has hosted numerous foreign leaders like President George W. Bush and Secretary of State Hillary Clinton. It is the location for countless Shinto weddings and provides a place for rest and relaxation for many Tokyoites. During the New Year, the shrine welcomes more than three million visitors who come to offer the year's first prayers (hatsumode).

The shrine is easily accessible via the JR Yamanote Line, exit Harajuku Station. It is also adjacent to the popular Yoyogi Park, making it easy to string together a visit to several places during your visit without feeling rushed.

Location(s):   1-1, Kamizono-cho, Yoyogi, Shibuya-ku, Tokyo

Web Page: http://www.meijijingu.or.jp/english/

Shinagawa-ku (品川区): Shinagawa Ward

Musashi Koyama Shotengai Shopping Mall

If you want to shop like the locals in Tokyo, avoid the trendy touristy places like Akihabara, Shibuya, and Omotesando and seek out a traditional shotengai (shopping mall). The shotengai are typically located near train stations and offer just about everything you would need at reasonable prices. Located in the Shinagawa district of Tokyo, you will find perhaps the most famous of these shotengai known as Musashi Koyama or as the locals call it, Musako.

Musashi Koyama opened in 1956 and stretches half a mile with approximately 250, mostly privately owned shops. The covered shopping arcade is just off of Musashi-Koyama Station, on the Tokyo-Meguro Line.

Inside the thriving shotengai, you will find ¥100 shops, sushi restaurants, cafés, clothing stores, appliance stores, real estate offices, video arcades, pharmacies, pachinko parlors, and shops selling all sorts of goods including Japanese pastries, vegetables, books, and kimonos!

Interestingly, the shotengai is frequented mostly by locals who know that the further you walk away from Musashi Koyama Station, the cheaper the goods offered seem to become. But the mall also attracts people from adjacent areas in search of privately owned shops, which are quickly disappearing from the Central Tokyo landscape.

Although Musashi Koyama may not be on most people's travel itineraries when visiting Tokyo, for those who dare to visit, it does afford an opportunity to experience a real slice of Tokyo life and perhaps walk away with one or two bargains in the process.

Location(s):   3-23-5 Koyama, Shinagawa-ku, Tokyo

Web Page: http://musashikoyama-palm.com/

Sumida-ku (墨田区): Sumida Ward

Ryogoku Kokugikan (両国国技館): Ryogoku Sumo Hall

If you plan on visiting Tokyo during the months of January, May, or September, you really should try to include a trip to the Ryogoku Kokugikan (Ryogoku Sumo Hall) to watch a sumo tournament.

Sumo, which originated in Japan, is a competitive, full contact sport where the rikishi (wrestlers) try to either force one another out of the circular dohyo (ring) or to touch the ground with anything other than the soles of their feet. A rikishi can also lose a match if he uses an illegal kinjite (technique) or if his mawashi (belt) comes completely undone. Watching a sumo tournament, one can't help but wonder how the mawashi manages to stay on despite all the tugging and pulling on it!

The matches take place in a ring called the dohyo, which measures 15 feet (4.6m) in diameter. The dohyo is constructed on top of a platform made of clay and sand. A new dohyo is built for each tournament. There is usually a structure resembling the roof of a Shinto shrine suspended over the dohyo.

The sport is interesting to watch as it spans many centuries and has preserved countless ancient traditions. Even today, it remains very ritualistic, incorporating such elements as using salt for purification, which dates back to when sumo was part of the Shinto religion. The wrestlers' lives are highly regimented also. They are required to maintain a communal lifestyle where all aspects of their daily lives are dictated by strict tradition.

Sumo has an exacting hierarchy where the wrestlers are ranked according to a system that dates back to the Edo period. In the top division (makunouchi), the ranks (in ascending order) are: maegashira, komusubi, sekiwake, ozeki, and yokozuna. Rikishi are promoted or demoted (except for yokozuna) based on their performance in six honbasho (Grand Sumo Tournaments) held throughout the year. In addition to the professional tournaments, exhibition competitions are held at regular intervals every year in Japan. Also, once every two years, the top ranked wrestlers visit a foreign country for such exhibitions.

Ryogoku is a district in Tokyo known as the heartland of sumo where rikishi are a common sight. Of the six professional Grand Sumo Tournaments held every year, Ryogoku Kokugikan stages three in January, May, and September. Opened in 1985, the hall has a seating capacity of 13,000 people. Although it is primarily used to stage sumo tournaments, over the years the venue has also hosted boxing, pro-wrestling, and live concert events. There is a Sumo Museum located on the first floor that displays items linked to sumo, like colored woodblock prints, banzuke tournament record books, and ceremonial aprons worn by the top-ranked rikishi.

The neighborhood is home to several dozen sumo stables where the wrestlers live and train. It is possible to observe sumo practice during the early morning hours but most require advance reservations. There are also several restaurants that feature chanko nabe on their menus. Chanko nabe is a hot pot dish containing a variety of vegetables, seafood, and meat that serves as the staple food for the rikishi. You will be interested to know that many of these restaurants are actually owned and managed by former wrestlers.

A day in Ryogoku will certainly prove to be an interesting one whether you are there to watch a tournament or just explore the area.

The hall is located just one minute away on foot from Ryogoku Station on the JR Sobu Line.

Location(s):   1-3-28, Yokoami, Sumida-ku, Tokyo

Web Page: http://www.sumo.or.jp/en/index

Sumida-ku (墨田区): Sumida Ward

Tokyo Skytree (東京スカイツリー)

Tokyo Skytree is a new television broadcasting and observation tower, which offers shops, restaurants, and an aquarium for visitors to enjoy. It is Tokyo's main landmark and the centerpiece of Tokyo Skytree Town in the Sumida Ward. Located not far from Asakusa, the tower stands at 634 meters (2,080 ft), making it the tallest building in Japan and the second tallest structure in the world after Burj Khalifa in Dubai, which stands at 829.8 meters (2,722 ft). The tower was completed on February 29, 2012 and its main purpose is to relay complete digital broadcasting signals since Tokyo Tower, which stands at 333 meters (1,093 ft), can no longer do so, because it is now surrounded by numerous high-rise buildings. The tower project was led by Tobu Railway and six broadcasting companies headed by NHK.

The base of Tokyo Skytree is constructed like a tripod, extending to a height of about 350 meters (1,150 ft), from which point the tower's structure is cylindrical, offering panoramic views of the Sumida River and the city below. There are observation decks at the 350-meter level (1,150 ft) and at the 450-meter level (1,480 ft). The lower level, the Tembo Deck, has the capacity to hold 2,000 visitors and spans three levels. The top level features tall windows that offer a 360-degree view of the city. There is a large digital touch panel display, which provides information on the various buildings that are visible from the tower. The middle level features a souvenir shop and Musashi Restaurant, which serves Japanese-French fusion cuisine. On the lower level of the Tembo Deck, visitors will find a café and a section of glass flooring giving them a direct view of the streets below.

From the Tembo Deck, visitors can board elevators to the Tembo Gallery located at the 450-meter level (1,480 ft), which can hold 900 visitors. The upper observatory features a spiral, glass-covered skywalk in which visitors ascend the last five meters (16 ft) to the highest point at the upper platform.

At night, Tokyo Skytree is illuminated using LED lights. There are two patterns used: iki (sky blue) and miyabi (purple).

As its opening approached, people reportedly waited in line for a full week to get tickets. By the opening, trips up the tower were fully booked for the first two months of operation. The tower opened to the public on May 22, 2012, drawing a crowd of tens of thousands, despite rainy conditions that blocked the views from the tower's observation decks. Strong winds also forced two elevators to be shut down, leaving visitors briefly stranded. According to Tobu Railway, 1.6 million people visited Tokyo Skytree during its first week of opening.

Although the number of visitors to Tokyo Skytree has declined somewhat since its opening, please do plan ahead for your visit to ensure that you will have an opportunity to visit the observation decks.

Location(s):   1-1-2 Oshiage, Sumida-ku, Tokyo

Web Page: http://www.tokyo-skytree.jp/en/

Taito-ku (台東区): Taito Ward

Asakusa District (浅草)

Located in Tokyo's Taito Ward, Asakusa was once considered the leading entertainment district. Today it is a notable tourist attraction known for its many temples and a place where one can get a genuine sense of what old Tokyo was like.

The 7th century Sensoji Temple is most popular of Asakusa's temples and easily recognized by its Furai Jin-mon (Gate of the Wind God and the Thunder God), adorned with a large red paper lantern that bears the inscription "Kaminari-mon (Thunder Gate)." The temple enjoys a constant flow of visitors and worshippers throughout the year.

Upon approaching the temple, tourists encounter a centuries-old shopping street known as Nakamise, where you can purchase traditional souvenirs and snacks from the local region. Next to the temple grounds is a small amusement park called Hanayashiki, which originally opened as a flower park in 1853 and is the oldest amusement park in Japan.

Aside from Sensoji Temple, visitors to Asakusa can enjoy a cruise down the Sumida River, which departs from a wharf located within a five-minute walk from the temple. Tokyo Skytree is only a 20-minute walk across the Sumida River from Asakusa.

Although it is relatively easy to get around Asakusa on foot, you may consider taking a guided tour of the area in one of the many rickshaws available. A 30-minute tour generally costs around ¥8,000.

An interesting fact about Asakusa is that the area was heavily damaged by U.S. bombing raids during World War II, particularly the March 1945 firebombing of Tokyo. Consequently, there are very few buildings dating back to the pre-1950s. However, one can still find traditional ryokans (guest-houses), homes, and small-scale apartment buildings scattered throughout the district.

With so many religious establishments, there are frequent matsuri (Shinto festivals) in Asakusa, as each temple or shrine hosts at least one matsuri a year, if not every season. The largest and most popular is the Sanja Matsuri in May, when roads are closed from dawn until late evening.

The district is also famous for its senbei (rice crackers), grilled on the spot, flavored with soy and usually wrapped in seaweed. There are many competing shops in the Nakamise arcade serving these delicious treats and the Japanese locals typically purchase packages of senbei as souvenirs for family and friends.

Regardless of what draws you to Asakusa, the district remains one of Tokyo's top destinations for foreigners and locals alike.

Location(s):   Taito-ku, Tokyo

Web Page: http://asakusa-nakamise.jp/e-index.html

Taito-ku (台東区): Taito Ward

Asakusa (浅草) District: Samba Carnival

Every year since 1981, together with samba teams from Brazil, about 4,700 lovers of samba dancing from all over Japan converge on Asakusa the last Saturday in August for what is known as one of the largest events in Tokyo. As a town that grew up around a temple, Asakusa observes many traditional festivals, but the Samba Carnival is a relatively new event. It started when the Mayor of Taito invited the winning group from that year's Rio Carnival to put on a display. The dance trend quickly caught on and samba became a part of Asakusa's rich tradition. As a matter of fact, the district is full of tributes to Brazilian culture and customs, including several of Japan's most popular samba schools.

During this one day event, 30 to 40 teams compete for prizes. The largest of these teams consist of 250 performers. The competition is usually broken into three tiers of dancers classified by their skill level and commitment to the highly technical art of samba dancing. The top league is comprised of dancers who are seriously committed to dancing, those who put on original dances with a high degree of technical skill, and musicians who can expertly play South American percussion instruments. The participants in leagues 2 and 3 are basically there to enjoy dancing the samba and participating in the costume parade.

The event characterized by its gorgeous costumes, intricate floats, and a healthy dose of sultry samba dancing draws more than 500,000 visitors annually. Considerable effort is put into making the costumes and floats. Colorful plumes and thousands of sequins are combined with an enormous amount of originality and creativity to produce fabulous outfits, some of which are so big you can hardly see the performers wearing them! Some teams try to achieve a glamorous spectacle while others go for the funny and ridiculous. Each group is accompanied by its own band, in which drums and Latin-American percussion instruments dominate. Most of the performers are young women, but there are kids, men, and older performers too. Every year, the winning team from the Rio Carnival is invited to Asakusa and they parade alongside the local teams.

A prize is awarded to the best team as determined by the judges and another based on mobile-phone voting by the general public. There are also extra prizes awarded by carnival sponsors. Although the parade is limited to Kaminarimon-dori and Umamichi-dori near Sensoji Temple, there is an overwhelming atmosphere of energy and exuberance throughout Asakusa on the day of the event.

To reach the event, use the Ginza or Toei Asakusa Subway Line exiting at Asakusa Station. Admission to the carnival is free.

Location(s):   Taito-ku, Tokyo

Web Page: http://www.asakusa-samba.org/

Inagi-shi (稲城市): Inagi City

Yomiuri Land (よみうりランド)

The beginning of the holiday season is always punctuated with brilliant light displays setting all of Japan aglow in splendor. One such illumination display takes place at Yomiuri Land in Inagi City, located just 30 minutes by train from central Tokyo.

Opened in 1964, Yomiuri Land is one of the larger and better known amusement parks near Tokyo. Situated on the hillside, it features three rollercoasters, a giant ferris wheel, and bungee jumping facilities. There are also smaller, kid-friendly rides for the younger members of your family as well as an onsen bath, which was added recently to attract older visitors to the park.

During the summer, Yomiuri Land's outdoor, beach-like pool and beer garden are popular with guests. The Giant Sky River (extra charge applies) standing at 82 feet (25 m) high and 1266 feet (386 m) long is the highlight. The park has a total of five pools, most of which get predictably crowded during the hot summer weekends.

Beginning in early November and running through February 15, the Yomiuri Land Jewellumination draws over 300,000 visitors to the park. The event utilizes over three million LEDs to light up the entire park. Even the popular Bandit rollercoaster is lit up! The park is illuminated from 4:00 PM to 8:00 PM daily but the hours are extended until 9:00 PM from December 13-25.

When you are at the park, be sure to scout out the park's mascot, named Land Dog. Popular with kids of all ages, he is supposed to be an alien who landed in Yomiuri Land on his spaceship.

Whether you are a thrill seeker and want to experience the Bandit, the Momonga, or the Miracle Wan Room, or you just want to slowly ride the ferris wheel taking in the breathtaking views of the park glistening with holiday lights below, Yomiuri Land has something for you.

Location(s):   4015-1 Yanokuchi, Inagi-shi, Tokyo

Web Page: http://www.yomiuriland.com/english/

Koganei-shi (小金井市): Koganei City

Edo Tokyo Open Air Architectural Museum
(江戸東京たてもの園)

Have you ever wondered what Tokyo would have looked like today if not for the random acts of nature such as earthquakes and floods and acts of man such as fires, air raids, and city redevelopment? Fortunately, the Edo Tokyo Open Air Architectural Museum, where various historic buildings have been preserved in their original state, can satisfy your curiosity.

The Museum located in Koganei, a suburb of Tokyo, features traditional buildings from the Meiji period (1868-1912) to more recent times, including the elegant home of former Prime Minister Takahashi Korekiyo, pre-war shops, a sento (public bath), western-style buildings, a farm house, and even a koban (police box). Visitors explore the structures and observe the changes in building styles, trends, and lifestyle that catalyzed the transformation of Tokyo into the metropolis it has become.

The Edo Tokyo Open Air Architectural Museum is divided into three distinct areas: center, east, and west, each with a specific theme (historical, suburban, and downtown). Visitors enter the museum through a ceremonial gate commemorating the 2600th anniversary of Japan. Once through the gate, guests can access the center area. Highlights here include the residence of former Prime Minister Takahashi Korekiyo and a traditional Japanese tea house complete with a beautiful garden.

The east area of the museum houses buildings from the late Meiji and early Showa periods including a replica of one of the first izakayas (Japanese-style bars). However, the main attraction seems to be a traditional Japanese sento.

172

The west area of the museum stands in stark contrast to the east and features homes and buildings of the Japanese elite, which reflect a strong western influence. These homes have gas and electric-powered kitchens and lavish western furniture, a luxury afforded only to the privileged. There is also a Showa period photo studio with all of its original equipment intact, where visitors can have their photos taken and developed. Finally, several beautiful Edo-period farmsteads can be seen where daily life is reenacted.

The museum is located in the western part of Koganei Park, Koganei City, just 25 minutes west of Shinjuku Station if traveling by train. Its hours of operation are 9:30 AM to 5:30 PM (4:30 PM from October to March).

Location(s):   3-7-1 Sakura-cho, Koganei-shi, Tokyo

Web Page: http://www.tatemonoen.jp/english/index.html

Tama-shi (多摩市): Tama City

Sanrio Puroland (サンリオピューロランド): Sanrio (Hello Kitty) Theme Park

Along with Tokyo Disneyland and Tokyo DisneySea, Sanrio Puroland, a theme park dedicated to Hello Kitty and various other characters developed by the company, is one of Japan's most popular attractions drawing over 1.5 million visitors annually. Located just 30 minutes from central Tokyo in Tama City, the park is easily accessible via the Odakyu Tama Line, the Keio Sagamihara Line, and the Tama City Monorail (Tama Center Station).

The huge five-story indoor theme park, which opened on December 7, 1990, includes a fully furnished Hello Kitty house (much like Mickey's and Minnie's houses at Disneyland), amusement park type rides, three theaters where various musical productions are presented, a film theater, and a gift shop offering unique and ultra kawaii (cute) Sanrio Puroland brand items and merchandise.

The park also offers several themed restaurants including a sweet shop, a cinnamon shop, a buffet style restaurant, and an automated cafeteria-style restaurant.

During the summer months, there are parades, concerts, and a daily fireworks display.

As Hello Kitty has been Sanrio's most universally popular character and the inspiration for hundreds of products that generate millions of dollars a year in global sales, the park enjoys a steady influx of visitors not only from all over Japan but also from overseas. For Hello Kitty lovers, there can be no better place than Sanrio Puroland!

Location(s):   1-31 Ochiai, Tama-shi, Tokyo

Web Page: http://en.puroland.jp/enjoy_en/

Points of Interest: Kanto Region

Tokyo Station

National Diet Building Tokyo

Tokyo Imperial Palace

Hamarikyu Gardens

Tokyo Tower

Tokyo Skytree

Sensoji Temple Asakusa

Asakusa Rickshaw Tour

Five-Story Pagoda Sensoji Temple Asakusa

Shops Leading Up To Sensoji Temple Asakusa

Shinjuku Gyoen National Park

Asahi Beer Building Asakusa

Sumida River Cruise Terminal Asakusa

Sumida River Cruise

Yakatabune Pleasure Boat Cruise Sumida River

Rainbow Bridge

Fuji Television Headquarters Odaiba

Replica of The Statue of Liberty Odaiba

Gundam Statue Odaiba

Odaiba Takoyaki Museum

Madame Tussauds Wax Museum Odaiba

Yodobashi Electronics Store Akihabara

Meiji Jingu Shrine Shibuya

Takeshita-dori Harajuku

Crepe Shop Takeshita-dori

Clothing Store Takeshita-dori

Wako Department Store Ginza

Yasukuni Shrine Chiyoda Tokyo

Yokohama Marine Tower

Minato Mirai Yokohama

Nippon Maru Minato Mirai Yokohama

Cup Noodles Museum Yokohama

Yokohama Chinatown

Yamashita Park Yokohama

Yokohama Doll Museum

Chubu Region

Aichi Prefecture (愛知県)

Inuyama-shi (犬山市): Inuyama City

Meiji Mura Museum (博物館明治村)

Located just an hour from Nagoya, you will find one of Japan's superb outdoor museums known as Meiji Mura (Meiji Village).

The architectural museum opened in 1965 and displays sixty-seven buildings from the Meiji period (1868-1912), the Taisho period (1912–1926), and the early Showa period (1926–1989). The Meiji period was of particular importance in Japanese history as it marked the end of the country's feudal age and was a time of rapid change. The structures from this period characteristically reflect the influences of Western architecture. Further, these are actual buildings that were moved and reconstructed on the 101-hectare (101 acres) property alongside Lake Iruka. Perhaps the most noteworthy of these is the reconstructed main entrance and lobby of Frank Lloyd Wright's landmark Imperial Hotel, which originally stood in Tokyo from 1923 to 1967. The main structure of the Imperial Hotel was demolished to make way for a new, larger version that stands across from the Imperial Palace today.

Other notable structures include Lafcadio Hearn's summer house from Shizuoka (1868), St. John's Church from Kyoto (1907), and Kyoto's old St. Francis Xavier Catholic Cathedral (1890). Interestingly, the cathedral is available to rent for weddings.

The goal of the museum is to preserve these early historic

examples of Western architecture mixed with Japanese construction techniques and materials. Nine of the buildings displayed here are designated as Important Cultural Assets and nearly all are registered as Tangible Cultural Assets. A majority of the buildings remain empty while others have displays showing the history of the building, period furniture, and other exhibits. There is a steam locomotive, a street car, several shuttle buses, and horse-drawn carriages that transport visitors within the grounds.

Aside from touring the buildings, visitors to the museum can enjoy performances by a kabuki troupe in the Kurehaza Theater and partake in sake tastings in Kyoto's former Nakai Brewery.

Meiji Mura is divided into five areas and touring the park will require a full day. You can reach the park from Nagoya Station via the Meitetsu Inuyama Line, exit Inuyama Station. From there, transfer to a Meitetsu bus to Meiji Mura. The journey will take approximately 20 minutes.

Location(s):   1 Uchiyama, Inuyama-shi, Aichi

Web Page: http://www.meijimura.com/english/index.html

Inuyama-shi (犬山市): Inuyama City

Okashi no Shiro (お菓子の城): Sweets Museum

Located just north of Nagoya in Aichi Prefecture is an amazing sweets museum called Okashi no Shiro. The museum is housed in a 19th-century Neo-Baroque style building and serves not only as a sightseeing spot but also as a hall for parties and weddings.

Inside, beside a winding staircase, you will find a 46-foot (14 m) tall sugar cake, said to be the tallest sugar cake in the world. There is also a Sweets Village featuring 200 works using sugar to depict famous castles and landmarks from around the world as well as various scenes from well-known fairytales.

The museum also houses two restaurants. Cupid's Flower Garden is an all-you-can-eat sweets buffet offering everything from cakes to ice cream, coffee, juice, tea, and the experience of creating your own crepes and parfaits. Cinderella's Restaurant offers a lunch buffet serving such delectable items as roast beef, pasta, pizza, desserts, and juice. Again, this is an all-you-can-eat buffet and there is no time limit enforced. Do note that the lunch buffet is open only on weekends, whereas the sweets buffet is open all week long.

Visitors to Okashi no Shiro can engage in various hands-on experiences, including baking cookies, biscuits, and breads. The museum grows its own fruits in their fruit garden and these can be used in the various baking classes. Another popular experience is dressing up in different costumes and having your photo taken on the museum grounds. Cinderella's Magic Salon offers at least 100 dresses/costumes available to rent as well as accessories such as shoes and floral bouquets. The Magic Salon offers rental tuxedos for men and they even have costumes for tiny infants!

Lastly, you can host your party, corporate event or wedding in Cinderella's Party Hall. The room can accommodate up to 300 people between the hours of 9:00 AM and 8:00 PM and the cost of rental is ¥4,200 per person.

The museum is open from 9:30 AM to 5:00 PM on weekdays (closed Wednesdays and Thursdays) and   9:00 AM to 6:00 PM on weekends. The admission fee is ¥1,200 for adults and ¥900 for children aged three years and older. In addition to the admission charges there are separate fees charged for the various activities so check the web page for specifics.

Location(s):   1-11 Shinkawa, Inuyama-shi, Aichi

Web Page: http://www.okashino-shiro.jp/english.html

Nagoya-shi (名古屋市): Nagoya City

<u>Atsuta Matsuri (Festival)</u>

The 1,900-year-old Atsuta Jingu Shrine is host to 70 festivals throughout the year but the largest and most auspicious of these is the Atsuta Matsuri (Shobu-sai). The shrine, hidden among 1,000-year-old cypress trees, is located in Nagoya in Aichi Prefecture. It is said to be the home of the legendary Kusanagi-no-Tsurugi or the Sacred Sword Kusanagi, one of the three Imperial regalia.

On June 5th of every year, the Atsuta celebration takes place with parades, taiko drumming, martial arts displays, and fireworks. The highlight of the festival is the five Kento Makiwara, large floats decorated with 365 lanterns. These floats are displayed at the entrance gates to the shrine and are lit up between 6:00 PM and 9:00 PM.

The Atsuta festivities begin at 10:00 AM with a special ceremony held in front of the shrine's main sanctuary. Here, the Emperor's messenger and the shrine's priests pay homage to the gods of the shrine. A special dance called the Atsuta Kagura is performed to the tune of Japanese flutes and taiko drums. It is said that this local dance has been performed at the shrine since the shrine's inception 1,900 years ago. The word kagura means god entertainment and refers to a form of Shinto theatrical dance that predates Noh (A major form of classical Japanese musical drama that has been performed since the 14th century). Visitors to the shrine during the matsuri will also have an opportunity to see kyudo (Japanese archery) and kendo (a type of Japanese fencing).

In the evening, night stalls line the temple grounds offering

203

delicious local delicacies and traditional matsuri fare. The fireworks take place at the Jingu Koen (Park) from 7:50 PM to 9:00 PM.

The festival is free to attend and the shrine can easily be accessed via the JR Tokaido Line from Nagoya Station to Atsuta Station.

Location(s):   1-1-1, Jingu, Atsuta-ku, Nagoya, Aichi

Web Page: http://www.atsutajingu.or.jp/jingu/shinto/reis ai.html/

Fukui Prefecture (福井県)

Fukui-shi (福井市): Fukui City

Eiheiji Temple (永平寺)

Located just nine miles east of Fukui City in Fukui Prefecture is Eiheiji Temple, the head temple of the Soto Sect of Zen Buddhism. The temple is a remarkable structure constructed entirely of wood with intricate frescoes decorating its inner walls. It was founded in 1244 by Dogen Zenji, the Buddhist scholar who introduced Soto Zen to Japan in 1228 after studying in China for several years. Eiheiji means the temple of eternal peace.

The temple complex consists of over 70 buildings and structures, each connected by covered walkways. The atmosphere of tranquility one finds here is further enhanced by a stream that flows through the inner courtyards.

It is important to note that unless you are admitted to the meditation programs, the only parts of the temple complex open to tourists are the Treasure Hall (a small museum containing scrolls and statues) and the Entrance Hall housing the information center.

Eiheiji is still an active monastery with about 150 practicing Zen monks. Visitors affiliated with a Soto Zen Buddhist organization can stay at the temple for one or more nights and follow the monks' daily routine.

A one-night stay costs ¥8,000 and includes dinner, a bath, and evening meditation on the first day. The second day starts early at 3:30 AM, and consists of a meditation session, morning service, and breakfast. Requests for overnight stays must be made in advance.

A single tatami mat, measuring 3 ft. by 6 ft. (1m by 1.9m), is laid in rows on a raised platform called tan in a common room. This is where each trainee eats, sleeps, and meditates.

Visitors are expected to dress modestly and keep silent. Each visitor receives a list of rules to which they must adhere. For example, photography of the priests-in-training is strictly prohibited.

The temple can be reached by bus from Fukui Station. There are four buses and the trip is approximately 30 minutes. You can also take a train to Eiheiji-Guchi and then transfer to a connecting bus, which takes about 15 minutes to reach the temple.

Location(s):   5-10 Shihi, Yoshida-gun, Eiheiji-cho

Web Page: http://www.sotozen-net.or.jp/soto/honzan

Katsuyama-shi (勝山市): Katsuyama City

Fukui Prefectural Dinosaur Museum (福井県立恐竜博物館)

When you think about Japan, what comes to mind? Mount Fuji, cherry blossoms, the temples of Kyoto, the ski slopes of Nagano, the bright lights of Tokyo? How about a dinosaur museum? That's right, the Fukui Prefectural Dinosaur Museum, located in Nagaoyama Park in Katsuyama City is about ten minutes by car from Echizen Railway Station. It is considered one of the three largest dinosaur museums in the world along with the Royal Tyrrell Museum of Paleontology in Canada and the Zigong Dinosaur Museum in China. The museum is an active international center of research on dinosaurs with a team of Japanese and foreign specialists in residence.

More dinosaurs have been unearthed in the Katsuyama area of Fukui than anywhere else in Japan. Excavations that began in 1989 have yielded such fossils as the Fukuiraptor, the Fukuisaurus, and the Fukuititan. As a matter of fact, dinosaurs are just about everywhere in town, on the traffic island outside Katsuyama Station and even on manhole covers.

The museum officially opened on July 14, 2000 and consists of four major departments: the exhibit, the educational, the service, and the research departments. Its 320,000 sq. ft. (97,536 m²) of display space feature over 30 complete dinosaur skeletons, plus many partials and other fossils, minerals, rocks, and related exhibits. The building also houses a restaurant, a gift shop, a library, and a special exhibit hall.

A long escalator takes visitors to the lower level where they can view Dino Street, a hallway displaying fossils of some of the earliest known life forms on earth. A bone bed is situated at the

207

end of the hallway and it is a replica of an actual site in Wyoming.

The main exhibition hall located on the floor above, is the museum's primary exhibition space and consists of various dinosaur fossils. Dioramas, including some with robotic dinosaurs, provide visitors with a conceptual look at the dinosaurs' habitats.

The second floor contains exhibits primarily focused on earth sciences, including plate tectonics, rock formation, and precious gems.

The third floor displays the history of life, showing a timeline from the formation of the earth to the present.

There is a Dino Lab with actual fossils on display, which visitors are permitted to handle. Additionally, there is a fossil preparation room where visitors can watch fossils being cleaned and preserved.

Outside, you can find replicas of dinosaurs and their fossils throughout the park grounds, including some cartoonish ones that offer excellent photo opportunities.

The museum is open from 9:00 AM to 5:00 PM. Admission is ¥720 for adults, ¥410 for high school/ college students, and ¥260 for primary/ secondary school students.

Location(s):   51-11 Terao, Muroko, Katsuyama-shi, Fukui

Web Page: http://www.dinosaur.pref.fukui.jp/en/

Gifu Prefecture (岐阜県)

Gifu-shi (岐阜市): Gifu City

Oda Nobunaga Festival

Located just two hours from Tokyo is the historic city of Gifu. On the first Saturday and Sunday in October, the city is host to the annual Nobunaga Festival.

Although he was born in Aichi, Oda Nobunaga, one of the samurai warlords of the Sengoku period, used Gifu Castle to launch his campaign for a unified Japan. He resided in Gifu for nine years until 1576, during which time he moved his headquarters to Azuchi (present day Shiga Prefecture). Just as he was about to realize his dream of unifying the country, Nobunaga was overthrown by his general in 1582 and forced to commit suicide. The event is known as the Honnoji Incident. He was 49 years old at the time of his death.

The Gifu Nobunaga Festival, one of Gifu's most famous festivals, honors the feats and achievements of Oda Nobunaga and draws spectators from all over Japan. As with most festivals in Japan, there are many enjoyable activities and events all weekend long in downtown Gifu City. The most notable activities are the memorial ceremonies that take place at Sofukuji, the Nobunaga family temple, and the samurai warrior processions down Nagarabashi-dori (Gifu's main street).

The procession features several of Japan's famous historic figures including Oda Nobunaga, Lady Nohime (his wife), Toyotomi Hideyoshi (who succeeded Nobunaga), and Luis Frois (Portuguese missionary who befriended Nobunaga). It starts at 12:30 PM from Gifu Station and ends around 2:30 PM at Gifu

City Hall. The entire festival runs from 10:00 AM to 5:00 PM and is free to attend.

The festival is definitely a must see if you want to get a glimpse into Japan's feudal past!

Web Page: www.gifucvb.or.jp/en/02_event/02_06.html

Gujo-shi (郡上市): Gujo City

<u>Gujo Hachiman Castle (郡上八幡城)</u>

Nestled away in the mountains of Gifu Prefecture just north of Nagoya is the unique town of Gujo Hachiman. With its beautiful scenery, small side streets preserved in their original state and the pristine Nagara River that runs through the town, Gujo Hachiman offers visitors a perspective into Japan of a bygone era. The town's many waterways still function in much the same capacity as they did in the 1600s. Local residents utilize them for washing rice, vegetables, and laundry. The townspeople cooperate to keep the canals/ waterways clean and the pure drinking water is a source of local pride.

The town is also known as the capital of plastic food (the replica food samples that you see in shop and restaurant windows throughout Japan). A local resident is credited with having pioneered the production of these familiar items and consequently to date, 80 percent of all plastic food samples are still produced in Gujo Hachiman.

There is a large summer dance festival known as Gujo Odori, which takes place in Gujo Hachiman for a period of thirty-one festival nights, between July and September. The dances continue all through the night during Obon, which is celebrated in mid-August. The summer dance festival originated over 400 years ago and continues strong today.

In early to late November, visitors flock to Gujo Hachiman for another reason. Perched atop a steep mountainside is the beautifully reconstructed Gujo Hachiman Castle, where one can find magnificent views of the surrounding mountains and valleys below. Unlike other castles in Japan, which are typically surrounded by sakura (cherry blossoms), this castle is surrounded by momiji (Japanese maple trees) which are ablaze with the brilliant colors of autumn at this time of year. Between November 8-16, from sunset until 9:00 PM, the momiji are illuminated, allowing spectators a unique opportunity to marvel at the colorful leaves at night.

Gujo Hachiman Castle hosts an annual Autumn Momiji Festival from November 1 to November 24, which features a reenactment of an early Edo period battle as well as a Japanese tea ceremony and taiko drumming.

Visitors to the castle are expected to pay a nominal fee of ¥310 to tour the castle itself but hiking up the mountain to just take in the beautiful scenery is free of charge.

Castle Hours are from 9:00 AM to 5:00 PM (March to May and September to October), 8:00 AM to   6:00 PM (June to August) and 9:00 AM to 4:30 PM (November to February). The castle is closed from December 20 to January 10.

Location(s):   659 Hachiman-cho, Yanagimachi, Gujo-shi, Gifu

Web Page: http://castle.gujohachiman.com/

Ishikawa Prefecture (石川県)

Kaga-shi (加賀市): Kaga City

Yamanaka Onsen (山中温泉)

Founded 1,300 years ago, Yamanaka Onsen is a small resort town along the Kasukenkai Gorge renown for producing the best hot spring waters in the region. Many famous writers and artists, including the famous Edo period poet and traveler Matsuo Basho, have visited the area. The town is also the birthplace of the prominent Japanese Iron Chef, Rokusaburo Michiba. It is a popular tourist spot for both Japanese and foreign travelers to the Ishikawa Prefecture.

The Kasukenkai Gorge runs parallel to the town just a few blocks from the town center. Several bridges including a beautiful wooden bridge at one end and a modern, quirky steel bridge (Ayatori) at the other, cross the gorge. A forested trail leads from either bridge down into the gorge and along the Daishoji River that runs through it, providing a tranquil escape from the town above.

Visitors can choose to patronize the public baths located in Yamanaka's downtown area or travel to the town's larger hotels and ryokans. The main street running through the town has been renovated with buried power lines and traditionally designed storefronts, which afford a quaint view of an old Japanese town.

Yamanaka Onsen is also famous for a variety of local crafts, including Yamanaka Lacquerware. The local lacquerware, characterized by delicate hand-engraved designs, has been produced here for over 400 years. Tourists can find out more about the lacquering process and purchase lacquerware products at the Yamanaka Lacquerware Traditional Industry Museum, which serves both as a shop and exhibition space as well as a training center.

The Yamanaka-bushi folk song, which originated in the port towns of Hokkaido, was brought to Yamanaka by traders stopping over at the nearby Hashidate Port. Sightseers can enjoy performances of the folk song on weekends at the Yamanakaza Theater.

Whether your intent is to stop over for the day to wander the trails and shops or stay at one of the many ryokans and enjoy the rejuvenating onsen waters, a trip to Yamanaka Onsen is highly recommended for those seeking to immerse themselves in Japanese culture and traditions.

Location(s):   Yamanaka Onsen Shimotanimachi, Kaga-shi

Web Page: http://www.yamanaka-spa.or.jp/global/eng/

Kanazawa-shi (金沢市): Kanazawa City

<u>Kenrokuen Garden (兼六園)</u>

Kenrokuen Garden located in Kanazawa City comprises one of the three great gardens in Japan along with the Korakuen Garden in Okayama, and the Kairakuen Garden in Ibaraki.

Kenrokuen actually translates to Six Attributes Garden and it once formed the outer garden of Kanazawa Castle. The garden was expanded over the years and opened to the public in 1871. For a small admission fee, visitors can enjoy the expansive 10 hectares (25 acres) filled with a variety of trees, ponds, waterfalls, and flowers.

Some of the major areas of focus during your visit should include the Kotoji Lantern, the Kasumiga-ike (Pond), the Karasaki Matsu, the Gankou-bashi (Bridge), the Kaisekito Pagoda, the Midori-taki (Green Waterfall), and last but not least, the fountain.

The Kotoji Lantern is easy to spot as it stands on two legs in Kasumiga-ike. The lantern is a modified version of the Yukimi Lantern, which you can find throughout Japan, and is used to light up the surface of the water. The pond and trees surrounding the lantern make this a very scenic and popular spot in Kenrokuen.

The Kasumiga-ike is the largest pond in Kenrokuen. In addition to the Kotoji Lantern, you will find the Uchihashi-tei tea house, the Niji-bashi (Rainbow Bridge), the Karasaki Matsu, and Horai Island here.

The Karasaki Matsu is a black pine tree, which was planted by the 13th Lord Nariyasu. It is said that he brought the seed from

215

the shores of Lake Biwa, the largest freshwater lake in Japan, located in Shiga Prefecture (west-central Honshu). The tree has beautiful, sprawling branches supported by posts to protect them from breaking, especially during the winter when there is heavy snowfall in the region.

The Gankou-bashi is a bridge made of 11 tomuro stones laid out to look like geese flying in formation. It is also called Tortoise Shell Bridge because of the shape of each step.

The 13-ft. (4m) tall Kaisekito Pagoda stands on an island in the center of Hisago-ike, another pond within Kenrokuen. Its six tiers are covered with moss and the stones have a worm-eaten look to them.

Near the pagoda, you will see the Midori-taki. The fall is formed by water flowing out of the Kasumiga-ike into Hisago-ike.

Finally standing approximately 12 feet (3.7 m) high is the garden's fountain, purported to be the oldest fountain in Japan. Water from the Kasumiga-ike feeds the fountain and it is said that its development was for the purpose of sending water to the secondary closure of the castle.

The beauty and tranquility found in a Japanese garden is unmatched and what better place to observe this for yourself other than one of the two great gardens in the country? The garden is open to the public from 7:00 AM to 6:00 PM (March 1 to October 15) and from 8:00 AM to 4:30 PM (October 16 to the end of February).

Location(s):   1-1 Marunouchi, Kanazawa-shi

Web Page: http://www.pref.ishikawa.jp/siro-
                   niwa/kenrokuen/e/index.html

Kanazawa-shi (金沢市): Kanazawa City

Myoryuji (妙立寺)：Ninja Temple

Kanazawa's Tera-machi (Temple District) is home to one of the most interesting temples in Japan. Constructed in 1585, Myoryuji, otherwise known as Ninja-dera (Ninja Temple), is an intricate structure with hidden rooms, secret passageways, concealed staircases, false doors, and other unusual features that have earned it the name, Ninja-dera. There are 23 rooms and 29 staircases to be exact.

The temple was originally situated near Kanazawa Castle but in 1643 it was relocated to Tera-machi just south of the castle. The temple was constructed in this manner in an effort to circumvent the strict building restrictions imposed by the shogun and served as a disguised military outpost. In essence, Myoryuji has nothing to do with ninjas at all but its design is aimed to guard against intruders or an attack.

During the Edo period, the Tokugawa Shogunate prohibited the construction of buildings higher than three stories. When viewed from the outside, the temple appears to be a two-story structure; however, it is actually a four-story building with a seven-layer internal structure. The temple is accessed through an unusual triangular entranceway. A small lookout room on top of the temple, which provides a view across the Kaga plain, was used to detect approaching armies.

There is a secondary entrance to the temple, which can be accessed by a short set of shoji lined steps. The semi-translucent paper steps allowed defenders inside the temple to see the shadows of invaders' feet on the steps. From that point they were able to attack the invaders from inside by poking spears up through the stairs. That same entrance features a trick sliding door and a secret passageway. From inside, if one slides the door open in one direction, it leads outside, but if the door is slid open in the other direction, it reveals a hidden staircase to a secret room. As long as the door to the outside is open (such as when invaders are letting themselves in), the door to that staircase is blocked and hidden.

Today, visitors to the temple can tour the grounds by guided tour. A reservation is highly recommended but you can still experience a guided tour without a reservation. Simply provide your name and you will be given a tour time, unless of course the temple is extremely crowded with visitors that day. Tours are conducted every 30 minutes between 9:00 AM and 4:30 PM.

Location(s):   1-2-12 Nomachi, Kanazawa-shi, Ishikawa

Web Page: http://myouryuji.or.jp/en.html

Kanazawa-shi (金沢市): Kanazawa City

Nagamachi (長町): Samurai District

The city of Kanazawa, located in Ishikawa Prefecture, was once known as the city of canals. These canals served both to supply water and provide a means for transporting goods. Nestled between two canals (Onosho and Kuratsuki) that flow below Kanazawa Castle, you will find Nagamachi, the samurai district. It was once home to the samurai under the control of the Maeda clan who ruled the area.

The samurai who resided in this district were from the middle and upper classes. Their carefully preserved houses surrounded by earthen walls and the old stone pavements make you feel as if you have been transported to the Edo period. People still reside in these houses but some, such as the Nomura family house, are open to the public. Visitors can also visit the Kaga Hanshi, a former stable with an adjacent garden and the Ashigaru Shiryokan, two reconstructed houses that are examples of the modest homes occupied by the foot soldiers or the lowest ranking samurai.

There are also several museums in the area worth visiting. Among them are:

Shinise Kinenkan Museum: A restored Edo period pharmacy that houses local Kanazawa crafts.

Maeda Tosanokami-ke Shiryokan: A museum dedicated to the Maeda family, which features samurai armor and other relics.

If you visit Nagamachi during the winter months you will find that the mud walls are covered with rolls of straw to protect them from the harsh Kanazawa weather. This method is also used to protect the trees in the nearby Kenrokuen Park.

Nagamachi is the perfect destination for those who are passionate about Japan's feudal past and the country's samurai heritage. The district is relatively close to Kanazawa Castle and Myoryuji (Ninja Temple), so why not combine your visit and enjoy a full day in Kanazawa?

Location(s): Nagamachi, Kanazawa-shi, Ishikawa

Nagano Prefecture (長野県)

Chikuma-shi (千曲市): Chikuma City

Mori Shogunzuka Kofun (森将軍塚古墳)

Located in Nagano Prefecture, Chikuma City has an incredible number of historic sites despite its small size. Among these is the Mori Shogunzuka Kofun, a 4th century megalithic tomb located in the hills of Chikuma City. There are approximately 30,000 kofun mound tombs in Japan dating from the 3rd century to the 7th century. Many of the tombs have distinctive, keyhole-shaped mounds that are unique to ancient Japan. The Kofun period (mid-3rd century to early to mid-6th century) derived its name from these tombs.

The Mori Shogunzuka Kofun measures approximately 100 meters (303 ft) long and was designated as a Historic Site in 1971. It was completely excavated, repaired, and rebuilt in the original shape between 1981 and 1991. During the excavation, a pit style stone chamber was found in the rear mound. The floor space of the chamber is presumed to be one of the largest in Japan. Unfortunately, it was plundered by pot hunters who only left behind some fragments of iron weapons, a bronze mirror, and some farming tools. There are 76 smaller tombs and 13 small tumuli surrounding the kofun. It is believed that these were constructed afterwards by the relatives and descendants of the chieftain buried in the main chamber.

At the base of the hill, you will find the Shinano no Sato Historic Park with a replica village from that period along with the Mori Shogunzuka Museum and the Nagano Prefectural Museum of History.

The Shinano no Sato Historic Park replica village features a series of accurately recreated pit-houses, primitive dwellings that were dug into the ground. Aside from providing shelter from Nagano's extreme winters, these structures were also used to store food and for cultural activities.

It is approximately a 20-minute walk from the village to the mound where the kofun is situated. The longer path to the top is comprised of steep slopes and attracts many hikers. The designated short cuts are even steeper and more precarious to navigate, so do use caution.

The village and kofun are open to the public free of charge. The museums contain exhibits of items unearthed during the excavations and provide a detailed look into what life was like during that period. A small admission fee is charged.

Web Page: http://www.city.chikuma.lg.jp/

(Chikuma City Web Page with link to Mori Shogunzuka Kofun/ English translation available)

Hakuba-mura (白馬村): Village of Hakuba

Located in the Northern Alps of Nagano Prefecture is one of Japan's most popular ski resort towns, Hakuba. With an annual snow fall of over 36 feet (11 m), the town was selected as the main venue for the 1998 Winter Olympics. Some of the Olympic facilities still remain in use today, including the Hakuba Ski Jumping Stadium and the Hakuba Olympic Village Memorial Hall, a small museum located within walking distance from the ski jump. Hakuba boasts more than ten ski resorts with a wide variety of terrains catering to everyone from beginners to experts and its bars and restaurants are some of the best you will find in the prefecture.

During the spring, summer, and autumn months known as the green season, visitors flock to Hakuba for its cool temperatures and popular water sports including boating, sport fishing, wakeboarding, and windsurfing. There are three freshwater lakes (Aoki-ko, Nakatsuna-ko, and Kizaki-ko), that attract fishermen from all over Japan. Most of the ski resorts operate their lifts during the summer months allowing visitors easy access to higher elevations. There is a trail popular with mountain bikers, which extends above the Hakuba Happo-one resort to a small pond offering spectacular views of the local alpine peaks. Just a few hours further up the trail lies the peak of Karamatsu-yama on the main ridge of the Northern Alps, a popular spot for hikers.

The top ski run located at the Hakuba Goryu Ski Resort transforms into an alpine garden during the summer and attracts many visitors. There is a trail from this area that takes you to a viewpoint just 50 minutes away. A little further, you will find the peak of Goryu-yama. From the Tsugaike Kogen Ski

Resort, you can take a ropeway to a wetland area, which has been designated as a National Treasure. From there, you can follow another trail leading up to Shirouma-yama.

Hakuba is also home to several onsens (Japanese hot spring baths), which can help take the chill away after a long day on the slopes. Onsens are a popular destination for many native Japanese and something to experience at least once if you are a visitor to this magnificent country! The following is a brief list of onsens in the area:

Echoland No Yu	http://www.wadanohousehakuba.com/EcholandOnsen.html
Tokyu Onsen (Tokyu Hotel)	http://www.hakuba-r.tokyuhotels.co.jp/english/
Shobei No Yu (Mominoki Hotel)	http://www.mominokihotel.com/index-e.html
Kurashita No Yu	http://www.kurashitanoyu.com/
Mimizuku No Yu	http://hakuba-happo-onsen.jp/mimizukunoyu/
Juro No Yu	http://mall.hakubamura.net/juro/

Hakuba is centrally located to Osaka, Nagoya, and Tokyo and easily accessible via the Hokuriku Shinkansen. During the winter months, a highway express bus operates six round-trips per day between Shinjuku and Hakuba. The one-way trip takes about four and a half hours and costs ¥4,850 yen.

Web Page: http://www.hakubatourism.jp/abouthakuba/
             (Hakuba Tourism)

Karuizawa-machi (軽井沢町): Town of Karuizawa

Rising 3,280 feet (1,000 m) above sea level, the resort town of Karuizawa in the highlands of Nagano Prefecture is the perfect destination to escape the heat and humidity that plagues Japan during the summer months. Easily accessible via the Hokuriku Shinkansen from Tokyo Station and with average summer temperatures hovering around 77°F (25°C), Karuizawa is the preferred destination of many of Japan's affluent, who own summer homes here. Even John Lennon and Yoko Ono spent time here in the 1970s!

Located at the foot of the active volcano, Mount Asama, Karuizawa offers cool, fresh mountain air and stunning views. The town was first discovered and promoted as a mountain resort by westerners living in Japan in the late 1800s. Today, what was once considered an upscale resort town for the rich and famous is easily accessible and can be enjoyed by everyone. The exclusive hotels and elegant second houses of the rich are still here, but the town also has a relaxed and casual atmosphere and is a joy to explore either on foot or by bicycle.

The main shopping street is known as Ginza-dori (the old Karuizawa Street/ Kyu-Karuizawa) and is located about a half mile north of the train station. The street is lined with cafés, restaurants, interesting souvenir shops, and food stalls. The street is known as Ginza-dori because branches of stores from Tokyo's famous Ginza district open here during the summer months. Also on this street, you will find a little bakery called France Bakery. It is a must see for any Beatles fan, as this is the bakery John Lennon frequented. Karuizawa is also famous for its food, especially its local fruit jams and honey. Definitely check out the famous croquettes and the local European-style sausages while you are here.

There is also a sprawling outlet mall called Karuizawa Prince Shopping Plaza near the train station (south exit side), where you can indulge in some retail therapy in any one of the 200 shops and restaurants. The surrounding area includes camp grounds, hiking trails, horseback riding trails, golf courses, and tennis courts and is perfect for those who love the great outdoors.

Japan's version of Germany's Romantic Road stretches over 217 miles from Ueda City in Nagano Prefecture through the mountains of Gunma Prefecture to Utsunomiya City in Tochigi Prefecture. Karuizawa is located along Japan's Romantic Road and is a nice place to enjoy the autumn colors around mid-October to early November.

Naka-Karuizawa is the secondary town center and, although it has fewer shops and restaurants than Kyu-Karuizawa, it contains several other interesting sites. In particular, Harunire Terrace is a trendy, upscale shopping and dining area built on a wooden terrace and surrounded by a forest. It features an array of restaurants and boutiques, housed in attractive rows of shops with wooden facades. But please take note that Harunire Terrace can get quite crowded during meal times, especially during the weekends. There are also several museums and parks with additional recreational spaces to take advantage of.

Shiraito Waterfall, which literally means "the waterfall of white threads," is 9 feet (2.9 m) high and 229 feet (70 m) wide. It is located in the forests north of downtown Karuizawa and is a popular sightseeing spot. John Lennon, Yoko Ono, and their son Sean were photographed here during their stay in Karuizawa.

Although Karuizawa is a favorite summer destination for many, keep in mind that it draws visitors year-round with opportunities to ski, golf, hike, or just relax in the cool and calm atmosphere.

Web Page: http://www.jnto.go.jp/eng/location/regional/n agano/karuizawa.html
(Japan National Tourism Organization/ Karuizawa)

Karuizawa Museums

Nagano's highland resort town of Karuizawa is just 70 minutes via the Hokuriku Shinkansen (bullet train) from Tokyo Station and offers much to see and do.

For art and history buffs, Karuizawa has a wide selection of impressive museums to choose among.

Exiting Karuizawa Station and heading southwest, you will find the Karuizawa Taliesin, one of Karuizawa's largest leisure parks situated near Lake Shiozawa (Shiozawa-ko in Japanese). The park is home to three museums, five historic buildings, a rose garden, and six restaurants and cafés. The three museums are the Musée Peynet, the Kouko Fukazawa Nonohana Flower Museum, and the Literary Museum of Karuizawa.

There are four museums in the world dedicated to the work of Raymond Peynet, a French graphic artist born in 1908. There are two museums in France (Antibes and Brassac les Mines) and two in Japan (Karuizawa and Mimasaka). The Karuizawa museum is housed in a building that was designed in 1933 by Czech-born U.S. architect Antonin Raymond. In front of the building, a bronze statue dedicated to Peynet's Lovers can be found. The facility also contains a pottery shop, restaurant, and boutique where books, pottery, posters, and jewelry are sold.

The Kouko Fukazawa Nonohana Flower Museum is an art gallery dedicated to the works of the painter Kouko Fukazawa (1903-1993). The gallery is housed in a stately, old wooden building that began life in 1911 as the Karuizawa Post Office.

Finally, the Literary Museum of Karuizawa contains a collection of manuscripts and correspondence from writers connected with Karuizawa. Completed in 1985, the building was designed by GK Sekkei, an architecture firm headquartered in Tokyo, formed by a group of students who studied under pioneering Japanese designer Koike Iwataro.

Just down the street from Karuizawa Taliesin, you will find the Karuizawa Picture Book Forest Museum. The building was constructed in 1886 by a Scottish missionary, A.C. Shaw, who sought inspiration from the Forest of Muse. Today, the museum houses 6,000 items consisting largely of western works of pictorial literature and children's books including a number of first editions and rare printings, which are spread across three buildings. The museum grounds also include a book shop, a garden shop, and a large central garden.

Venturing north of Karuizawa Station, you will encounter the Karuizawa New Art Museum (KaNAM). The museum is dedicated to post-war Japanese and foreign modern art. The glass building was designed by Japanese architect, Rikuo Nishimori, and opened in 2012. The white supports on the exterior and interior represent the local forests. The museum includes an art shop and an Italian restaurant, Ristorante Pietrino.

Located near the Sengataki Waterfall, you will find the Sezon Museum of Modern Art. The museum houses a collection of modern art works by world-famous artists from the early 20th century to the present. The museum's collection consists of 500 pieces that are selectively exhibited to the public during spring and summer. For your convenience, you will find a terrace café and a museum gift shop on the premises as well.

Finally, a museum worth the trip is the Hiroshi Senju Museum. Hiroshi Senju is an internationally renowned painter who has created large-scale paintings for locations such as the Grand Hyatt Tokyo and Haneda Airport. The building was designed and built by the architect Ryue Nishizawa and can best be described as a clean, elegant collection of exhibition spaces harmoniously set among beautiful natural backdrops both inside and out.

This is just the tip of the iceberg as there are a number of smaller museums that house private collections and cater to many different interests. Karuizawa is a lush, cool, and beautiful place to visit where many of Japan's wealthy own elegant summer homes. The central part of the town is stylishly laid out with restaurants, cafés, and boutiques and is worth visiting once you have toured the various museums in the area. The best way to tour Karuizawa is to plan an overnight stay and take full advantage of everything this resort town has to offer.

Location(s):   217 Shiozawa, Kitasaku-gun, Karuizawa-machi,
                    Nagano
                    (Karuizawa Taliesin)

Web Page: http://www.karuizawataliesin.com/

Matsushiro-machi (松代): Town of Matsushiro

<u>Matsushiro Underground Imperial Headquarters</u>
(松代大本営跡)

Over a million people visit the capital city of Nagano in Nagano Prefecture annually. The city was built around Zenkoji Temple, one of Japan's most popular temples and in 1998, hosted the Winter Olympic Games. Located just half a mile south of Nagano City, you will find the pleasant, former castle town of Matsushiro. The city is recognized for its samurai houses, gardens, museums, and for a tourist attraction known as the Matsushiro Underground Imperial Headquarters.

The Imperial Headquarters is a massive underground bunker complex built during World War II. As the tide of war began to turn, an absolute national defense zone was set by the military in September 1943 identifying an area that they had to secure at any cost. However, when Saipan, Mariana Islands, the most important strategic point within the zone fell in July of 1944, the decision was made to transfer the Imperial Palace, the army headquarters, and other important governmental departments to Matsushiro.

Construction of the bunker began on November 11, 1944 and continued until Japan's surrender on August 15, 1945. At the time, construction was 75 percent complete with 63,040 sq. ft. (5,857 m²) of floor space excavated. In total, 7,000 Koreans and 3,000 Japanese laborers worked three eight-hour shifts and later two twelve-hour shifts to build the complex at a cost of ¥200,000,000. The complex, designed specifically to withstand B-29 bombings, was an interlinked series of tunnels underneath several mountains. The plan was to have the facilities for the

Imperial General Headquarters and Palace constructed under Mount Maizuru, the military communications under Mount Saijo, government agencies, NHK and central telephone facilities under Mount Zozan, the residences of the Imperial Family under Mount Minakami, and the Imperial Sanctuary under Mount Kobo.

Although the bunker was never used as originally intended, it was utilized by other agencies after the war. In 1947, the Meteorological Agency set up a seismographic office in the concrete building that was constructed at Mount Maizuru. An assortment of seismographs and equipment was installed making it the largest office of its kind in Japan. In 1967, the Matsushiro Earthquake Center was set up following a local earthquake. In 1990, parts of the Mount Zozan bunker were opened by the Nagano Municipality, and Shinshu University set up an astronomical observatory inside.

Today, the complex is administered by Nagano City's Sightseeing Bureau. Visitors are permitted to explore the first 500 meters (1,640 ft) of tunnels under Mount Zozan; the rest of the facility is off limits to the public. Comprised mostly of those interested in war-time history and school children learning about the local history, the complex hosts over 100,000 visitors annually.

Location(s):   Nishijo 479 – 13, Matsushiro-machi, Nagano

Web Page: http://www.matsushiro.org/daihonei/

Nagano-shi (長野市): Nagano City

Chibikko Ninja Mura (チビッ子忍者村): Kids' Ninja Village

Say the word "ninja" and you will instantly have the undivided attention of locals and tourists alike in Japan. Legends surrounding ninja culture are well known around the world and one of the best places to learn about these stealthy fighters is Nagano, where deep within the forested mountains, ninja masters perfected their craft. The Togakushi area of Nagano is the legendary home of the Togakure School of Ninja, which was active during Japan's Sengoku period or the Warring States period. Today, the area is home to the Togakure Ninpo Museum and the Chibikko Ninja Mura (The Children's Ninja Village).

It is said that during the 12th century, a warrior from Nagano fled to Iga in Mie Prefecture after fighting on the losing side of the war between the Minamoto and the Taira clans. Iga was considered the birthplace of the ninja and the warrior acquired his skills there before returning to Nagano to start his own school. The Togakure Ninpo Museum memorializes the local Togakure School of Ninja. Located just an hour by bus northwest of central Nagano City, the museum includes several buildings that showcase the tools and weapons used by the Togakure Ninja. There is also an interesting photo exhibit of the ninja practicing various techniques of warfare.

One of the buildings is a ninja house, appearing rather ordinary on the outside but built with numerous secret doors, passages, and contraptions on the inside. There is also a shuriken (throwing star) range. For a nominal fee, visitors can try their hand throwing shuriken at target boards.

The Children's Ninja Village is a ninja theme park featuring a maze, a ninja slalom, obstacle courses, and jungle gyms, where visitors can pretend to undergo ninja training. You can really get into the spirit by renting ninja costumes in either red or black, children or adult's sizes, before taking part in your training. The costumes have to be returned before departing the park but the souvenir shop has ninja costumes for sale so you can relive the ninja experience after returning home.

If you get hungry, there is a restaurant on the premises serving tasty hot dogs, burgers, curry, and soft- serve ice cream. The menu also includes a variety of ninja- themed sweets that are particularly popular with visitors.

The park operates from late April through late November between the hours of 9:00 AM and 5:00 PM. It is closed on Thursdays except during summer vacation from mid-July to the end of August, when it is open daily. The area is prone to heavy snowfall, necessitating the closure of the park during the remainder of the year.

Location(s):   3193 Togakushi, Nagano-shi, Nagano

Web Page: http://www.ninjamura.com/english

Obuse-machi (小布施町): Town of Obuse

Nagano Prefecture located in the Chubu region has some of the world's most impressive highland areas. Many visitors to the prefecture come for its mountain resorts and hot springs. However, visitors to Obuse, a town located in the Kamitakai district, are drawn there for quite a different reason.

Located 150 miles (241 km) north of Tokyo, Obuse is an artistic town known for its galleries, museums, and craft shops. The town was the home of Katsushika Hokusai, a renowned Edo period (1603-1867) woodblock painter, best known for his ukiyoe woodblock print, The Great Wave off Kanagawa, who spent the later years of his life here. It is said that Hokusai created many of his finest works while working at his studio in Obuse. A nice selection of Hokusai's woodblock prints, watercolors, painted manuscripts, and two festival floats are on display at the Hokusai Museum (Hokusai-kan), one of three major museums in town.

The other major museums in Obuse include the Obuse Museum Nakajima Chinami Gallery and the Takai Kozan Memorial Museum. The Obuse Museum was established in 1992 and displays 400 pieces from Japanese painter Chinami Nakajima. Nakajima is best known for his flower and bird motifs as well as for his very striking wood block prints. Sculpture and metal works by Fuminori Haruyama are also included in the museum's holdings. The Takai Kozan Memorial Museum is the restored former residence of Takai Kozan, a wealthy local merchant, who sponsored Hokusai to come to Obuse. During the Edo period, his home was known as the cultural salon, drawing countless contemporary intellectuals. Katsushika Hokusai, Sakuma Shozan, Kusaka Genzui, and Fujimoto Tetsuseki were all regular visitors to the home. The museum has sketches by Hokusai and houses the Hekiiken studio built specifically for the artist. Takai was also a talented artist in his own right and his sketches and calligraphy are also on display along with brushes and other personal possessions.

For the grownups, Obuse has several sake shops and wineries worth visiting. European grapes, such as Merlot, Chardonnay, and Pinot Noir are produced in Nagano as the region's climate is very similar to the areas of Europe where these grapes originated. The town's two major sake breweries are Masuichi and Matsubaya.

Finally, Obuse is known for its delicious chestnuts and the confections that are created from them. As a matter of fact, the town's sidewalks were created using the wood from old chestnut trees.

Nagano is accessible from Tokyo Station via the Hokuriku Shinkansen (bullet train). The journey takes 1 hour and 20 minutes. From Nagano City, take the Nagano Dentetsu (local train) to Obuse, an additional 30 minutes' travel.

Web Page: http://www.town.obuse.nagano.jp/

http://www.book-navi.com/hokusai/hokusai-e.html (Hokusai Museum)

http://www.obusewinery.com/ (Obuse Winery)

Shinano-machi (信濃町): Town of Shinano

<u>Lake Nojiri (野尻湖)</u>

Lake Nojiri (Nojiri-ko), an ancient glacial lake, is located about 12 miles (19 km) north of Nagano City in the town of Shinano, Nagano Prefecture. It is Nagano's second largest lake next to Lake Suwa and the spot where Japanese residents have been secretly sneaking off to for years and where many own summer houses in the kokusaimura (international village) area.

Following Japan's long isolation period, Christian missionaries living in Japan would run off to Nagano's Northern Alps to escape the region's hot summers. Later, during the Taisho period, many of these foreign missionaries began to come to Lake Nojiri instead to avoid the growing crowds at Karuizawa. Subsequently, an international village arose on the shores of the lake, which is still a popular summer resort today.

When you visit the area, you will find a lively and diverse foreign community, friendly locals, great fresh food, and a host of water sports that draw locals and foreigners alike. During the summer months, water skiing, swimming, golfing, wakeboarding, wind-surfing, pleasure boating, cycling, hiking, and fishing are very popular. In late summer, visitors can witness over a million cosmos flowers in bloom in Kurohime Kogen (Kurohime Plateau). The flowers bloom in just about every color of the rainbow and are a spectacular sight. The lake is also host to the Lake Nojiri Hanabi Matsuri (fireworks festival), which takes place every year at the end of July. In the winter months, visitors can try their hand at Japanese smelt fishing in a heated boat while sipping warm shochu (A Japanese distilled beverage typically distilled from rice, barley, sweet potatoes, buckwheat, or brown sugar).

For the history buffs, the Togakushi Shrine nestled among 900-year-old cedar trees is just a 30-minute drive from Lake Nojiri. Approximately one hour away, you will find the Zenkoji Buddhist Temple. Built in the 7th century, it is perhaps most famous for its involvement in the battles between Uesugi Kenshin and Takeda Shingen in the 16th century, when it served as one of Kenshin's bases of operations.

In 1948, a tooth fossil of an Asian straight-tusked elephant (known as the Naumann Elephant) was discovered at Lake Nojiri. Consequently, there is a museum that exhibits the Naumann Elephant fossils as well as fossils of big-horned deer that roamed the area 40,000 years ago during the Jomon period. You will also find an assortment of stone and bone tools on display. (Address: 287-5 Nojiri)

You can access Lake Nojiri via the Hokuriku Shinkansen (bullet train) from either Tokyo or Ueno Stations. By car, take Route 18 or the Joshin-etsu Expressway between Nagano and Joetsu City and look for the turn-offs to Lake Nojiri.

Location(s):   Shinano, Kamiminochi-gun, Nagano

Suwa-shi (諏訪市): Suwa City

<u>Lake Suwa Fireworks</u>

Lake Suwa (Suwa-ko) located in the central part of Nagano Prefecture is the 23rd largest lake in Japan with an area of 13 square kilometers (5 mi²) compared to the 670 square kilometers (259 mi²) occupied by Japan's largest fresh water lake, Lake Biwa, located in Shiga Prefecture. An interesting phenomenon takes place at Lake Suwa during winter, something that is referred to as Omiwatari (The God's Crossing). There is a natural onsen (hot spring) located under the lake's surface that causes pressure ridges to form on the surface of the lake. When the lake's surface freezes during winter, the warm onsen waters beneath the lake circulate, forming these ridges, which can reach heights of 30 centimeters (12 in) or more!

That is not the only thing Lake Suwa is famous for. During mid-August of each year, a grand fireworks festival is held in the Kamisuwa district. Fireworks festivals during the summer months are highly regarded in Japan, just like the blooming sakura (cherry blossoms) in the spring. Hanabi means flowers of fire and like the cherry blossoms their existence is very brief. Hailed as the largest fireworks festival in the world with 40,000 shells detonated, the Lake Suwa Fireworks Festival draws over 350,000 spectators. (The largest fireworks festival in Tokyo, held over the Sumida River uses only 20,000 shells.)

The event, which began shortly after World War II in an effort to uplift spirits in postwar Japan, lasts two hours. The finale features a 2 kilometer (1.2 mi) long waterfall of cascading sparkles, which draws gasps from the spectators as the sounds of the detonating shells echo off the surrounding Japanese Alps.

Lake Suwa is accessible via the JR Chuo Line. Exit at Kamisuwa Station and your destination is a short 8-minute walk from that point.

Web Page: http://www.suwako-hanabi.com/

Suwa-shi (諏訪市): Suwa City

Suwa Onbashira Festival

Japan is known for its festivals and events such as the Enshu Arai Tezutsu Hanabi (Arai Hand-held Cannon Fireworks Festival), is a true demonstration of masculinity. However, in my opinion, one of the most dangerous demonstrations of masculinity is a 1,200-year old matsuri celebrated in the Suwa Region of Nagano Prefecture.

The Onbashira (御柱) is a festival held every six years in Lake Suwa, which draws over 500,000 spectators. The matsuri lasts ten weeks (April 1 to June 15) and consists of two segments: Yamadashi and Satobiki. The literal translation of "Onbashira" is "the honored pillars" and entails men riding massive logs measuring 55 feet (17 m) in length and weighing 20,000 pounds (9,072 kg), as they slide down perilous slopes toward Suwa Taisha.

Following a Shinto purification ceremony, carefully selected logs are chopped down using axes that are specially manufactured for this occasion. During Yamadashi, teams of men drag the logs down the mountain towards Suwa Taisha, which is one of the oldest shrines in existence. The event during which the men prove their bravery by riding the logs down the treacherous, rough terrain is known as Kiotoshi.

The second part of the festival known as Satobiki involves parading 16 logs through the narrow streets and symbolically placing them into the corner posts of the foundations of the four shrine buildings at Suwa Taisha. The idea is that by replacing the pillars every six years, the area around the shrine is renewed spiritually. For those of you who were watching, you may recall that this ritual was performed as part of the opening ceremonies of the 1998 Nagano Winter Olympics.

The journey from the mountain side to the shrine is approximately six miles and requires three days to complete.

The Onabashira has been held without fail for 1,200 years. The most recent festival was in 2016 with the next one slated for 2022. If you would like to watch this amazing event in person, do note that participation in Onbashira is not open to outsiders!

Location(s):   Suwa Taisha, Nagano

Web Page: http://www.go-nagano.net/shisetsu-
                       detail?shisetsuid=6022004

Niigata Prefecture (新潟県)

Myoko-shi (妙高市): Myoko City

Myoko Happiness Illumination

There are countless, marvelous holiday illumination events taking place in Japan during the winter months, but do you know that there is an equally grand illumination event that takes place during the summer? Located in Myoko-shi, Niigata, the Myoko Happiness Illumination is a large-scale summer illumination event that runs from early August through mid-November.

The event takes place at the APA Resort Joetsu Myoko, located in Myoko City. The resort is popular for its indoor and outdoor onsens (hot spring baths), an 18-hole golf course, and its stunning mountain scenery. The Myoko Happiness Illumination event takes advantage of the resort's vast grounds to create amazing images using 1.2 million bidirectional LED lights. The illumination event also features the Gate of Happiness, the Wishing Bell, and the world's largest tunnel of light measuring 984 feet (300 m).

At the 8th hole on the golf course, there is a three-dimensional illumination display called dragon eggs. It is a fantastic light and sound show that is designed to stimulate all five of your senses.

Visitors can also take advantage of the various food and souvenir booths set up nearby and enjoy some limited edition and local specialties.

The event hours are 5:00 PM to 10:00 PM and there is an admission charge of ¥1,000 (¥900 if tickets are purchased in advance).

If you are fortunate enough to visit Japan during the summer months, do take advantage of the fabulous fireworks displays that Japan is known for and include a visit to this amazing illumination event as well.

The resort is accessible from Tokyo via the Marunouchi Line toward Ikebukuro; from there transfer to the Hokuriku Shinkansen towards Nagano, and then transfer to the JR Shinetsu Main Line towards Naoetsu. Disembark at Sekiyama Station. The entire journey requires approximately four hours.

Location(s):   1090 Okemi, Myoko-shi, Niigata

Web Page: http://www.apahotel.com/myoko/

Sado Island (佐渡ヶ島)

Earth Celebration Music Festival

Every year since 1988, Sado Island in Niigata Prefecture has been the host of Earth Celebration, an international music festival held to celebrate global culture. The event is organized by Kodo, a professional taiko drumming troupe based on Sado Island.

Since their debut at the Berlin Festival in 1981, Kodo has single handedly popularized taiko drumming, both in Japan and abroad. They regularly tour Japan, Europe, and the United States and since their debut they have given over 4,000 performances. Although the main focus of the performance is taiko drumming, other traditional Japanese musical instruments such as fue and shamisen are included during the traditional dance and vocal performances.

Earth Celebration is a three-day event held in mid to late August in Ogi Town located on the southern coast of Sado Island. Thousands of people come from all over Japan and overseas to attend the event, whose central attraction is its three main concerts, one held each night of the festival at Shiroyama Park. The first night's concert features Kodo, while the second night's concert features various guest performers. The third night is a collaboration featuring both Kodo and the guest performers.

In addition to the main concerts at night, there are a number of events that take place during the day. Special performances, called fringe concerts, are held at various venues around town, with many taking place at the Kisaki Shrine. The festival program also features numerous workshops, such as taiko drum and Japanese flute making, taiko drumming, and traditional

Sado dance. These workshops require advance registration and most include a participation fee of ¥3,000 - 5,000.

Other festival activities include boat rides around Ogi Harbor in taraibune (tub-shaped boats characteristic of Sado Island) and the Ogi Okesa dance, which follows the concert on the second night. This traditional Sado dance is performed by Ogi townspeople and everyone is invited to participate. Harbor Market takes place every day from 10:00 AM to 10:00 PM at Ogi Harbor. Dozens of small shops and food stands create a small tent city where you can shop and enjoy food from around the world.

General admission is ¥5,200 per day, students aged 15-24 is ¥3,500 per day (¥3,800 at the door), and children (14 and under) are admitted free.

Web Page: http://www.kodo.or.jp/ec/

Shizuoka Prefecture (静岡県)

Kosai-shi (湖西市): Kosai City

Enshu Arai Tezutsu Hanabi: Arai Handheld Cannon Fireworks

Summer in Japan means festivals and just about every city and town has one. But no summer in Japan would be complete without fireworks. Japanese hanabi (fireworks), which many argue are the world's most gorgeous and elaborate, are displayed each year during July and August in festivals held throughout the country. However, nothing compares to the Enshu Arai Tezutsu Hanabi – Arai Handheld Cannon Fireworks.

Arai (新居町) was a town located in the Hamana district of Shizuoka Prefecture. On March 23, 2010, Arai was merged into the city of Kosai and thus no longer exists as an independent municipality. The Hamana district was dissolved as a result of this merger but the fireworks festival is still referred to as the Arai Handheld Cannon Fireworks Festival. The tradition has been carried over from generation to generation for well over 300 years. All of the cannons are hand made by each of the villagers according to instructions handed down by their elders.

The tezutsu (cannons) are constructed by cutting bamboo, wrapping them in tatami mats, clearing the inside of the bamboo tubes, and finally, on the day before the fireworks, a specialist adds the chemicals for the firework itself.

Enshu Arai Tezutsu Hanabi is an integral part of the Suwa Shrine Festival. On the evening of the fireworks, a special fire is lit at Suwa Jinja and candles ignited by this fire are handed over to the leaders of each fireworks group. They carry the lit candles in lanterns to their respective groups and use them to carefully light the cannons.

The climax of the festival is the Sarutahiko Enka. One man dressed like a tengu (goblin with a long nose) along with 1,000 participants ignite their handheld firework cannons and dance in the sparks created. Large columns of sparks light up the night sky. It is truly amazing!

Additional information about the festival can be obtained from The Japan National Tourist Organization (10th floor, Tokyo Kotsu Kaikan Bldg., 2-10-1, Yurakucho, Chiyoda Ward, Tokyo; (03) 3201-3331).

Location(s):   Arai Elementary School, Arai-cho, Kosai, Shizuoka

Susono-shi (裾野市): Susono City

<u>Fuji Safari Park (富士サファリパーク)</u>

When most people think of safaris, I am almost certain that no one would think of the lowlands around the snow-capped peak of Mount Fuji in Japan! Yet, the Fuji Safari Park in Susono City located at the foot of Mount Fuji in Shizuoka Prefecture offers just that!

The Fuji Safari Park opened in 1980 and was the first safari-style attraction of its kind in Japan. The park is divided into two zones: The Safari Zone and The Free Contact Zone. The latter is a zoo with enclosures for smaller mammals and a petting station. The Safari Zone is divided into seven sections that house bears, lions, tigers, cheetahs, elephants, and rhinos. Visitors can tour these sections in several ways including their own car, a rental vehicle, or a bus.

The buses are decorated to resemble animals and contain wire netting over the windows. Passengers are provided with vegetables, pellets, and meat that they can feed to the animals at close range. There is an additional charge for taking the bus, which includes the food to feed the animals. If you drive your own car through the park, you are instructed to keep your car windows and doors locked at all times and it is easy to understand why. If you encounter a problem, rangers in SUVs are present to help. It takes approximately 30 minutes to drive through each of the seven sections. There are 4WD sport utility vehicles equipped with a navigation system available to rent as well. The rental fee is ¥5,000 and the vehicles seat up to seven passengers. A valid driver's license recognized by Japan is required for renting these vehicles.

From April through October, the park offers a night safari. Visitors are provided with night vision equipment to observe the animals in their nocturnal setting.

For an additional fee, visitors can participate in horse drawn cart rides, pony rides, and have their pictures taken with baby animals. There are also cat, dog, and rabbit houses, and a guinea pig area where visitors can spend time holding and playing with the different animals.

If you get hungry, there is a large canteen-type family restaurant on the premises. There are also several food stalls selling everything from hot dogs to shaved ice. If you choose to pack your own picnic lunch, there are many benches and outdoor seating where you can enjoy your meal.

And, you need not leave the park empty handed as there is a nice souvenir shop too.

The safari park is easily accessible via the Tokaido Shinkansen, exit Mishima Station. From there, it is about a 30-minute ride to the park.

Location(s):   2255-27 Aza Fujiwara, Susono-shi, Shizuoka

Web Page: http://www.fujisafari.co.jp/english/

Yamanashi Prefecture (山梨県)

Fujiyoshida-shi (富士吉田市): Fujiyoshida City

Fuji-Q Highland (富士急ハイランド)

Located just at the foot of Mount Fuji is one of Japan's most popular theme parks, Fuji-Q Highland. The park owes its popularity to its roller coasters and anime-themed rides and attractions. The theme park's centerpiece is the Fujiyama roller coaster which opened in 1996. It stands at 259 feet (79 m) tall and can reach speeds of 80 miles (129 km) per hour. At the time of its opening, it was considered the world's tallest and fastest roller coaster. In 2001, the park introduced Dodonpa, which was capable of reaching speeds of 106 miles (171 km) per hour, making it the park's fastest roller coaster and the world record holder for the fastest acceleration. Five years later, in 2006, the park opened yet another roller coaster called Eejanaika. This roller coaster is only the second 4th dimension roller coaster ever constructed, the first one being X² at Six Flags Magic Mountain in California. Eejanaika is 249 feet (76 m) tall and accelerates to speeds of up to 78 miles (126 km) per hour. In 2011, the park once again introduced a new roller coaster, this time, unveiling the Takabisha, the steepest roller coaster in the world with a 121-degree free fall. It stands at 141 feet (43 m) high and can reach speeds of 62 miles (100 km) per hour.

In addition to the roller coasters, there are several large-scale entertainment attractions including the Haunted Hospital, which is the second largest haunted attraction in the world. It takes approximately one hour to tour the old hospital and the pavilion. The Gundam Crisis and Evangelion World attractions are immersive anime-themed displays that include life size models of robots and various characters.

The park also has the standard theme park rides such as the tea cups, ferris wheel, pirate ship, and the drop tower type rides. There are countless restaurants, souvenir shops, and carnival boardwalk type games scattered throughout.

For younger kids, there is an area modeled after the Thomas the Tank series called Thomas Land, which includes both the Thomas and Percy train rides, a 3D theater, and a variety of smaller rides.

During the winter months, the park is home to one of the largest ice skating rinks in the world.

For those of you who are not adrenaline junkies, there is The Fujiyama Museum, an art museum displaying a wide variety of paintings and other illustrations of Mount Fuji. The museum is located on the Fuji-Q Highland park grounds and is free to enter for park attendees who have unlimited ride tickets.

Fuji-Q is open from April 1 to September 30 from 9:00 AM to 5:00 PM during the weekdays and 9:00 AM to 8:00 PM on weekends and holidays. During the summer, the park opens at 8:00 AM and closes at 9:00 PM.

Location(s):   5-6-1 Shin Nishihara, Fujiyoshida

Web Page: http://www.fujiq.jp/en/

Hakone-machi (箱根町): Town of Hakone

Most first time visitors to Japan seek out Tokyo as their destination without even considering venturing outside of the city's borders. Even if you only have a day or two to spare, it would be advantageous to visit Hakone-machi, where you can enjoy the spectacular mountain scenery, world-class art museums, traditional ryokans (inns), onsens (hot springs), and get a feel for the Japanese countryside. The town of Hakone, located in Kanagawa Prefecture, is a popular destination for Japanese and international tourists alike with easy access from Tokyo. During the holidays, the area tends to be quite congested, particularly since Hakone's focal point, Mount Fuji, was named a UNESCO World Heritage site in June 2013. To beat the crowds, plan your trip during the week and enjoy all the town has to offer at a more leisurely pace.

The fastest way to reach Hakone-machi from Tokyo is to take the Tokaido Shinkansen Kodama train from Tokyo to Odawara. From there, you must transfer to the Hakone-Tozan Line to reach Hakone-Yumoto. The one-way trip will last approximately one hour.

Hakone-machi is part of the Fuji Hakone Izu National Park. Spanning 474 square miles (1,228 km²) and incorporating the Yamanashi, Shizuoka, and Kanagawa Prefectures, the park consists of Mount Fuji, Fuji Go-ko (Fuji Five Lakes), Hakone-machi, the Izu Peninsula, and the Izu Islands.

Mount Fuji is the highest mountain in Japan rising to an elevation of 12,389 feet (3,776 m). Still considered an active volcano, it last erupted in 1708. Mount Fuji's exceptionally symmetrical cone, which is snow-capped several months a year, is a well-known symbol of Japan, frequently depicted in art and photographs and the object of pilgrimage for centuries.

Fuji Go-ko or the Fuji Five Lakes are situated in an arc around the northern half of Mount Fuji and were formed when the lava flow spread across the area damming up rivers. The five lakes include Lake Kawaguchi, Lake Motosu, Lake Sai, Lake Shoji, and Lake Yamanaka. Lake Kawaguchi is the most famous of the five lakes, and its image is usually featured on posters and commercials for the Fuji Five Lakes region. It is the only lake in the Fuji Five Lakes area that has an island. Lake Motosu is the ninth deepest lake in Japan and along with Lake Sai and Lake Shoji, was formed by lava flowing across what is now known as Aokigahara Jukai Forest. The three lakes remain connected to this day by underground waterways. Lake Yamanaka is the easternmost and largest of the five lakes. Standing at 3215 feet (980 m) above sea level, it is the third highest lake in Japan.

Of course, no visit to Hakone-machi would be complete without stopping off at one of the many hot springs in the area. More than a dozen springs supply the numerous bath houses and inns with hot water. Travelers to the area for just a day can enjoy bathing in one of the public bath houses or ryokans for a fee. The fees range from ¥500-2,000. Those who choose to spend the night at one of the inns can enjoy the onsen without charge.

Lake Ashino, a caldera lake, is known for its great views of Mount Fuji. Several pleasure boats and ferries traverse the lake and visitors can also take advantage of the fishing and hiking opportunities available here.

In addition, Hakone-machi is also home to various museums. The Hakone Open Air Museum, the Narukawa Art Museum for Modern Japanese Paintings, the Pola Museum of Art featuring Western paintings, and the Venetian Glass Museum are just a few.

Finally, Hakone Jinja (shrine), located on the south shore of Lake Ashino, is a beautifully picturesque Shinto shrine. Its buildings are hidden by a dense forest but the huge torii (gate) stands prominently in the lake. Take the path that leads from the torii up to a series of steps flanked by lanterns through the forest to the shrine's main building, which sits peacefully among the tall trees. The shrine is beautiful throughout the year and is particularly breathtaking when shrouded in mist.

So be daring and venture beyond Tokyo to take in the sites and natural beauty of Hakone-machi. The memories will stay with you for a lifetime!

Web Page: http://www.town.hakone.kanagawa.jp/

Hayakawa-cho (早川町): Town of Hayakawa

<u>Nishiyama Onsen Keiunkan (西山温泉慶雲館): The Oldest Hotel</u>

In the southern alps of Yamanashi Prefecture, nestled in lush valleys in the very heart of nature, you will find the oldest hotel still in operation according to Guinness World Records. The hotel was first classified as the oldest hotel in history in 2011 and the title was renewed in September of 2013.

The Nishiyama Onsen Keiunkan began operating in 705, catering to everyone from ancient samurai to modern tourists including Takeda Shingen, Tokugawa Ieyasu, and numerous Japanese emperors. Fifty-two generations of the same family have operated the hotel since its founding, growing the space and modernizing it slowly with each passing epoch.

The natural hot springs in the area feed the inn's daily water needs. The numerous open-air and communal hot spring baths, as well as the showers, baths, and sinks in each of the guest suites are fed by pure, hot spring water, which is neither treated nor heated by any artificial means.

There are only 35 guest suites, each consisting of two large, Japanese-style rooms. The Minobu River runs right behind the hotel and guests can glimpse views of the river from a number of the hotel's rooms. The cost to rent one of the suites is ¥32,000 per night, but this is considered an ultra-luxurious establishment.

Unlike other typical onsens that operate during certain hours, the baths at Nishiyama Onsen are open 24 hours a day. The onsen water is of the highest quality and the views of the valley from the baths are amazing.

Meals are served kaiseki-style, which is essentially a traditional Japanese multi-course meal. It typically consists of an appetizer, sashimi, a simmered dish, a grilled dish and a steamed course. The chef can elect to include additional dishes at his discretion. Further, kaiseki meals represent a type of art form that seeks to balance taste, texture, appearance, and colors of food. To achieve this, only fresh seasonal ingredients are used and are prepared in ways that aim to enhance their flavor. Local ingredients are often included as well. Finished dishes are artfully presented on plates that are chosen to enhance both the appearance and the seasonal theme of the meal. Dishes are beautifully arranged and garnished, often with real leaves and flowers, as well as edible garnishes.

The success of this hotel is its ability to adapt to the requirements of each era and to renew their services with modern means. Although it is a ryokan with traditional tatami mat-floored rooms, it is mixed with elements of modern hotel design appealing to a wide range of guests.

Location(s):   825 Yujima, Minamikoma-gun, Hayakawa-cho

Web Page: http://www.keiunkan.co.jp/

Katsunuma-cho (勝沼町)： Town of Katsunuma: Japan's Wine Country

Wine enthusiasts traveling to Japan may be surprised to learn that Japan's wine-making dates back to the Meiji period, when Japan first opened its doors to the Western world. In modern day Japan, quality wines are produced in several areas including Nagano, Hokkaido, Niigata, and Katsunuma.

Katsunuma, located in the eastern part of Kofu Valley in Yamanashi Prefecture, is the center of viticulture in Japan. Known as the Town of Grapes and Wine, the distinctive Koshu grapes have been grown here for more than 1,200 years. There are presently more than 30 wineries in the region. Wine aficionados from all over Japan and abroad come to visit these wineries and enjoy the unique wines produced in Katsunuma.

The wineries range from the larger, more famous ones like Suntory, Chateau Mercian, and Grace to much smaller and less well known wineries such as Domaine Chateraise, Chateau Soryu, L'Orient, and Asaya.

Japan's unique wine is made from the Koshu grapes and the process is pretty arduous. You simply cannot crush and ferment this grape. Due to Japan's humid climate, wine makers have to extract the sugar from the Koshu grapes, make sure all of the percentages are just right, and then go through the fermenting process. As a result, one gets a white wine that pairs perfectly with Wa Shoku (Japanese cuisine)! Japanese producers also produce red wines and other whites. I found their Cabernets to be very light on the palate and sweeter than California wines.

If you want to visit the Katsunuma wine country, it is only an hour and a half away from Tokyo. Unfortunately, the area is

260

considered to be the countryside and English is not commonly spoken here. When you arrive at Katsunuma-budokyo Station, the main mode of transportation is by taxi. Another option would be to rent a car from Tokyo and drive to Katsunuma.

Most tastings are complimentary, but bottle purchases are recommended.

If you have time, visit Budo No Oka, situated on top of a hill with breathtaking views. This is a huge complex that includes a hotel, onsen, vineyard, restaurants, gift shop, and tasting cave.

Location(s):   5093 Hishiyama, Katsunuma-cho, Koshu-shi
                  (Budo No Oka)

Web Page: http://budounooka.com/

Points of Interest: Chubu Region

Matsumoto Castle Nagano

Zenkoji Temple Nagano

Matsushiro Castle Nagano

Olympic Stadium (1998 Winter Olympics) Nagano

Mount Shirouma Hakuba Nagano

Mori Shogunzuka Kofun Nagano

265

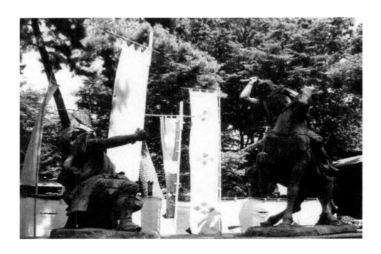

Kawanakajima Battlefield Nagano

Ueda Castle Nagano

Lake Ashi, Mount Fuji Hakone

Lake Suwa Fireworks Festival Nagano

Kansai Region

Introduction to Kansai (関西地方)

The Kansai Region, which is sometimes referred to as the Kinki Region (近畿地方), is situated in the south central part of Honshu, Japan's main island. It is comprised of the prefectures of Mie, Nara, Wakayama, Kyoto, and Shiga and has a reputation for being the cultural and historical heart of Japan. It is also the second most densely populated area of the country after Greater Tokyo.

There is a deep running rivalry between the Kansai and the Kanto Regions. Kanto is considered to be the symbol of standardization in Japan, whereas Kansai is representative of its counterculture. Kanto people are seen as sophisticated, reserved, and formal while Kansai people are thought to be pragmatic, entrepreneurial, and possessing a strong sense of humor. The Kansai people also speak a distinct Japanese dialect commonly called Kansai-ben.

Kansai is well known for its food, especially Osaka. There is a popular saying, "Kyotoites are ruined by overspending on clothing; Osakans are ruined by overspending on food" (京の着倒れ, 大阪の食い倒れ). Popular Osakan dishes include: takoyaki (balls of grilled, savory batter with pieces of octopus inside), okonomiyaki (savory pancakes with cabbage, meat or seafood, flavored with Japanese Worcestershire sauce and mayonnaise), kitsune udon (literally means fox noodles, udon noodles served in hot soup and topped with seasoned aburaage/ deep fried tofu), Osaka zushi (pressed sushi or box sushi as it is sometimes called), and kushikatsu (seasoned, skewered, grilled meat). Other regional delights include yudofu (a popular dish in Kyoto, this is tofu simmered in hot water with kombu/ seaweed and eaten with various dipping sauces). Kansai is also the home of many Wagyu brands of beef including Kobe, Matsusaka, and Omi and the region produces 45 percent of all sake in Japan!

Two Nippon Professional Baseball teams call Kansai their home, the Hanshin Tigers and the Orix Buffaloes. The Hanshin Tigers are one of the oldest professional clubs in Japan. They played their first season in 1936 as the Osaka Tigers and assumed their current team name in 1961. The Orix Buffaloes team was formed following the 2004 season by merging two teams, the Orix BlueWave of Kobe and the Kintetsu Buffaloes of Osaka.

Lake Biwa, the largest freshwater lake in Japan, can be found in the Kansai Region as well as four of Japan's national parks and six of the seven top prefectures in terms of national treasures.

There are three major airports in the Kansai Metropolitan Area: Kansai International Airport, Osaka International Airport which only serves domestic flights, and Kobe Airport.

The Tokaido Shinkansen (bullet train) line from Tokyo serves Osaka, Kyoto, and Kobe.

Web Page: http://www.jnto.go.jp/eng/location/routes/rtp/kansai/
(Japan National Tourism Organization / Kansai)

Hyogo Prefecture (兵庫県)

Himeji-shi (姫路市): Himeji City

Himeji Castle (姫路城)

Located in central Himeji City in Hyogo Prefecture, Himeji Castle is the largest and most visited castle in Japan. It was registered in 1993 as one of the first UNESCO World Heritage Sites in the country. Himeji City is just 30 miles (48 km) west of Kobe and about 400 miles (644 km) west of Tokyo.

The castle originated as a hilltop fort constructed by Akamatsu Norimura in 1333. The fort was dismantled and reconstructed as a castle in 1346. Later in 1581, it became a three-story castle under the direction of Toyotomi Hideyoshi. In 1601, Ikeda Terumasa demolished the entire structure, rebuilding in its place a five-story main tower with three smaller towers.

The castle is constructed out of wood with white plaster walls. It stands on a hill 150 feet (46 m) above sea level. The top of the main tower stands 302 feet (92 m) above sea level.

Amazingly, the castle remained intact for over 400 years. During the Meiji period, many Japanese castles were destroyed as they were reminders of Japan's feudal past. Himeji Castle was abandoned in 1871 and some of the castle corridors and gates were destroyed to make room for Japanese army barracks. The castle complex was slated for demolition by the government, but due to the efforts of an Army Colonel named Nakamura Shigeto, it was spared. Today, you will find a stone monument placed within the castle complex at the first gate, the Diamond Gate, honoring Nakamura.

In 1945, at the end of World War II, Himeji City was heavily bombed. Although most of the surrounding area was burned to the ground, Himeji Castle managed to survive intact. Then, in 1995, the city was substantially damaged by the Great Hanshin Earthquake and once again the castle survived virtually undamaged.

Today, the castle is regarded as one of the finest surviving examples of a prototypical Japanese castle, consisting of 83 buildings with a remarkably advanced defensive system. The complex defensive design is like a labyrinth and even with the route clearly marked, many visitors to the castle are easily lost.

The castle has undergone a three-year restoration. In June of 2014, the main keep was unveiled showing the public what the castle looked like in its original state. The castle was fully re-opened on March 27, 2015.

Location(s):   68 Hommachi, Himeji, Hyogo

Web Page: http://www.city.himeji.lg.jp/guide/castle.html

Himeji-shi (姫路市): Himeji City

Himeji Castle: Yukata Festival

Most visitors to Himeji City are drawn there because of the beautiful Himeji Castle and Engyoji Temple on Mount Shosha, but did you know there is another attraction Himeji is known for, which draws over 200,000 visitors to Hyogo's second largest city? It is the Himeji Yukata Matsuri, which takes place in late June. The tradition goes back to a ceremony that took place about 260 years ago when the lord of Himeji Castle moved the Osakabe Shrine to downtown Himeji. Himeji Castle was built on the former grounds of the shrine; therefore, common folks could not visit or pray at the shrine. Moving the shrine to downtown Himeji meant that everyone could easily have access to the shrine and a celebration ensued. However, the ceremony took place on such short notice that the citizens of Himeji did not have enough time or money to prepare their formal kimonos. Instead, they were permitted to wear their summer yukatas and thus the Yukata Festival began.

In the beginning, the event was simply referred to as the Yukata Matsuri but since more and more yukata festivals were popping up across Japan, it was eventually renamed the Himeji Yukata Matsuri. The event runs three days and consists of a yukata parade, a yukata fashion show, and various live dance and musical performances. It is considered the oldest and largest festival of its type in Japan with over 800 vendors. You can even gain free access to Himeji Castle if you are dressed in a yukata!

The yukata differs from the kimono in that it is made from a light cotton material with bright colors and patterns and is typically worn during the summer months. Although it is common to see men and women wearing yukatas during the summer festivals, the garment represents the main component of this particular festival and it is estimated that 70 percent of all festival goers at the Himeji Yukata Matsuri attend wearing their yukatas. Of course, if you do not own a yukata, you can rent one at the Jokamachi Style shop near Himeji Castle as well as other places around town.

The festival runs from 4:30 PM to 9:30 PM and is free to attend. Access to the festival is relatively easy as the city lies along the Sanyo Shinkansen line. The destination is approximately 40 minutes from Kobe and three hours from Tokyo.

Location(s):   33 Tatemachi, Himeji-shi, Hyogo
                 (Osakabe Shrine)

Web Page: http://www.hyogo-
                 tourism.jp/english/whatsnew/index.php?id=149

Himeji-shi (姫路市): Himeji City

Himeji Engyoji Temple (書寫山圓教寺)

If you have ever been curious about the Japan/ Hollywood connection, one place you may consider visiting is the Himeji Engyoji Temple in Himeji City.

Situated above Mount Shosha, the location served as Katsumoto's (Ken Watanabe's character) temple in the film, *The Last Samurai* (2003), starring Tom Cruise. The plot was inspired by the 1877 Satsuma Rebellion led by Saigo Takamori. It was the last armed uprising against the new government and ended with Takamori's death. Filming took place in various places including New Zealand, California, and Japan (Kyoto and Himeji).

Access to the temple is easy via the Mount Shosha Ropeway (書写山ロープウェイ). From the ropeway station, it is a 10 to 15-minute walk uphill to reach the Niomon Gate.

The temple is a sprawling monastic complex that was founded in 966. It is the 27th temple along the Saigoku 33 Temple Pilgrimage. The Daikodo, the main temple building, dates back to the 15th century. Major restoration work took place in 1956 but the structure remains all original. The Maniden is another impressive building within the complex. Rebuilt in 1932, it stands high atop the forest, similar to the viewing stage at Kiyomizu Temple in Kyoto. Be sure to visit the other buildings comprising the three main buildings (Mitsunodo) where the monks lived. Along with the Daikodo, there is the Jikido, which served as the lodging and dining hall and now exhibits temple treasures, and the Jogyodo, which was used as a lecture hall.

Temples such as this and particularly of this scale are no longer found in Japan. Visitors can elect to spend the night in the temple lodgings, attempt to hand copy one of the sutras, or simply relax and meditate in this calm and beautiful setting. In order to spend the night, reservations must be made at least three days prior to your visit.

So, come and see for yourself why this amazing location was chosen for *The Last Samurai* and visit the places where Ken Watanabe and Tom Cruise delivered their lines.

The temple complex is open from 8:30 AM to 5:00 PM.

Location(s):   2-12 Gokenyashiki, Himeji, Hyogo

Web Page: http://www.shosha.or.jp/

Kobe-shi (神戸市): Kobe City

Kobe Port Tower (神戸ポートタワー)

Most visitors to Kobe are immediately drawn to the most striking feature of the city's skyline, the Kobe Port Tower. Completed in 1963, the hyperboloid lattice structure stands at approximately 354 feet (108 m) high and offers a spectacular view of the bay area and its surroundings. Kobe is one of Japan's busiest ports and there are always interesting things to see along the waterfront.

The Kobe Port Tower is the first tower in the world with a pipe structure. It resembles a Japanese drum, is painted a burnt orange, and is illuminated each night, making it a very interesting piece of architecture. The tower's observation deck is located at the 295-foot (90 m) level and on a clear day visitors can glimpse views of Osaka, Mount Rokko, and the Kansai International Airport from its large windows. The structure stands in Meriken Park and is not far from the Kobe Maritime Museum.

Designed by the Nikken Sekkei Company, the tower's unique structure allowed it to survive the 1995 Great Hanshin Earthquake. There is a rotating cafe on the observation deck level that provides diners with a 360-degree view of the city below. If you are inclined to bring home a little souvenir, there is a gift shop that can satisfy your needs.

The tower is open to the public seven days a week between 9:00 AM and 9:00 PM (March through November) and 9:00 AM and 7:00 PM (December through February). There is a nominal admission charge of ¥600 for visitors who are high school age and older. Elementary school and junior high school students are admitted for ¥300. You can access the Kobe Port Tower from the JR Kobe or the Hanshin Railway, exit Motomachi Station. From that point, your destination is 15 minutes on foot.

Location(s):   2-2 Hatoba-cho,Chuo-ku, Kobe-shi, Kobe, Hyogo

Web Page: http://www.kobe-meriken.or.jp/port-tower/

Kyoto Prefecture (京都府)

Kyoto-shi (京都市): Kyoto City

<u>Aoi Matsuri: Hollyhock Festival</u>

The Aoi Matsuri, held annually on May 15, is one of the three main festivals that take place in Kyoto. Aoi is the Japanese term for Hollyhock. The festival dates back to the 7th century and it is said that it started as a way to appease the gods after a severe storm destroyed the harvest. The flower was believed to protect against natural disasters and was used as a decoration throughout the festival. The festival is officially called Kamo Matsuri due to its association with the two Kamo Shrines: Shimogamo Shrine (Lower Shrine) and Kamigamo Shrine (Upper Shrine).

The festival features a parade with over 500 participants dressed in costumes from the Heian period (794-1185). The parade begins at 10:30 AM at the southern gate of the Imperial Palace of Kyoto. Around 11:15 AM, the procession crosses over the river located in front of the Shimogamo Shrine. Once at the shrine, there is a two-hour ritual before the procession departs for the Kamigamo Shrine.

Each year, a new Saio is elected. The Saio was traditionally a young female member of the royal family who served as the high priestess of the Kamo Shrines. Today, the Saio is an unmarried woman who goes through a purification ceremony before the festival and is carried on a palanquin during the procession. The other main figure of the festival is the Imperial Messenger who leads the parade on horseback.

It is an amazing spectacle to watch as men on horseback, others carrying enormous arrangements of flowers, ornately decorated ox-drawn carts and women dressed in traditional aristocratic costumes parade past you. Paid seating is available at the Imperial Palace and at the Kamo shrines as well as along the parade route. Otherwise, you would need to arrive significantly early to obtain a good spot without paying.

The Imperial Palace is five minutes on foot from Imadegawa Station on the Karasuma Subway Line.

Location(s):   3 Kyoto-Gyoen Kamigyo-ku, Kyoto-shi, Kyoto
                 (Kyoto Imperial Palace)

Web Page: http://sankan.kunaicho.go.jp/english/guide/ky
                 oto.html

Kyoto-shi (京都市): Kyoto City

Fushimi Inari Taisha (伏見稲荷大社)

Over the years, there have been a number of interesting locations in Japan that served as the backdrop for several Hollywood films.

One such place is the Fushimi Inari Taisha, a Shinto shrine located in Fushimi-ku, Kyoto. The shrine is famous for the thousands of vermilion torii (gates) lining the paths on the hill on which the shrine is situated. It is also famous for being featured in the film, *Memoirs of a Geisha* (2005). The film was based on a novel by U.S. author Arthur Golden (1997) and told in first person perspective the experiences of a fictional geisha working in Kyoto before and after World War II.

The shrine is dedicated to Inari, the Shinto god of rice, and is often associated with wealth. The kitsune (foxes) are believed to be Inari's messengers, hence you will encounter numerous kitsune statues on the shrine grounds. The torii are all donated by individuals, families, and organizations. The gates are considered offerings to the shrine. You will find the donator's name and the date of the donation inscribed on the back of each gate. The cost of the gates begins around ¥400,000 for a small sized gate and can run over ¥1,000,000 for a large gate.

At the shrine's entrance stands the Romon Gate, which was donated in 1589 by Toyotomi Hideyoshi. Hideyoshi was a famous daimyo (feudal lord), warrior, general, samurai, and politician during Japan's Sengoku (Warring States) period and is regarded as Japan's second great unifier. At the very back of the shrine's main grounds is the entrance to the torii-gate-covered hiking trail, which starts with two dense, parallel rows of gates called Senbon Torii (thousands of torii gates). After trekking through the torii lined hiking paths, you can stop at the various food stalls that specialize in kitsune udon, a popular noodle dish named after the god's messengers.

The hike to the summit and back will take two to three hours. Along the way, you will find countless smaller shrines with stacks of miniature torii gates that were donated by visitors on a smaller budget.

The shrine with its many torii seems almost a surreal place that was created by Hollywood but in fact it is very real and dates back to even before the capital of Japan was moved to Kyoto.

Fushimi Inari Taisha is located just outside JR Inari Station, the second station from Kyoto Station along the JR Nara Line. The shrine is also just a short walk from Fushimi Inari Station along the Keihan Main Line.

Location(s):	68 Fukakusa Yabunouchicho, Fushimi-ku, Kyoto
Web Page:	http://inari.jp/

Kyoto-shi (京都市): Kyoto City

Gion Corner: Kyogen Traditional Comic Theater

There are four forms of traditional Japanese theater which include: Kabuki, Noh, Bunraku, and Kyogen.

Noh is the oldest theater art form still regularly performed today. Its stories are derived from traditional literature and it features only male actors. Noh integrates elaborate masks, costumes, and various props in a dance-based performance, requiring highly trained actors and musicians. Emotions are conveyed using stylized gestures and masks are utilized to represent the various roles such as ghosts, women, children, and elderly people.

Kyogen, which literally translates to "mad words" or "wild speech," developed alongside Noh and was performed along with Noh, serving as a break between acts. To this day, it retains close ties with Noh and is sometimes designated as Noh-Kyogen. Kyogen, like Noh, features only male actors; however, that is where the similarity ends. While Noh theater is formal, symbolic, and solemn, Kyogen is comical, satirical, and presents humorous stories of daily life. Its primary goal is to make its audience laugh. The performers do not wear extravagant costumes, makeup, or masks. Instead, they are dressed in simple kimonos and are accompanied by a chorus.

It is said that Kyogen was a major influence on the development of Kabuki theatre. It was adopted as the official form of entertainment during the Edo period and was subsidized by the government. Further, since Kyogen was performed along with the Noh, it was patronized by the upper class.

There were once three schools of Kyogen that included the Sagi School, the Okura School, and the Izumi School. The Sagi School was closed down leaving only the Okura and Izumi schools to quietly cultivate their art. After World War II, many forms of Japanese traditional arts were revived. Consequently, Kyogen's popularity increased once again and today it is performed and practiced regularly throughout the country and is featured on television programs. In 2001, Kyogen was designated by UNESCO along with Noh as one of the Masterpieces of the Oral and Intangible Heritage of Humanity.

One interesting fact is that during the post-war period, foreigners were allowed to participate in Kyogen as amateur performers. Today, foreigners who reside in Japan and possess sufficient Japanese language skills are afforded the opportunity to practice this traditional art form with amateur troupes.

There are many places to see Kyogen performed including Tokyo and Osaka but what better place to enjoy this traditional art form than in a town that is dotted with traditional Japanese houses and where geisha and maiko roam the streets? Gion Corner, located within the Gion district of Kyoto, presents several of Japan's traditional performing arts including the Kyo-mai dance performed by maiko dancers, Gagaku court music and Bunraku puppet theater all on one stage. While you are there, be sure to visit the Maiko Gallery where videos of dances, maiko kanzashi (hair decorations), and other items are on display.

Admission to Gion Corner is ¥3,150 for adults, ¥2,200 for audience members between the ages of 16-22, and ¥ 1,900 for those between the ages of 7-15.

The theater is easily accessible from JR Kyoto Station, via city bus 206 or 100. Get off at the Gion bus stop and the theater is five minutes on foot from that point. Alternatively, you can take the Keihan Line train to Gion Shijo Station and again the theater is only a five-minute walk.

Location(s):   570-2 Gionmachi Minamigawa,
                      Higashiyama-ku, Yasaka Hall, Kyoto

Web Page: http://www.kyoto-gioncorner.com/

Kyoto-shi (京都市): Kyoto City

<u>Kiyomizu-dera (清水寺)</u>

In the 2005 film, *Memoirs of a Geisha*, a majority of the filming took place in California; however, there were a few scenes that were filmed in Japan. One such location was the famous Kiyomizu Temple or Kiyomizu-dera, located in eastern Kyoto.

The temple was founded in 778 and takes its names from the waterfall located within the complex (Kiyomizu translates to pure water). The buildings you see today were constructed in 1633 by the order of Tokugawa Iemitzu, who ruled from 1623 to 1651. He was known for enacting the Sakoku Edict of 1639, which closed off Japan to foreigners. Disobeying these edicts was punishable by death and it wasn't until the 1850s when Japan once again opened its ports to foreigners.

An interesting fact about the temple complex is that not a single nail was used to construct the various structures. The main hall of the complex has a large veranda supported by tall pillars and it juts out over the hillside offering visitors breathtaking views of the city below. Below the main hall is the Otowa Waterfall. Water from this fall is believed to have wish-granting powers.

The temple complex incorporates several other shrines; among them is the Jishu Shrine dedicated to the god of love. There are a pair of love stones located at this shrine. Those visitors who successfully walk between them with their eyes closed are granted their wish of finding love.

Other structures on the temple grounds include the Okunoin Hall, which resembles the main structure, but on a smaller scale and includes a viewing stage as well. The three-storied Koyasu

Pagoda is located in the far southern end of the temple grounds and is often visited by expectant mothers praying for an easy and safe childbirth.

The temple is part of the Historic Monuments of Ancient Kyoto and a UNESCO World Heritage site. There are countless shops and restaurants surrounding the temple that have been catering to tourists and pilgrims over the years and are worth visiting.

Location(s):   1-294 Kiyomizu, Higashiyama-ku, Kyoto

Web Page: http://www.kiyomizudera.or.jp/lang/01.html

Kyoto-shi (京都市): Kyoto City

<u>Nanzenji (南禅寺)</u>

When visiting Kyoto's many temples, it is a good idea to include Nanzenji Temple, located at the base of the Higashiyama Mountains. Established in 1291, it is the head temple of one of the schools within the Rinzai sect of Japanese Zen Buddhism. Like other temples in Kyoto, Nanzenji began life as a retirement villa for Japanese emperor Kameyama in 1274 and was later converted into a Zen temple.

The temple was burnt down in 1393 and then rebuilt. However, it was destroyed by fire once again in 1447. It was leveled during the Onin War of 1467 and reconstructed in 1597. The large complex has over time included between nine and twelve sub-temples, including the central temple.

Nanzenji's central temple grounds are open to the public free of charge, but separate fees apply for entering the temple buildings and the sub-temples. The massive two-story Sanmon Gate, which visitors encounter first upon entering the complex, was built in 1628 to commemorate the dead at the siege of Osaka. It includes a balcony from which visitors can glimpse views of Kyoto.

Standing behind the gate is the Hatto (Dharma Hall), a large lecture hall, which is not open to the public.

Past the Hatto is the Ohojo (Abbot's Large Quarters), which was brought over from Hideyoshi's Fushimi Castle and dates back to the 1590s. The Ohojo is renowned for its dry stone garden. Also highly regarded are the paintings on the sliding doors, which include realistic depictions of tigers on gold leaf. Visitors enter

287

the Ohojo building complex through the former temple kitchen, where they can also find a small tea room to their right with a view of a miniature waterfall.

Outside the Ohojo, visitors will come across a large brick aqueduct that passes through the temple grounds. Built during the Meiji period, the aqueduct is part of a canal system that was constructed to carry water and links Kyoto and Lake Biwa. There are foot paths alongside the canal that lead into the surrounding forest.

Nanzen-in is located near the aqueduct. It is a 1703 reconstruction of the original retirement villa of Emperor Kameyama, which was the first building at the Nanzenji complex. Beyond that you will find the sub-temples of Konchi-in, Tenju-an, and Choso-in, all open to the public although Tenju-an is only open during the spring and fall.

Nanzenji is a beautiful spot to observe the changing of the leaves in autumn and consequently gets extremely busy from mid to late November.

It is relatively easy to reach the temple complex as it is just a short walk from Keage Subway Station on the Tozai Line.

Location(s):   86 Nanzenji Fukuchicho, Sakyo-ku, Kyoto

Web Page: http://kyoto.asanoxn.com/places/higashiyama
                 _nth/nanzenji.htm

Kyoto-shi (京都市): Kyoto City

Randen Arashiyama Station (嵐山駅)： Kimono Forest

Many tourists flock to Kyoto to experience its countless temples and shrines. After all, having served as the capital of Japan for over one thousand years, there is quite a bit of history and culture to draw both tourists and native Japanese to this beautiful city. But located on the western outskirts of Kyoto is another area worth seeing, called Arashiyama.

Arashiyama, whose literal translation is Storm Mountain, is home to numerous temples and shrines, but its star attraction is the famed Arashiyama Bamboo Forest. Walking down the central path through the forest is rather awe-inspiring and otherworldly. One feels a sense of inner peace while standing amidst these towering bamboo giants, sheltered from all that is wrong in this world.

Drawing inspiration from the forest, an artist, Yasumichi Morita of GLAMOROUS Co. designed Arashiyama Station on Kyoto's Keifuku Arashiyama Line (commonly called the Randen Line) to invite visitors to the Arashiyama area not only to enjoy the beauty of its bamboo forest but also to marvel at the Kimono Forest created on the grounds of the station.

The Randen Line's Kimono Forest consists of 600 poles, each 6.5 feet (2m) high, wrapped with Kyoto Yuzen kimono fabrics. The poles are illuminated by LED lights at night and provide a completely different atmosphere compared to the daytime display. The textiles were designed by Kyoto's Kamedatomi, a textile factory dating back to the Taisho period. There are 32 different patterns on display, each carefully selected by the artist himself.

The renovation of the station was completed in July of 2013 and the ticket barriers were removed allowing everyone to be able to enter the station and marvel at its Kimono Forest and patronize the new shops. At the end of Kimono Lane, you will find a small fountain and the station's so-called power spot, the Ryu no Atago. The water springs from 160 feet below ground and its source is said to be none other than the sacred Mount Atago. People come to this area to pray and to dip their hands in the cold water, which is believed to relax and restore.

So, the next time you are in Kyoto, take a side trip to Arashiyama to experience the Bamboo Forest and the Kimono Forest for yourself. It is a remarkable experience that should not be missed.

You can access Arashiyama Station via the Keifuku Arashiyama Line from Omiya Station in central Kyoto. The travel time is approximately 20 minutes.

Location(s):   20-2 Sagatenryuji Tsukurimicchicho Ukyoku, Kyoto-shi, Kyoto

Web Page: http://randen.keifuku.co.jp/en/index.html

Kyoto-shi (京都市): Kyoto City

Saihoji (西芳寺)：Moss Temple

Kyoto is a great place to visit during the sakura (cherry blossom) season and during autumn, when the momiji (Japanese maple trees) are ablaze with beautiful hues of gold and red. The many temples that crisscross Kyoto afford ample opportunities to walk the grounds and commune with nature. But Kyoto also has another natural attraction that lures people by the thousands each year. This is Kyoto's famous moss temple, Koke-dera (苔寺) or (Saihoji).

The original temple is said to have been established by the monk, Gyoki during the Nara period. Over time, the temple fell into disrepair and in 1339 it was revived as a Zen temple and renamed Saihoji. The temple grounds are covered with more than 120 types of moss, resembling a beautiful green carpet. It is said that the moss came into existence following the floods during the Edo period. The garden, situated on the eastern temple grounds, is arranged as a circular promenade surrounding a pond, shaped like the character for kokoro (heart). Within the pond, there are three small islands: Asahi (sunrise) Island, Yuhi (sunset) Island, and Kiri (mist) Island.

There are three tea houses within the garden. Shonan Tei was built in the 14th century but subsequently destroyed. The tea house you see today is the reconstructed version. Shoan Do was constructed in 1920 and houses the wooden image of Sen Shoan after whom the teahouse derives its name. Tanhoku Tei was donated to the temple in 1928.

The garden is acclaimed by many to be one of Kyoto's most beautiful gardens. After visiting this magnificent place, it won't

291

come as a surprise that the temple and grounds were registered as a UNESCO World Heritage Site in 1994.

However, a word of caution when visiting Koke-dera. In an effort to protect the moss, the temple has required advance reservations since 1977. Requests must be submitted in writing and should include your name and mailing address, your preferred date of visit, and the number of people in your party. The best times to view the garden are during the rainy season (mid-June through mid-July) and in autumn, when the red and gold of the momiji contrast nicely with the lush green of the velvety moss. There is an entrance fee of ¥3,000 payable in cash and all visitors are asked to participate in a ceremonial ritual prior to accessing the outdoor area.

Location(s):   56 Jingatani-cho, Matsuo, Nishikyo-ku, Kyoto
                  615-8286

Web Page: http://aquadina.com/kyoto/spot/7003/

Kyoto-shi (京都市): Kyoto City

<u>Toei Uzumasa Eigamura (東映太秦映画村): Kyoto Studio Park</u>

For movie buffs, the Toei Uzumasa Eigamura, also known as the Kyoto Studio Park, is a must see on your next visit to Japan! Of course, there is the Universal Studios Theme Park in Osaka, but the attraction in Kyoto is set in the Edo and Meiji periods and features various traditional buildings that are occasionally used as backdrops for filming historical movies and TV dramas. As a matter of fact, the Kyoto Studio Park is the only theme park in Japan where visitors can actually observe the filming of a movie or TV drama.

The Uzumasa area of Kyoto was once home to several movie studios, which earned it the nickname, Hollywood of Japan. However, the film industry soon fell into decline with the advancement of television and the theme park was constructed as a way to preserve the traditions of the Japanese movie industry.

The park consists of streets depicting various town settings and includes a replica of the Nihonbashi Bridge and part of the Yoshiwara Red Light District. Visitors can enter a Samurai-style residence and visit the Edo period law courts. You can even go inside of a period jail cell and see what it was like to be a criminal in Japan at the time.

The attendants are all clothed in period costumes that add to the atmosphere. The park is also home to a ninja maze, a 3D Theater, a haunted house, video arcades, restaurants, and souvenir shops, all designed to make your visit truly enjoyable. For ¥8,500 – ¥16,000, guests can don historic costumes and have their photos taken. Costumes are also available for rental while strolling the park. Sometimes it is difficult to discern the actors and staff members from the guests!

The center of Main Street is the setting for the acrobatic Samurai Show and the Chanbara Show, which demonstrate traditional Japanese sword fighting. Location Studio is set up as a movie school, where a director, a samurai, and a villain explain to the audience how a scene is developed. It is both humorous and informative, so do make a point of checking it out. Understand that some of the shows require an additional fee, so be certain to check the schedule when you arrive.

The Movie Cultural Hall is set inside of a European-style building from the Meiji era and recalls the history of the Japanese movie business. It is an informative and fun place to visit. The SFX Pool is a special effects pool complete with its own dinosaur-like beast. Here, technicians have the ability to produce artificial rain and waves with the push of a button, creating either a raging sea or a tranquil flowing river instantly.

The park is a five-minute walk from Uzumasa Station of the Keifukyu Arashiyama Line or a 15-minute walk from JR Hanazono Station. Hours are from 9:00 AM to 5:00 PM. During the week the park is usually crowded with students on school excursions so plan your visit accordingly.

Location(s):   10 Higashi-Hachigaokacho, Uzumasa, Ukyo-ku, Kyoto

Web Page: http://www.toei-eigamura.com/en

Uji-shi (宇治市): Uji City

Byodoin Temple (平等院)

When visiting the many temples and shrines that Kyoto is famous for, you must make a point of including the beautiful Byodoin Temple, located in the city of Uji. It was originally constructed as a villa for Fujiwara-no-Michinaga in 998. Following Fujiwara's death in 1052, his son converted the building into a Buddhist temple. The Phoenix Hall or Hodo was constructed in 1053 and it is all that remains today of all of the magnificent buildings that once stood on the grounds.

The temple complex was once much larger and the beach surrounding the pond stretched to the Uji River. Unfortunately, most of the buildings were burned down during the civil war of 1336.

The Phoenix Hall houses a large wooden statue of Amida Buddha seated on a high platform. The sculpture is constructed from Japanese cypress and is covered with gold leaf. The statue measures approximately 10 feet (3m) high from its face to its knees. Fifty-two wooden statues of bodhisattvas, said to express heaven, surround the statue. Phoenix Hall was declared a UNESCO World Heritage Site in December of 1994 and is commemorated on the back of the Japanese ten-yen coin.

The temple also possesses what is considered to be one of the most famous bells in Japan. Designated as a National Treasure, the temple bell bears no inscriptions, only reliefs of maidens and lions. The bell's design is thought to be of Korean influence.

On the temple grounds, you will find a fan-shaped lawn where Minamoto-no-Yorimasa took his own life after being defeated by the rival Taira clan. Minamoto was a prominent Japanese poet and a warrior. His ritual suicide by seppuku is the earliest recorded instance of a samurai's suicide in the face of defeat.

Interestingly, there is a replica of Byodoin located at the Valley of the Temples in O'ahu, Hawaii. It was constructed in 1968 to commemorate the 100-year anniversary of the first Japanese immigrants to Hawaii.

Byodoin Temple in Uji is a ten to 15-minute walk from Uji Station on the JR Nara Line. Alternatively, you can take the Keihan Uji Line from central Kyoto (Shijo Station) to Uji. The trip takes 30 minutes and the temple is a five-minute walk from the station.

The temple is open to the public from 8:30 AM to 5:30 PM. There is an admission charge of ¥600.

Location(s):   116 Ujirenge, Uji 611-0021

Web Page: http://www.byodoin.or.jp

Nara-shi (奈良市): Nara City

Heijo-kyu (平城宮): Nara Imperial Palace

Nara became the capital of Japan in the year 710 and remained so for 84 years. Today, its vast collection of historic treasures makes it a popular tourist destination for Japanese and non-Japanese alike.

During the period in which Nara served as the capital city, it was called Heijo-kyo and the Imperial Palace was known as Heijo Palace. The design of the palace grounds was based on Chang'an, the capital of China during the T'ang Dynasty. The entire palace compound occupied an area approximately 1,100 yards (1,006 m) from north to south and 1,300 yards (1,189 m) from east to west. The primary buildings included Daigoku-den where governmental affairs were conducted; Chodo-in where formal ceremonies were held; and, Dairi, the Emperor's residence. The palace was surrounded by walls 30 feet (9.5 m) tall, but was accessible through 12 gates; the main gate was the Suzakumon. The Suzakumon was situated at the southern end of the complex, directly to the south of the Daigoku-den.

When the capital was moved to Heian-kyo (Kyoto) in the 8th century, Heijo Palace was simply abandoned. Over the years the ravages of time and the elements slowly destroyed the buildings. By the beginning of the Kamakura period in the late 12th century, there was practically nothing left standing above ground. However, those sections that lay underground were preserved and were re-discovered by modern archaeologists. The site is officially designated as an Imperial Property; therefore, no new buildings or developments can be established without prior Imperial approval. Archaeological and restorative efforts of the site began in 1955 and the grounds were opened to the public in 1998. Heijo Palace along with the surrounding area was established as a UNESCO World Heritage Site the same year.

Three major structures of the former palace complex have been reconstructed in recent decades. Among them is the Daigoku-den, the largest building on the palace grounds, which was reconstructed for the occasion of the 1,300th anniversary of the Nara Capital and opened to the public in April 2010. Its ceiling is decorated with animals from the lunar calendar. A throne stands in the center of the hall and is housed within a hexagonal compartment that opens towards the south.

The other full-scale reconstructions involved the Suzakumon and the East Palace Garden (Toin Teien), which features a pond, streams, and bridges. It was used by the Imperial family for banquets.

Scattered across the palace grounds are various building foundations such as the imperial living quarters and administrative offices. At the northeast corner of the palace grounds stands the Excavation Site Exhibition Hall, where exposed excavation sites were left open for the public to view. At the western end of the grounds is the Nara Palace Site Museum, which houses artifacts, models, photographs, and maps.

The palace is just 15 minutes on foot heading east from Yamato-Saidaiji Station. There is limited parking available and visitors are encouraged to use public transportation. Heijo Palace grounds are open year-round with the exception of public holidays and during the observance of the New Year (December 29 to January 3). Hours of operation are 9:00 AM to

4:30 PM.

Location(s):   Sakicho, Nara-shi, Nara Prefecture

Web Page: http://www.nabunken.go.jp/heijo/museum/in
                dex.html

Osaka Prefecture (大阪府)

Osaka-Shi (大阪市): Osaka City

Abeno Tennoji Illuminage

Just next to Tennoji Station in Osaka, you will find an urban oasis similar to New York's Central Park or London's Hyde Park, called Tennoji Koen or Tennoji Park. It first opened in 1909 and is home to the Tennoji Zoological Gardens, the Chausuyama Tomb, and the Osaka Municipal Museum of Art.

Annually, beginning in early November, Tennoji Koen hosts the Abeno Tennoji Illuminage, a light show featuring three million colored LEDs. The highlights of the light display include a 320-foot (98 m) rainbow promenade (a tunnel lit up with all seven colors of the rainbow), and a 55-foot (17 m) tall Christmas tree, called the Wonderland Tree. The illumination event supports the reconstruction efforts in the Tohoku region following the Great East Japan Earthquake in 2011.

The Abeno Tennoji Illuminage, which runs through January 31, draws large crowds and is popular among young couples as it offers an ideal dating spot this time of the year. The lights are switched on at 5:30 PM and remain illuminated until 9:30 PM.

The park is just a 10-minute walk from JR Osaka Loop Line Tennoji Station. Admission to the park is ¥1,000 for adults and ¥500 for children (Children under 3 are admitted without charge.).

So if you happen to be in the Kansai region, why not stop off at Tennoji Park and enjoy some winter time magic? Not all large scale illumination events are restricted to Tokyo and her suburbs.

Location(s):   1-108 Chausuyama, Tennoji-ku, Osaka-shi

Osaka-Shi (大阪市): Osaka City

<u>Amerikamura (アメリカ村): American Village</u>

Osaka city, located in the Kansai region and the second largest city in Japan, is a fun place to visit as there seems to be no end to the many culinary, shopping, and entertainment experiences. Among these is an area known as Amerikamura, which is to Osaka what Harajuku and Shinjuku are to Tokyo.

Amerikamura literally translates to American Village and is referred to as Amemura by the locals. Located near Shinsaibashi, it is a fun place to visit, mingle with the younger generation, and take in performances by local entertainers. The area came into existence in the 1970s when several warehouses were renovated to sell imported goods from the United States. Today, Amemura is famous for its vibrant nightlife, unique fashion, bars, galleries, and much more.

Centered on Sankaku Koen (Triangle Park), the district is always crowded with people who work in the area, musicians, artists, and expatriates. There are several Western fashion retail outlets like Adidas and Ed Hardy and numerous secondhand shops selling everything from the prized branded goods to random trinkets. If you are hungry, stop by the many food stalls selling typical street food found in other parts of Osaka, such as takoyaki. You will also find several American stands selling things like hot dogs and fries.

If you are visiting Dotonbori, the popular tourist destination in Osaka, why not swing by Amemura as well? The two areas are right next to one another. Otherwise, Amemura is only a five-minute walk from Shinsaibashi Station (Midosuji Subway Line) and easily identifiable by its small-scale reproduction of the

Statue of Liberty that peers down on the streets below.

Web Page: http://americamura.jp/en/index.php

Osaka-Shi (大阪市): Osaka City

Dotonbori (道頓堀)

Osaka is a bustling metropolis, famed for its unique entertainment district and principal tourist destination, Dotonbori. Set along the Dotonbori-gawa canal, this neighborhood is the place to go in Osaka for fantastic food, theater, and entertainment.

Dotonbori dates back to 1612, when a local businessman named Yasui Doton began the project of expanding the Umezu River with the hope of increasing commerce in the area. The project was interrupted when Doton died during the Siege of Osaka, but his cousins took over the project and the canal was finally completed in 1615. By 1662, the area was well known for its Kabuki and Bunraku theaters as well as several restaurants and cafés that cropped up to cater to the tourists and theater goers.

Today, the traditional arts theaters are gone but the area continues to be a popular entertainment and nightlife district characterized by its eccentric atmosphere and large, illuminated signboards. The most recognizable of these illuminated signboards is the Glico Confectionary Company's display of a runner crossing the finish line. First installed in 1935, it is considered an icon of Osaka and recently underwent its sixth update, where the historic neon lights were replaced by LED lights.

Like the Glico running man display, the Kuidaore Taro or Kuidaore Ningyo, as it is sometimes known (a mechanical drum-playing clown), is an easily recognized icon of Dotonbori. It once stood in front of the now-closed Kuidaore Restaurant providing the perfect photo opportunity for visitors to Osaka's famous neighborhood. Kuidaore Taro was first placed in front of the restaurant in 1950 and remained there until after the restaurant's closing in 2008. For a year after the closing, it was loaned out for various events across the nation. When it was returned to Osaka in 2009, it found a permanent home in front of a large commercial complex, which stands near the former Kuidaore Restaurant location.

Other well-known signs in the area include the Kani Doraku Crab, a 6.5 meter (21 ft) mechanical crab in front of the Kani Doraku Restaurant, which moves its arms and eyestalks, a squid that puffs steam, and oni (demons) that are illuminated at night.

Dotonbori is a great place to visit if you are hungry; its streets are lined with countless places to eat and drink. The local specialties consist of takoyaki (battered balls filled with diced or minced octopus) and okonomiyaki (a pancake like indulgence packed with pork, vegetables, or seafood). Both items can be purchased fresh from street stands for only a few hundred yen. Another item, which Dotonbori is known for is, fugu (pufferfish). This poisonous and potentially lethal fish is served in many restaurants as a delicacy, and if it isn't prepared properly it can result in severe illness or even death. However, this danger doesn't stop the locals from eating it. Some of the restaurants which serve fugu on their menus display a giant pufferfish outside their shop.

At night, Dotonbori really comes alive with an amazing mixture of light and sound as thousands flock to the area to enjoy a bite to eat, sing a little karaoke, play video games, or visit one of the many pachinko parlors. No trip to Osaka would be complete without experiencing this amazing place. Dotonbori is easily accessible by train via the Midosuji Line to Nanba Station.

Location(s):   Dotonbori, Chuo-ku, Osaka-shi

Web Page: http://www.dotonbori.or.jp/en/

Osaka-Shi (大阪市): Osaka City

<u>Osaka Castle (大坂城)：3D Mapping Illumination Event</u>

Constructed in 1583 by Toyotomi Hideyoshi, Osaka Castle is one of Japan's most famous castles having once played a major role in the unification of Japan. The castle was destroyed several times by fires and the air raids of World War II only to be reconstructed where today it stands as one of the most important Tangible Cultural Properties of Japan.

In the winter of 1614, Tokugawa Ieyasu attacked Toyotomi Hideyori, the son and rightful heir to Hideyoshi and the last remaining threat to Ieyasu's rule, which started the Siege of Osaka. Although the Toyotomi forces were outnumbered approximately two to one, they managed to fight off Tokugawa's 200,000-man army. Afterwards, Tokugawa had the castle's outer moat filled with sand negating one of the castle's main outer defenses. During the summer of 1615, Hideyori began to restore the outer moat, which outraged Tokugawa. He sent his armies to Osaka Castle again and this time the castle fell and Toyotomi Hideyori and his mother committed seppuku. There is a stone on the castle grounds that marks the place where the pair ended their lives.

Visitors to the castle can learn more about the history of the castle when they visit the Osaka Castle Museum. Various artifacts, panel screens, and a diorama on the 7th floor offer an insight into the over 400-year history of the castle as well as provide a glimpse into the life of Toyotomi Hideyoshi. The panel screen presentations are subtitled in English, Chinese, and Korean.

The year 2014 marked the 400-year anniversary of the Siege of

Osaka and various events and festivities to commemorate the event took place in and around the castle.

One such event was the 3D illumination of the castle, which began on December 14, 2014 and continued through February 16, 2015. The event was a collaboration between the Osaka Government Tourism Bureau and the illumination engineers at Huis Ten Bosch Park in Nagasaki. The main tower of Osaka Castle was turned into a massive canvas colored by a brilliant lightshow choreographed to music. In addition to the 3D illumination, the Nishinomaru Garden was decorated with lights drawing over 590,000 spectators to the event.

After touring the castle and museum, stop by the Osaka Castle Park, a 106-hectare (262 acre) oasis whose scenery changes with each season, drawing droves of visitors year-round. Established in 1931, the park is not only home to 600 cherry trees but also a beautiful spot to enjoy the changing of the autumn leaves.

Location(s):   2, Osakajo, Chuo-ku Osaka-shi, Osaka

Web Page: http://www.osakacastle.net/english/

Osaka-Shi (大阪市): Osaka City

<u>Tsuruhashi (鶴橋): Koreatown</u>

Similar to the Japanese enclaves that exist outside Japan, numerous Koreatowns have also been established outside of the Korean peninsula. During the time when Korea was under Japanese rule, approximately 2.4 million Koreans immigrated to Japan. Some came due to economic reasons and some were forced to move during World War II to work as laborers. Although many departed after the war, others remained and were joined in the 1950s by a wave of refugees from Jeju Island after a communist uprising there. Today, Koreans are the second largest ethnic minority living in Japan after the Chinese, and Osaka is home to the largest Korean population followed by Tokyo.

Tsuruhashi in Ikuno-ku is the center of Osaka's Koreatown and it is well known for its many Korean restaurants, shops, and super markets. The residents hail from all over the Korean peninsula and from many different eras. Some of Tsuruhashi's inhabitants are from South Korea, some are from North Korea and others were brought or have family who were brought to Japan during a time when Korea was a unified nation.

The area is easily accessible via the JR Loop line, the Kintetsu Nara and the Osaka lines, or the Sennichimae Subway line. In the area surrounding Tsuruhashi Station, there is a labyrinth of 800 market stalls that offer all sorts of imported items and amazing Korean food, all at reasonable prices. Also there is an entire side street devoted to Korean BBQ or yakiniku as it is referred to in Japan. Each restaurant offers various cuts and types of meat at different price points. Alongside the Korean restaurants, you will also find Japanese restaurants offering okonomiyaki (tepan fried batter with vegetables, pork or seafood), kushi-katsu (deep fried skewers), sashimi, and sushi. If you are interested in kimchi, you will find a variety of stalls offering every type of kimchi available including soft-shelled crab kimchi, cucumber kimchi, and celery kimchi. There are shops selling brightly colored Korean hanbok (traditional Korean dress), table ware, raw fish, meat, and vegetables, which are hard to find elsewhere.

Tsuruhashi is a dark and dank area, reminiscent of pre-war Japan, comprised of narrow streets and alley ways teaming with tourists who come there to simply feast and stroll. It is where Korean traditions have been preserved and passed down alongside Japanese traditions and customs, and it is definitely worth visiting if the opportunity arises.

Location(s):   1-chome Tsuruhashi, Ikunoku, Osaka-shi, Osaka

Web Page: http://www.ikuno-koreatown.com/

Osaka-Shi (大阪市): Osaka City

Universal Studios Japan

(ユニバーサル・スタジオ・ジャパン)

When you visit Japan, visiting an American-based establishment is probably the furthest from your mind; however, you may find it interesting to see how the foreign businesses operate in Japan. There are always subtle and sometimes not so subtle differences when catering to the Japanese market.

One such place is Universal Studios Japan, which opened in the Osaka Bay area in March of 2001. It was the first theme park under the Universal Studios brand to be built in Asia and receives over 10 million visitors a year, making it the second most visited amusement park after Tokyo Disney Resort.

The park sits on 390,000 square meters (4,197,925 yds²) and is similar to the Universal Orlando Resort, containing selected attractions from that resort and Universal Studios Hollywood. The attractions are arranged in eight distinct areas of the park. The newest area, The Wizarding World of Harry Potter, was modeled after the ones in Universal Orlando and Universal Studios Hollywood. It opened on July 15, 2014 with its flagship attraction, Harry Potter and the Forbidden Journey. Although a majority of the attractions here are the same as the ones found in the U.S., there are also attractions that are unique to Universal Studios Japan such as Hogwarts Express Photo.

Each area is broken down as follows:

1. Hollywood

2. New York

3. San Francisco

4. Jurassic Park

5. Amity Village

6. Universal Wonderland

7. Waterworld

8. The Wizarding World of Harry Potter

The area designated as Hollywood features Hollywood Dream (The Ride) and Space Fantasy (The Ride) as well as various 4D attractions. From there, you can move on to New York and enjoy the Amazing Adventures of Spiderman ride or move to the theater to watch *Terminator 2*. There are various stage and street shows in this area. San Francisco is right around the corner where you can experience Back to the Future (The Ride) or come face to face with an inferno in Backdraft. Visitors can go back in time when they visit the Jurassic Park area and ride the Jurassic Park ride or see how they react when they encounter carnivorous velociraptors prowling the streets. Who can remember the popularity of the movie *Jaws*? The 1975 American thriller directed by Steven Spielberg and based on Peter Benchley's novel of the same name caused so many people to fear the water! Visit quiet Amity Village and take part in the boat tour where things become rather unsettling fairly quickly. Rounding the park, we have Universal Wonderland, home to Snoopy Studios, Hello Kitty Fashion Avenue, and Sesame Street Fun World. Finally, there is a live theater presentation in Waterworld with amazing stunts and breathtaking action.

The park also features a nighttime parade called The Magical

Starlight Parade showcasing numerous illuminated floats. Please note that there is an extra charge to access the special viewing area.

Just outside the park's gates is Universal Citywalk, a shopping and dining area, which also features multiple official Universal hotels. When visiting the Citywalk, make sure to stop by at the Osaka Takoyaki Museum featuring various vendors of the dish, which was invented in Osaka 75 years ago!

The theme park is easily accessible via the JR Yumesaki Line; the entrance gate to Universal Studios Japan is a five-minute walk from Universal City Station.

Location(s):   2-1-33 Sakurajima, Konohana-ku, Osaka-shi, Osaka

Web Page: http://www.usj.co.jp/e/

Shiga Prefecture (滋賀県)

Hikone-shi (彦根市): Hikone City

Hikone Castle (彦根城)

Any visit to Shiga Prefecture has to include a tour of Hikone Castle. It is one of only four Japanese castles to be declared a National Treasure. The other castles are Himeji, Matsumoto, and Inuyama. Located near Lake Biwa, Japan's largest lake, it is one of twelve remaining original castles in Japan; this means it survived the post-feudal era without undergoing destruction and reconstruction.

The castle took twenty years to construct and was completed in 1622. With its beautiful ivory-white walls surrounded by a double moat, the castle served 14 generations of feudal lords for nearly 260 years without suffering any attacks. When the Meiji era began in 1868, many castles were scheduled to be dismantled and only upon the request from the emperor himself, Hikone Castle was kept intact. Today, it remains one of the oldest original castles in Japan.

Hikone Castle's three-storied castle keep (The Tenshu) is relatively small but displays a unique design that combines multiple architectural styles. The approach to the castle keep is quite interesting. It includes a spiral ramp, which accesses a wooden bridge designed to be destroyed easily in the event of an attack. The castle's expansive grounds include the Genkyu-en Garden, the Housho-dai Tea Room, the Tenbin Yagura Turret, the Umaya (Horse Stable), the Jihosho (Time-keeping Bell), and the Hikone Castle Museum.

Like many castles in Japan, the grounds of Hikone Castle

become a popular cherry blossom viewing spot during spring. Hikone's cherry trees reach full bloom about a week later than those in nearby Kyoto, around early to mid-April and draw visitors from all over Japan.

Visitors to the castle can take part in the 90-minute castle tour, which covers most of the important parts of the castle area, including the Genkyu-en Garden. The garden was constructed in 1677 and is modeled after a detached palace belonging to Emperor Genso of the Tang Dynasty in China.

The Hikone Castle Museum displays artwork belonging to the Hikone Clan, including Hikone Folding Screens and samurai warrior armor.

Hikone City can be reached via the Tokaido Main Line. Hikone Castle is just 15 minutes on foot from Hikone Station.

Location(s):   1-1 Konki-cho, Hikone-shi, Shiga

Web Page: http://www.hikoneshi.com/en/castle/

Points of Interest: Kansai Region

Kitano Tenmangu Shrine Kyoto

Fushimi Inari Taisha Kyoto

Sagano Bamboo Forest Arashiyama Kyoto

Kiyomizu-dera Kyoto

Historic Gion District Kyoto

Osaka Castle

Dotonbori Hotel Osaka

Osaka Bay

Kobe Port Tower

Heijo Palace Nara

Byodoin Temple Uji City

Himeji Castle Hyogo

Shirahama Beachfront Resorts Wakayama

Chugoku Region

Introduction to Chugoku (中国地方）

Chugoku Region is the westernmost area of Honshu, Japan's largest island. It consists of the prefectures of Hiroshima, Okayama, Shimane, Tottori, and Yamaguchi. The area is further sub-divided into the heavily industrialized Sanyo Region and the more rural Sanin Region.

The region is considerably more laid-back than the eastern part of Honshu and attractions include the UNESCO World Heritage Sites of Itsukushima Shrine on Miyajima Island and the Hiroshima Peace Memorial (Atomic Dome). Chugoku is also home to one of the Three Great Gardens of Japan, Korakuen Garden.

Popular dishes in this region include okonomiyaki, Matsuba-gani, katsuo no tataki, and sanuki udon. The okonomiyaki made in Hiroshima is quite different from the dish you will find anywhere else in Japan. Instead of pancake like batter cooked on a hot iron griddle, Hiroshima style starts with a crepe-like thin pancake on the griddle that is topped with heaps of shredded cabbage and other toppings such as Matsuba-gani (snow crab), katsuo no tataki (seared bonito), tempura bits or seafood. On the side, yakisoba noodles are cooked along with a fried egg before all the ingredients are assembled in layers. Tottori Prefecture is famous for Matsuba-gani and boiled crab commands high prices. Kochi Prefecture is famous for bonito fishing and katsuo no tataki is a general term used to describe this fish seared over a flame. It is often served with lots of sliced garlic, thin sliced onions, shiso, green onion, myoga, and lemon with a generous amount of soy sauce mixed with yuzu citrus. Sanuki style udon is served al dente with a simple soy sauce or broth.

Hiroshima Airport serves the greater Chugoku Region. The Sanyo Shinkansen line links Hiroshima, Okayama and other major towns to Kyushu in the southwest and Kansai (Osaka) to the east.

Web Page: http://chugoku-navi.jp/english/

Hiroshima Prefecture (広島県)

Hiroshima-shi (広島市): Hiroshima City

Hiroshima Castle (広島城)

The city of Hiroshima developed as a castle town as did many other towns throughout Japan. Hiroshima Castle, constructed on a plain in 1589, served as the city's physical and economic center. Today, visitors to the castle will find the reconstructed five-story keep surrounded by a moat. Although the castle survived the Meiji restoration when many castles were destroyed, it did fall victim to the atomic bomb, which was dropped on the city in 1945. The castle was reconstructed thirteen years later from reinforced concrete and houses a museum, which chronicles the castle's and Hiroshima's history. A second reconstruction effort was undertaken in 1994 during which time the second layer of defense surrounding the castle known as the Ninomaru was reconstructed using traditional methods.

The castle originally had three concentric moats, two of which were filled in during the late 19th and 20th centuries. Within the castle walls, you will find three trees that survived the atomic bomb. One is a eucalyptus, the other a willow, and the third one is a holly. In addition, there is a concrete bunker from which the first radio transmission was broadcast following the detonation of the atomic bomb.

Situated next to the castle is the Gokogu Shrine. During the second week of January, the Tondo Matsuri where the previous year's amulets are burned takes place here.

In October, the annual Hiroshima International Food Festival is held around the castle moat. The huge two-day festival is a food lover's paradise and showcases local food and beverages from all twenty-three cities and towns across the prefecture. Admission is free and visitors pay only for the food they consume.

The castle is a 15-minute walk from the Peace Park and worth visiting if you are in the area.

Location(s):   21-1 Moto-machi Naka-ku Hiroshima-shi

Web Page: http://visithiroshima.net/things_to_do/attracti ons/historical_places/hiroshima_castle.html

Hiroshima-shi (広島市): Hiroshima City

Hiroshima Heiwa Kinen Koen (広島平和記念公園): Hiroshima Peace Memorial Park

Located in central Hiroshima, Hiroshima Peace Memorial Park is a sobering reminder of Hiroshima's tragic past following the world's first atomic bomb attack. The purpose of the park is not only to memorialize the victims of the bomb, but to also raise awareness of the horrors of nuclear war and advocate world peace. Before the war, the area, which the park currently occupies, was the political and commercial heart of the city. This is why it was targeted for the atomic bomb. Four years following the attack, it was decided that the area would be dedicated to peace and it would serve as a memorial for the thousands of victims. Over a million visitors from all over the world visit the park each year. On August 6, 2015, the park commemorated the 70th anniversary of the dropping of the atomic bomb on the city.

Officially opened on April 1, 1954, the park spans over 120,000 square meters (1,291,669 ft²) and is lined with trees and walkways. It contains several memorials and a museum, including the Memorial Centograph, the Flame of Peace, the Children's Peace Monument, the Atomic Bomb Dome (Genbaku Domu), the Rest House, and the Hiroshima Peace Memorial Museum.

The Memorial Cenotaph located near the center of the park is an arched tomb for the victims of the bomb. A stone chest below the arch holds a register that contains all the known names of those who lost their lives as a result of the bombing. Engraved on the cenotaph are the words, "Let all souls here rest in peace, for we shall not repeat the evil." A memorial ceremony takes place here annually on the anniversary of the bombing.

The Flame of Peace is a memorial symbolizing two hands held with palms facing upward. It was designed to call attention to the victims of the bombing who were unable to satisfy their thirst for water. The flame has been burning since August 1, 1964 and will be extinguished once all of the nuclear weapons on earth have been destroyed.

The Children's Peace Monument was built to memorialize all the children who died as a result of the atomic bombing of Hiroshima. The monument features Sadako Sasaki holding a golden crane above her head. She was a young girl who developed leukemia from exposure to radiation from the atomic bomb at the age of 11. She is known for attempting to fold 1,000 origami paper cranes so that her wish to become healthy again would come true. In Japan, the crane is a symbol of longevity and happiness, and it is said that the gods will grant a wish to anyone who folds a thousand paper cranes. Sadly, she died having completed her 644th crane, but her classmates folded the rest, with which she was buried. The monument was built with donations from school children.

The Atomic Bomb Dome (Genbaku Domu) is the skeletal ruins of the former Industrial Promotion Hall. The bomb is believed to have exploded almost directly above the building and it is one of the very few structures left standing near the epicenter of the blast. It was left as is after the bombing in memory of the casualties. The dome is on the UNESCO World Heritage List.

The Rest House is another building that survived the atomic bomb. The building, constructed in 1929, was originally the

Taishoya Kimono Shop. It was used as a fuel distribution station after 1944 and when the bomb was dropped in 1945, it crushed the roof, destroyed the interior, and burned everything consumable except what was in the basement.

The Hiroshima Peace Memorial Museum is the primary museum in the park dedicated to educating visitors about the bomb. It contains exhibits and information covering the buildup to war, the role of Hiroshima in the war up to the bombing, and extensive information on the bombing and its effects, along with substantial memorabilia and pictures from the bombing.

The Hiroshima Peace Memorial Park is open all year. The Peace Memorial Museum is open:

8:30 AM to 6:00 PM (March – November)

8:30 AM to 5:00 PM (December – February)

8:30 AM to 7:00 PM in August during summer

It is closed from December 29 to January 1

The park memorializes the important turning point in a devastating war and should be on your list of places to visit when in Hiroshima. It is only through awareness and education that we can prevent such a tragedy from happening again.

Location(s):   1-2 Nakajimacho, Naka-ku, Hiroshima-shi,
                Hiroshima

Web Page: http://www.pcf.city.hiroshima.jp/top_e.html

Hiroshima-shi (広島市): Hiroshima City

Mazda Museum

Toyota plays a huge role in Nagoya's economy and Mazda has a similar impact in Hiroshima. Although Mazda (pronounced Matsuda in Japan) is not as large as Toyota, it produces over a million vehicles annually and is an innovative player in the Japanese auto industry.

The Mazda Motor Corporation was founded in Hiroshima in 1920 and its headquarters, development laboratories, factories, shipping facilities, and museum are still located there.

The museum provides an overview of Mazda's history including a look into the technology of its automobiles. Visitors are also provided access to the assembly line, where they can see a variety of different car models being produced. To visit the museum, reservations are required in advance. Guided tours are offered weekdays at 9:30 AM and 1:00 PM in Japanese and at 10:00 AM in English. Each tour lasts approximately 90 minutes and reservations can be made up to a year in advance.

Visitors to the museum first gather at the Mazda headquarters and sign in at the front desk. When the tour is scheduled to begin, a Mazda tour guide directs visitors on to a bus to take them to the museum building nearby.

The tour begins with a historical overview of the Mazda Company from its early days, when it was manufacturing three-wheeled trucks, to the present day. Highlights include the Mazda Cosmo (the world's first rotary engine car) and the 4-rotor Mazda 787B. From there, you will be taken to see how the design and build processes work at their Ujima plant. The tour concludes with a view of Mazda's attempts at making hydrogen fueled cars and some of their concept vehicles. At the end of the tour, there is a shop featuring Mazda-branded merchandise.

The Mazda facility is accessible via the JR Sanyo line from Hiroshima station going east, exit at Mukainada Station. From there the headquarters are a five-minute walk.

Location(s):   3-1 Mukainada-cho, Shinchi

Web Page: http://www.mazda.com/en/about/museum/guide/

Hiroshima-shi (広島市): Hiroshima City

Shukkeien Garden

While wandering through Hiroshima and taking in all the historic sites, do not neglect to visit Shukkeien Garden located just 15 minutes on foot from Hiroshima Station. The garden is considered to be one of the great Japanese gardens and played an important role during the atomic bombing of the city.

Constructed back in 1620 just after the completion of Hiroshima Castle, it is a shrunken scenery garden consisting of valleys, mountains, waterfalls, and forests represented in miniature throughout the garden's landscape. Situated around the garden's main pond are a number of tea houses where visitors can enjoy ideal views of the surrounding scenery.

Shukkeien was originally constructed as the garden of Asanu Nagaakira's (the feudal lord of Hiroshima) villa. In its center is Takuei Pond, which contains over ten small rock islands. There is a bridge spanning the center of the pond known as Koko-kyo (Straddling Rainbow Bridge). The original bridge over the pond was demolished and what you see today is the reconstructed version. Gardens of this type first appeared during the Muromachi era (1336 to 1573).

The main tea house is called the Seifukan. There is a window located on its east wall which perfectly frames the bridge spanning the pond. Many newlywed couples come to this spot to have their photographs taken. As a matter of fact, the garden enjoys over 180,000 visitors annually and is a very popular attraction in Hiroshima.

On a sad note, the garden is located only three quarters of a mile from the hyper center of the atomic bomb. Hence, all of the structures in the garden were destroyed and the vegetation burned with the exception of one tree that withstood the blast. Those who were injured by the bomb took refuge in the garden and died there. Their remains were interred within the garden.

Location(s):   2-11 Kaminobori-cho, Naka-ku, Hiroshima City

Web Page: http://visithiroshima.net/things_to_do/attracti
ons/parks_and_gardens/shukkeien_garden.ht
ml

Okayama Prefecture (岡山県)

Okayama-shi (岡山市): Okayama City

<u>Korakuen Garden (後楽園)</u>

Located next to Okayama Castle on the north bank of the Aashi River is Korakuen Garden, one of Japan's official three great gardens (Kenrokuen in Kanazawa and Kairakuen in Mito are the other two). The name Korakuen translates to "pleasure afterwards". It is based on a famous Confucian quote stating that a wise ruler must attend to his subjects' needs first and afterward attend to his own.

The garden was constructed by Ikeda Tsunamasa, the fourth lord of Okayama Castle. Construction of the garden began in 1687 and was completed 13 years later. The park was designed in the Chisan Kaiyu style (scenic promenade) and presents its visitors with a new view at every turn of the path. The path running through the garden connects to vast lawns, ponds, waterfalls, hills, tiny shrines, tea house, and streams. There is even a miniature maple forest, a lotus pond, and a greenhouse filled with orchids and cacti.

Korakuen Garden was opened to public in 1884 and continued to attract visitors until the bombing attack of World War II. When the war ended, the garden was restored to its former glory based upon old records.

The garden spans approximately 133,000 square meters (1,431,600 ft²), with the grassy area covering approximately 18,500 square meters (199,132 ft²). The length of the stream which runs through the garden is about 640 meters (2,100 ft). It features a central pond called Sawanoike (Marsh Pond), which contains three islands (Nakanoshima, Misoshima, and Jarijima), all purported to replicate the scenery around Lake Biwa near Kyoto.

A local ordinance prevents the construction of high-rise buildings that would encroach on the beautiful scenery. There are two entrances to the garden: across from the Okayama Prefectural Museum and across from the Moon-Viewing Bridge. Park hours are 7:30 AM to 6:00 PM (April – Sept.) and 8:00 AM to 5:00 PM (Oct. - March).

Location(s):   1-5 Korakuen, Okayama-shi, Okayama

Web Page: http://www.okayama-korakuen.jp/english/

Okayama-shi (岡山市): Okayama City

Okayama Castle (岡山城)

A visit to Okayama Prefecture would not be complete without a stopover at Okayama Castle, nicknamed Crow Castle because of its black exterior. One other castle, Matsumoto Castle located in Nagano Prefecture, has a black exterior and also bears the nickname Crow Castle. Constructed in 1597, the original castle was destroyed during World War II. The current castle is a concrete reconstruction, which was completed in 1966. Two of the watch towers, which survived the bombing of 1945, are now listed by the National Agency for Cultural Affairs as Important Cultural Properties. In 1996, as part of the castle's 400th anniversary celebrations, the castle's rooftop gargoyles were gilded. The castle is air-conditioned and has elevators that make it easy to navigate.

Okayama Castle is located on the Asahi River, which was once used as a moat. Korakuen Garden, one of the top three gardens in Japan, is located just across the river. The main building of Okayama Castle is six stories tall. The interior of the main building is rather modern and displays exhibits on the history and development of the castle. On the castle grounds, you will find other reconstructed buildings and unearthed foundations, which help give one a sense of the former extent of the castle's complex of buildings.

The castle is open from 9:00 AM to 5:30 PM daily. (Except for Dec. 29-31). Admission is ¥800 for those 15 years of age or older and ¥120 for children aged 6-14. It is easily accessible via the Sanyo Line. Get off at Okayama Station and the castle is a 20-minute walk or 10 minutes by bus.

Since Korakuen Garden is so close, why not combine a visit to the castle and the garden and enjoy the majestic remnants of feudal Japan in Okayama City?

Location(s):   2-3-1 Marunouchi, Okayama-shi, Okayama

Web Page: http://okayama-
                   kanko.net/ujo/english/index.html

Kurashiki-shi (倉敷市): Kurashiki City

The old merchant quarter known as Bikan Chiku (Bikan Historical Area) is a famous sightseeing area in Kurashiki City located in Okayama Prefecture.

Kurashiki is approximately ten miles from Okayama City, the prefectural capital of Okayama. Many of the city's former white-walled store houses have been transformed into museums, boutique shops, and cafés. As a matter of fact, Kurashiki loosely translates as "town of storehouses". The city was fortunate enough to escape the ravages of World War II and as a result, many of the original storehouses, mills, and shops remain in beautiful condition.

The city's preserved canal area dates back to the Edo period (1603-1867), when Kurashiki served as an important rice distribution center. The canal area is a ten-minute walk from Kurashiki Station's south exit.

Right outside the north exit of Kurashiki Station you will find the shuttered remains of an amusement park once referred to as the Copenhagen of Japan. With a beautiful collection of trees, flowers, and rides intended to recreate Denmark's Copenhagen, Tivoli Park was, for many years, the second most popular tourist attraction in Kurashiki (after Bikan Chiku). Due to mounting financial troubles, the park was shuttered at the end of 2008.

Kurashiki is also the home of Japan's first Western art museum, the Ohara Museum of Art. Established in 1930 by Magosaburo Ohara, it displays paintings by El Greco, Monet, Matisse, Gauguin, and Renoir.

Moving away from the Bikan Chiku area, you will find a modern

Kurashiki just like any other modern city in Japan, but still there exists this rare piece of old Japan, one that gives a sense of where people lived and worked.

Web Page: https://www.kurashiki-tabi.jp/for/en/city.html

Takahashi-shi (高梁市): Takahashi City

Takahashi city, located in Okayama Prefecture, is a castle town that once thrived at the foot of Matsuyama Castle (Bitchu Matsuyama Castle). Today, visitors can travel down carefully preserved historic streets close to the castle and drop in on the samurai and merchant houses that have been restored and are now open to the public.

Bitchu Matsuyama Castle, designated as such in order to differentiate it from Matsuyama Castle in Shikoku, is one of Japan's few remaining original castles that survived orders to be demolished during the early Meiji era. It was originally constructed in 1240 when castles served primarily as defensive fortresses. Accordingly, it was built on a steep mountain that is difficult to attack. Atop Mount Gagyu, the castle stands at an elevation of approximately 1,410 feet (427 m), making it Japan's highest castle.

Even today, Matsuyama Castle is not easily accessible. Visitors can take a taxi up most of the way, but there is a point at which you must walk as no vehicles are allowed on the path leading to the castle. The ascent to the castle will take you 20 minutes from the nearest parking lot and the path will wind through the ruined foundations of former castle structures leading to multiple successive circles of defense before reaching the innermost castle grounds and the castle keep.

The inside of the castle is only two stories high and relatively small. There are few artifacts inside; however, the uniqueness of the castle and the beauty of the surrounding area more than make up for it. Views of the town below can be enjoyed from several points along the way and also through the yasama (slits in the castle walls used by archers) on the top floor of the castle keep.

Unfortunately, despite all of its beauty and outstanding features, Bitchu Matsuyama Castle is one of the least visited of all the original castles.

From the castle grounds, you can get a great view of the Orii Samurai Residence. This is one of two samurai residences (the other is the Haibara Residence) open to the public in Takahashi City. It was constructed about 170 years ago and visitors can access the main building and garden. Within the main building, life-sized dolls are arranged to provide visitors with an opportunity to see what daily life may have been like in a samurai house during the Edo period.

The Orii Residence is open daily from 9:00 AM to 5:00 PM (Except December 29-January 3, when the residence is closed to visitors).

Takahashi is a pedestrian-friendly city listed as having one of the top ten beautiful streets in Japan. The best time to visit is during the spring when the cherry trees are in full bloom.

Matsue-shi (松江市): Matsue City

Matsue Castle (松江城)

Constructed in 1611, Matsue Castle is one of twelve original castles remaining in Japan, and it is the main attraction of Matsue City in Shimane Prefecture. What is meant by original is that the castle has not been destroyed by fire, war, or other causes and is completely original in its wooden form. A majority of castles in Japan today are concrete reconstructions of the originals.

The castle was abandoned in 1871 and all the buildings with the exception of the main keep were torn down, as were many other castles in Japan during the Meiji restoration. Fortunately, the castle underwent reconstruction and repair work in the 1950s and further restorations were completed in 2001, bringing it to its present form today.

The castle's black painted wood walls give it an ominous look and the five-story keep actually conceals a sixth floor. Several defensive features such as small windows and hidden openings from which stones could be dropped were incorporated into the castle's design. However, the castle never faced an attack, which probably accounts for its condition.

Within the castle, there are displays of arms and armor, a pictorial display of the castle's history, photos of all the castles throughout Japan, and miniature replicas of the layout of Matsue, chronicling the changes over time. The original shachi (mythical dolphins) from the castle's roof are also on display within the castle. It was believed that the shachi protected a castle from fire and were common in castle construction and design. From the top floor, there are beautiful views of the city and surrounding area including Lake Shinji, Japan's seventh largest lake.

Visitors to the castle can enjoy a pleasure boat trip around the extensive castle moat. The moat is part of Jozan Koen (park), which now houses the Matsue Historical Museum. The former home of Lafcadio Hearn and the Lafcadio Hearn Memorial Museum, and some samurai residences dating to the Edo period are located just north of the castle moat.

A short distance from the castle, you will find the Gessho Temple. Here, the graves of all nine Matsudaira lords (the rulers of the castle) are located and worth visiting.

The castle is 30 minutes on foot from JR Matsue Station. International visitors who show their passport will receive a 50 percent discount on the entrance fee.

Location(s):   1-5 Tonomachi, Matsue-shi, Shimane

Web Page: http://www.city.matsue.shimane.jp/kankou/jp
/e/castle.htm

Matsue-shi (松江市): Matsue City

P. Lafcadio Hearn Former Residence

If Matsue Castle is the main attraction in Matsue City, the former residence of Lafcadio Hearn and the Lafcadio Hearn Memorial Museum can be considered the second and third main attractions of the city. Patrick Lafcadio Hearn (1850 – 1904), known also by his Japanese name, Koizumi Yakumo, was an international author who wrote several books about Japan, notably *Kwaidan: Stories and Studies of Strange Things*. Of Irish decent, Hearn was born in and named after the island of Lefkada, one of the Greek Ionian islands. His mother was a Greek woman named Rosa Antoniou Kassimatis and his father was a military surgeon stationed in Lefkada during the British occupation of the islands.

In 1890, Hearn traveled to Japan with a commission as a newspaper correspondent that was soon terminated. Fortunately, he gained a teaching position during the summer of 1890 at the Shimane Prefectural Common Middle School in Matsue. He remained in Matsue for fifteen months, during which time he married Koizumi Setsu, the daughter of a local samurai family, with whom he had four children. In 1896, he became a naturalized Japanese citizen, assuming the name of Koizumi Yakumo and accepted a teaching position in Tokyo.

Hearn obtained another teaching position in Kumamoto in late 1891, where he spent the next three years of his life and completed his book, *Glimpses of Unfamiliar Japan* (1894). 1896 found Hearn teaching English literature at the Tokyo Imperial University, a job he had until 1903. He was fortunate enough to become a professor at Waseda University in 1904, but he passed away due to heart failure soon after. His grave is located at the Zoshigaya Cemetery in Toshima, Tokyo.

In the late 19th century, Japan was still largely unknown and exotic to westerners. Through his works, Hearn offered the West some of its first descriptions of pre-industrial and Meiji era Japan. Consequently, his books are considered to have historical value.

Although he remained in Matsue for only fifteen months, he managed to become the city's favorite son. Because of Hearn's Irish heritage, there are many cultural connections between Matsue and Ireland; an Irish festival and a parade are held annually to commemorate this relationship.

Hearn's old residence, a charming samurai house and garden, attracts many visitors. It was in this house that he began writing two of his most famous books, *Kwaidan* and *Glimpses of Unfamiliar Japan*, in which he describes many of his experiences in Matsue. Virtually next door, is the Lafcadio Hearn Memorial Museum, which displays a selection of Hearn's original manuscripts, his desk, quills and inkpot, and a number of his beloved Japanese tobacco pipes. The Museum was established in 1933 and attracts approximately 150,000 visitors a year.

Hearn's former residence is located in the samurai district north of Matsue Castle. There is an admission charge of ¥300 each for the museum and residence (Foreign visitors receive 50 percent off admission).

Location(s):   Kitahori-cho, Matsue, Shimane

Web Page: http://www.city.matsue.shimane.jp/kankou/jp
/e/lafcadio.htm

Yasugi-shi (安来市): Yasugi City

Adachi Museum of Art

Yasugi City, located in the eastern portion of Shimane Prefecture, was an ancient steel producing center. Today, visitors are drawn to the town for the highly regarded Adachi Museum of Art established in 1980 by businessman Adachi Zenko. Born in Shimane, Adachi was well known for his passion for collecting art. He opened the museum as a way of showing gratitude to his hometown and hoping to enhance the cultural development of the prefecture.

The museum houses a collection of nearly 1,500 20th century paintings, ceramics, and artwork that are rotated seasonally. Its permanent exhibit features the works of Yokoyama Taikan (real name, Sakai Hidemaro), who is credited with helping create the Japanese painting technique of Nihonga. The museum also boasts an award-winning garden, which has been named the best garden in Japan by the *Journal of Japanese Gardening* since 2003. The only down side is that the meticulously sculpted garden can only be viewed from behind the museum's large windows. There are some sections of the garden where there are walking paths but these take you away from the core of the garden.

Photography is permitted inside the museum except in certain sections that are specifically marked. For ¥500, you will be provided with a recorded tour in English highlighting the exhibits and garden. However, English descriptions are provided on each of the exhibits making the recording somewhat unnecessary.

The museum is easily accessible by train from Matsue Station, exit Yasugi Station. From that point there are free shuttle buses that run once every hour. There are also limited express trains from Okayama which stop at Yasugi Station before continuing on to Matsue.

Location(s):   320 Furukawa-cho, Yasugi-shi, Shimane

Web Page: https://www.adachi-museum.or.jp/en/

Tottori Prefecture (鳥取県)

Tottori-shi (鳥取市): Tottori City

<u>Tottori Sakyu Illusion</u>

Located two and a half hours from Osaka by train, the city of Tottori is situated along the coast of the Sea of Japan and is perhaps most famous for its sand dunes. The dunes are the largest in Japan and stretch 1.5 miles (2.4 km) from north to south and 10 miles (16 km) from east to west. The dunes were created over thousands of years, as sand from the nearby Sendaigawa River was washed out to sea and eventually re-deposited along the coast by the ocean's currents. Today, the constant movement of the tides and the coastal winds continuously shape the sand dunes and provide an ever-changing landscape.

The dunes offer many activities in which visitors can participate including camel and horse-drawn cart rides, paragliding, and sandboarding (a variation of snowboarding). Just a short walk from the dunes, you will find The Sand Museum. This unique museum displays large sand sculptures by artists from around the world and is an amazing place to visit. The exhibits change annually and last from mid-April to early January of the following year.

The Tottori Sand Dunes, which are part of the Sanin Kaigan National Park, draw visitors from all over Japan throughout the year, but for one month each year visitors can immerse themselves in the magical world of lights as the dunes are transformed into a world of illusion. The Tottori Sakyu Illusion, which takes place from the end of November through December 25, utilizes over 300,000 light bulbs and illuminated sand sculptures to create a world of light emerging from the darkness of the dunes.

The event has two venues: the Tottori Sakyu parking lot and the Tottori Sakyu Kodomonokuni, which is 15 minutes on foot from the parking lot. Visitors are admitted to both venues from 6:00 PM to 10:00 PM, free of charge. During the month of December, the city provides free shuttle service from Tottori Station to the dunes parking lot.

The Tottori Sakyu Illusion is a great way to usher in the holidays and should not be missed.

Location(s):   689-0105 Fukubechoyuyama, Tottori-shi, Tottori

Web Page: http://www.tottori-sakyu.jp/

Yamaguchi Prefecture (山口県)

Iwakuni-shi (岩国市): Iwakuni City

Iwakuni City, located in southeastern Yamaguchi Prefecture, is perhaps best known for its unique Kintai Bridge. Constructed in 1673, the bridge consists of five wooden arches, which span the Nishiki River. The bridge was declared a National Treasure in 1922 and is a very popular tourist destination, particularly during the blossoming of the sakura trees and the changing colors of the Japanese maples in autumn.

Kikkou Park is another popular tourist attraction that includes the Kintai Bridge. Recently, the park has become known for one other popular item, soft serve ice cream! Several different ice cream shops line the front of the park, but the most interesting is the Sasaki Kojiro and Musashi ice cream shops, which both claim to serve the best ice cream in Japan. For those who are unfamiliar, Sasaki Kojiro was a prominent swordsman most remembered for his death while battling Miyamoto Musashi in 1612. Legend has it that Musashi fought over 60 battles and was undefeated. Kojiro was regarded as his most formidable opponent.

The ice cream shop competition is fierce and revolves around which shop offers the greatest variety of soft serve ice cream flavors. The shops were featured on popular Japanese variety shows such as The Sekai Gyoten News and offer such unusual flavors as wasabi, curry, ramen, garlic, soy sauce, tomato, and habanero to name a few. Customers can also combine flavors to achieve their own unique creation. The Kojiro shop offers 50 flavors of soft-serve ice cream while Musashi lists 100 unique flavors. It is rumored that the Musashi shop kept adding to its menu in order to outdo the Kojiro shop.

There is even a ranking of ice cream flavors based on women's and men's preferences. For women it is: (1) Cleopatra's Tears, (2) Acerola Berry, (3) Golden Kiwi, (4) Chestnut, and (5) Tiramasu. For men, the list includes: (1) Hokkaido Vanilla, (2) Hokkaido Vanilla-Chocolate Swirl, (3) Banana Cocoa, (4) Cleopatra's Tears, and (5) Iwakuni Renkon (Lotus), which happens to be a local specialty.

Iwakuni is easily accessible by the JR Sanyo Shinkansen from Hiroshima. The 15-minute trip will cost ¥1,620 for a non-reserved seat. Alternatively, the city can be reached by local train on the JR Sanyo Main Line via Hiroshima. The trip takes 50 minutes and costs ¥760. Most travelers will combine a trip to Hiroshima, Miyajima, and Iwakuni.

Web Page: http://kintaikyo.iwakuni-city.net/en/summary.html

(Kintaikyo Bridge)

Mine-shi (美祢市): Mine City

Akiyoshidai Plateau/ Akiyoshido Cave

When traveling in Yamaguchi Prefecture, one of the places that you should definitely try visiting is Mine City, home to Akiyoshido Cave, the largest and longest limestone cave not only in Japan but in Asia. The cave, which contains 5.5 miles (8.9 km) of passage ways and is 328 feet (100 m) wide, was named by Emperor Hirohito in 1926 when he was still the crown prince. Today, visitors can enter a section a little over half a mile (1 km) long, which has been designated as a public sightseeing course.

The cave is part of the Akiyoshidai Plateau, an area dotted with limestone pinnacles. The plateau is believed to be a 300-million-year-old coral reef, which over time was eroded by rain. Both the cave and the plateau are designated as a quasi-national park.

Akiyoshido Cave is relatively easy to navigate as there are paved pathways and ample lighting. The temperature inside the cave is a constant 63°F (16°C) throughout the year making for a comfortable environment. Once inside, visitors will be treated to breathtaking limestone terrace pools filled with water, stalactites that form natural sculptures, and underground waterfalls. For an additional ¥300, they can traverse an adventure path, which is a bit difficult to navigate but offers a splendid view of the cave from a higher vantage point. The cave is home to six types of cave bats including the miniopterus fuliginosus also known as the Eastern Bent-Winged Bat, which measures between 4 and 5 inches (10-13 cm) in length.

There are three entrances to the cave system: Akiyoshido Visitor Center (Akiyoshido front entrance), Kurotani Visitor

Center (Kurotani), and Akiyoshidai Visitor Center (via elevator). The Akiyoshido entrance is the closest to the bus terminal and main parking lots while the Kurotani entrance is often utilized by tour groups. From the elevator entrance, it is a 5 to 10-minute walk to an observation deck. Visitors can glimpse nice views of the Akiyoshidai Plateau from this pathway. Buses run between the cave's three entrances. They run relatively frequently on weekends and holidays but are often infrequent during weekdays.

The cave is open year-round between 8:30 AM and 4:30 PM. Getting to the cave is straightforward using buses, which depart from both Yamaguchi Station and Shin-Yamaguchi Shinkansen Station and drop passengers off at the cave entrance. There are also buses departing from Shimonoseki. The journey from these stations to the cave usually takes one hour so plan accordingly.

Location(s):   Shuhocho Akiyoshi Takinokuchi, Mine,
                      Yamaguchi

Web Page: http://english.karusuto.com/

Points of Interest: Chugoku Region

Kurashiki City Okayama

Korakuen Garden Okayama

Bitchu Matsuyama Castle Okayama

Hiroshima Genbaku Dome

Miyajima

Kintai Bridge Iwakuni

Shikoku Region

Introduction to Shikoku (四国)

Consisting of four prefectures as denoted by its name: Ehime, Kagawa, Kochi, and Tokushima, Shikoku is the smallest and least populated of the four main islands of Japan. Located just south of Honshu, Japan's main island, Shikoku is the only Japanese island without any volcanoes.

The region is famous for its 88-temple pilgrimage, Japan's most famous pilgrimage route, and Awa Odori, a dance festival that takes place in Tokushima Prefecture during Obon (August 12-15). Awa Odori is the largest dance festival in Japan, drawing over 1.3 million visitors annually.

Life in this area is slow-paced and the climate is mild. Visitors to Shikoku can enjoy rafting and canoeing on one of the two major rivers, Yoshino-gawa (吉野川) and Shimanto-gawa (四万十川).The Seto Inland Sea/ Seto Naikai (瀬戸内海) is ideal for fishing and diving while the swells of the Pacific in Kochi make it a surfer's paradise.

While visiting Shikoku, be sure to sample the udon for which it is famous. Udon is a thick wheat flour noodle often served hot in a mildly flavored soup. The simplest form is known as kake udon, featuring a broth known as kakejiru, consisting of dashi (soup stock), shoyu (soy sauce), and mirin (a type of rice wine similar to sake but with a lower alcohol content). The most common form of dashi or soup stock used in Japan is derived from boiling kombu (kelp) and kezurikatsuo (shavings of katsuobushi – preserved skipjack tuna) and then straining the resultant liquid. Kake udon is often served with thinly chopped scallions and can include other toppings such as tempura (usually prawns that have been battered and deep fried), kakiage (mixed tempura fritter) or aburage (deep fried tofu seasoned with sugar, mirin, and shoyu).

Sanuki udon, another type of udon dish, is produced in Kagawa Prefecture, formerly known as Sanuki Province. This type of udon noodle is characterized by its square shape and flat edges.

In Kochi Prefecture, you will find that katsuo no tataki is very popular. This dish includes skipjack tuna or katsuo that is finely chopped and mixed with spring onion and rice vinegar. Outside the Kochi area, the fish is sliced and seared. Another regional item you will find in the Kochi area is sawachi ryori, which is sashimi or sushi served on a huge plate called sawachi.

Finally, in the Tokushima area, you will discover that sudachi is quite common. This is a small citrus fruit similar to a lime that is grated and added to dishes to give them a distinctive taste known throughout Tokushima during the summer months.

Although Shikoku lacks an international airport, it does have four regional/domestic airports: Tokushima Airport, Takamatsu Airport, Kochi-Ryoma Airport, and Matsuyama Airport. All of these airports have flights to Tokyo and other major Japanese cities such as Osaka, Nagoya, Sapporo, and Fukuoka.

You can also reach Shikoku via the three expressways connecting it to Honshu known as the Honshu–Shikoku Bridge Project. The three expressways include the Kobe-Awaji-Naruto Expressway (Eastern Shikoku), the Seto-Chuo Expressway (Central Shikoku), and the Nishiseto Expressway (Western Shikoku).

There are also a number of ferries that link Shikoku to various destinations including Honshu, Kyushu, and various islands around Shikoku.

Web Page: http://www.tourismshikoku.org/

Ehime Prefecture (愛媛県)

Ehime-shi (宇和島市) Ehime City

<u>Uwajima</u>

Uwajima is a coastal town in southern Ehime Prefecture, facing the Bungo Channel, which separates Kyushu from Shikoku. Although most travelers bypass it en route to Matsuyama, the town offers an interesting detour for its age old traditions of pearl farming and bloodless bullfighting. It also draws a steady trickle of travelers to its Shinto fertility shrine and attached sex museum. Now I have your attention!

Many Shinto shrines once had a connection to fertility rites. Of those that remain, the Taga Shrine is one of the best known. Taga Shrine is situated north of Uwajima's city center and people visit the shrine to pray for longevity, good health, and in particular, fertility. It features an improbably large phallus carved from a log alongside the main building and numerous statues and stone carvings throughout. Next to the shrine is a three-story sex museum featuring erotica from all corners of the world. There is an entry fee of ¥800 and if you wish to photograph the displays, you are required to pay ¥20,000. Minors under the age of 20 are not allowed to enter the museum.

Uwajima is also one of the top pearl producers in Japan. Shinju Kaikan, located at 3-58 Takakushi, is a pearl souvenir shop, which also has a restaurant and hotel on the premises. Here you can have pearl jewelry custom created to fit any budget.

The city also has an intimate relationship with bulls. It is one of nine locations to watch bull fighting in Japan. The bull fight (bull sumo) tournaments are held in January, April, July, August, and October. The Uwajima Bull Fighting Arena can't be missed since it is situated atop one of the hills above the city. The arena has a roof, allowing the fights to take place during inclement weather. It is here where enormous black bulls square off against each other and fight until one of them breaks off and runs away. The bulls are categorized in a similar hierarchical structure as sumo wrestlers, each with a rank that befits their past performances. The rank names mimic those used in sumo with the exception of the highest ranked bulls being referred to as "champions" rather than "yokozuna".

And let's not forget Uwajima Castle. Although small and modest, it is an original castle dating back to 1665. Visitors can approach the castle's keep from either the north or the south. The respective routes travel uphill on stone steps winding past moss covered stone walls and require 10 to 15 minutes to traverse. Once inside you will find that the castle's authentic wooden interior is relatively well-preserved. If you climb up the steep wooden stairs to the top floor, you will be rewarded with excellent views of Uwajima. The castle also has an interesting collection of portraits, swords, and armor that belonged to past feudal lords and are worth seeing.

Before you leave, be sure to try the local dish, tai meshi, which consists of red snapper and rice. It is delicious.

Web Page: http://www.uwajima.org/

Kagawa Prefecture (香川県)

Marugame-shi (丸亀市); Marugame City

Marugame Castle (丸亀城)

The cherry blossom is particularly significant in Japanese culture as it represents the end of dormant winter and the beginning of new life and the spring growing season.

Following the weather report on evening news broadcasts, the Sakura Zensen (the Cherry-Blossom Front) is presented. The blooms begin to open in Okinawa first during February and the front typically reaches Kyoto and Tokyo at the end of March or the beginning of April. It then proceeds north, arriving in Hokkaido a few weeks later. The Japanese pay close attention to these cherry blossom forecasts. They will go to parks, shrines, and temples with family and friends and hold a flower viewing party (hanami).

There are countless places all over Japan to observe the blossoming sakura trees and one exceptionally beautiful spot is Marugame Castle, also known as Kameyama Castle, located in Marugame, Kagawa Prefecture.

Kagawa Prefecture, located on the island of Shikoku, is the smallest prefecture in Japan. Marugame is a port city in western Kagawa Prefecture and it is located just west of the Seto Ohashi Bridge, which connects Shikoku to Japan's main island of Honshu. For many centuries, Marugame's location along the Seto Inland Sea has made it a key player in maritime trade and transportation. Marugame Castle was constructed high up on a hill overlooking the city in an effort to help control the area. The castle is one of twelve original castles in Japan today (castles whose keeps have survived the post-feudal period intact).

The castle was constructed between 1597 and 1602 by the feudal lord, Ikoma Chikamasa, who also built Tamamo Castle in nearby Takamatsu. However, the construction of the castle violated a policy that limited the number of castles per province and was torn down in 1615. When the province split in 1660, Marugame Castle was rebuilt. Over the centuries many of the castle buildings were destroyed by fires and now only the original keep and several of the castle gates remain.

Today, the castle is a part of Kameyama Park and houses a small museum. The castle grounds are very popular during the spring as 1,000 cherry trees are planted around the walls and the keep. They bloom from late March through early April and an annual festival is held on the site during the first two weeks of April.

The castle is a 15-minute walk from Marugame Station. It is accessible from Tokyo via the Marunouchi Line to the Tokaido / Sanyo Shinkansen and transferring to the Yosan Line Limited Express. The entire journey takes approximately five and a half hours.

Location(s):   Ichibancho, Marugame-shi, Kagawa

Kochi Prefecture (高知県)

Kochi-shi (高知市): Kochi City

Katsurahama Beach/ Sakamoto Ryoma Memorial Museum/ Kochi Castle

On the southern coast of Shikoku lies the capital city of Kochi. Small and friendly, the city was voted one of Japan's most livable cities and offers several attractions worth visiting. Kochi is the home town of Sakamoto Ryoma (1836-1867), an important historical figure who played a key role in the Meiji Restoration. The Sakamoto Ryoma Memorial Museum, located atop a hill on Katsurahama Beach, showcases the life and times of this Japanese hero. You will also find a large statue of Ryoma on the beach itself overlooking a lovely, scenic area.

Katsurahama is a picturesque beach located just south of city center. Due to strong currents, swimming is not permitted on this beach, but visitors do not mind as there are so many points of interest in and around the area. On a rocky point just above the beach, you will find the small Katsurahama Shrine. This vantage point offers an excellent spot for viewing some of the most beautiful sunsets Japan has to offer.

The Sakamoto Ryoma Memorial Museum is interestingly housed in a very modern building. It has several fascinating exhibits including his pistol and swords, written documents, a letter written by him just two days prior to his assassination, and several blood-splattered screens and scrolls from the soy sauce shop he was staying in at the time of his murder.

Sakamoto Ryoma was born in Kochi in 1835 and was one of the architects of modern Japan. He was instrumental in negotiating an alliance between the Choshu and Satsuma clans, which helped bring an end to Japan's feudal age in 1868. He left Kochi at the age of 28 and worked tirelessly all over Japan to reform the national political and economic system. He formulated an "Eight-Point Program" for the modernization of Japan, a political guideline for the new government and cabinet. Unfortunately, in November 1867, Ryoma was assassinated in Kyoto by the Shinsengumi secret police at the age of 33. He had lived to see only a month of the drastic change Japan was undergoing. The Meiji Restoration was near at hand, but he never saw the modern Japan he had struggled so hard to build.

The museum, located at 830 Urado-shiroyama, Kochi City, is open year-round from 9:00 AM to 5:00 PM. Admission is ¥500 for adults and students (excluding university students) are admitted free.

Kochi Castle is perhaps the town's biggest attraction and is completely original. First constructed between 1601 and 1611 by Yamauchi Katsutoyo, the castle burnt down in 1727 and was rebuilt between 1729 and 1753. A unique feature of Kochi's castle is that its donjon (main tower) was not only used for military purposes, but also as a residence. In most other castles, the lords usually resided in separate palace buildings rather than in the castle keep.

In an effort to help preserve the original state of the eight traditional tatami rooms, you will be required to take off your shoes before entering the palace. However, if you have been in Japan long enough, you will find this is a common practice. Visitors can only view the rooms from a walkway along the perimeter and consequently the castle tour will be fairly quick. After touring the castle, you may want to make your way to the large grassy area, which is ideal for picnics and springtime cherry blossom viewing. The castle grounds are part of a public park where local music events and festivals are held and you may be lucky enough to visit the castle during one of these times and enjoy the offerings.

South of the castle on Kenchomae-dori near the banks of the Kagami River, you will find the carefully preserved samurai barracks of the castle guards, known as the Kyu-Yamauchi-ke Shimo-Yashiki-Nagaya. You can tour these barracks free of charge.

Kochi is known for its local tuna fish and healthy vegetables grown in the surrounding countryside. There are many covered arcades such as Ohashi-dori and Obiyamachi, where you can find a number of good restaurants, bars, and izakaya serving dishes made with these local ingredients.

The city is easily accessible via the JR express trains to JR Kochi Station from Takamatsu (two and a half hours) and Matsuyama with a change at Uwajima. There are also intercity buses available from Tokyo, Nagoya, Osaka, Okayama, Hiroshima, Fukuoka, Kobe, Matsuyama, Tokushima, and Kyoto.

| Location(s): | 2-6-33 Kamimachi, Kochi-shi, Kochi |
| Web Page: | http://www.ryoma-kinenkan.jp/en/ (Sakamoto Ryoma Memorial Museum) |

Tokushima Prefecture (徳島県)

Naruto-shi (鳴門市): Naruto City

Naruto Whirlpools

Tokushima Prefecture, located in Shikoku, is best known for the Awa Odori Festival, which takes place in August and for Naruto no Uzushio (whirlpools of Naruto).

Naruto is located in the northeastern part of Shikoku Island and the whirlpools can be seen in the Strait of Naruto beneath the Onaruto Bridge, which connects Tokushima with Awaji Island. The whirlpools are created by large volumes of water moving between the Seto Inland Sea and the Pacific Ocean with the changing of the tide. The current in the strait is the fastest in Japan and the fourth fastest in the world. The whirlpools occur approximately every six hours and can typically be seen once in the morning and once in the afternoon. They vary in size depending on the intensity of the tides and tend to be larger during the spring months. Under ideal conditions, whirlpools as large as 65 feet (21m) in diameter can be formed. Alternatively, on calm days or outside peak times, there really isn't much to see. It is imperative to check the whirlpool schedules before planning a visit to Naruto.

The whirlpools do not pose a threat to the various sight-seeing boats that get right up next to the swirling waters. There are two companies who operate sightseeing cruises in Shikoku: Uzushio Kisen and Uzushio Kankosen. The first company operates small boats, which depart from a pier just outside of Naruto Park. The latter operates medium-sized boats (Aqua Eddy) and large boats (Wonder Naruto) from a pier a little further away.

You can also view the whirlpools from an enclosed walkway, the Uzu no Michi, which extends under the Onaruto Bridge. There are glass observation windows installed in the floor of the walkway, from which visitors can observe the whirlpools from 147 feet (47m) above the strait.

The Koen Mizuno Ryokan (http://koen-mizuno.com/), with its expansive Japanese-style rooms offering magnificent views of the sea, is yet another option for enjoying the whirlpools at a more relaxed pace.

One to two buses per hour run from Naruto Station to Naruto Park requiring about 25 minutes. You can also take a bus to Naruto Park from Tokushima Station. The buses run hourly beginning at 9:00 AM and the trip will take approximately an hour and a half.

Web Page: http://www.uzunomichi.jp/english/

Tokushima-shi (徳島市): Tokushima City

<u>Awa Odori Festival</u>

Tokushima City is the site of one of the most famous dance festivals held across Japan during Obon, the annual Buddhist event to honor the dead. Awa Odori (阿波おどり) dates back to the year 1578 and is still extremely popular today, drawing over 1.3 million tourists annually to the four-day festival, August 12-15.

Awa is the old feudal name for Tokushima Prefecture and odori means dance. Drawing its name from the lyrics of a well-known song, Awa Odori is also referred to as the "Fool's Dance."

踊る阿呆に – The dancers are fools

見る阿呆 – The spectators are fools

同じ阿呆なら – Both are fools alike so

踊らな損、損 – Why not dance?

Although there are events scheduled during the daytime, the main attraction doesn't start until 6:00 PM and runs until 10:30 PM. The city center shuts down and is turned into a large dance stage. There are seven different stage areas with either free or paid seating. The paid seating areas tend to draw the professional groups, while the free areas will have more casual dancers. You can also find numerous food and game stands that are common to Japanese festivals.

Groups of choreographed dancers and musicians known as ren (連) dance through the streets, accompanied by the shamisen lute, taiko drums, shinobue flute, and the kane bell. Performers wear traditional Obon dance costumes and chant and sing as they parade through the streets.

The ren distinguish themselves with difficult variations of the otherwise simple dance steps and with colorful costumes. Women wear yukatas (cotton kimonos) while men wear happi coats (traditional Japanese straight-sleeved coat worn over shorts or pants).

Men and women dance in different styles. The men dance in a low crouch with knees pointing outwards and arms held above the shoulders. The women's dance uses the same basic steps, but due to the restrictive yukata only the smallest of steps can be taken and the hand gestures are more restrained and graceful, reaching up towards the sky. Children and adolescents of both sexes usually dance the men's dance. The dances are intended to welcome the souls of deceased ancestors.

Tourists and visitors may find it difficult to secure a hotel within Tokushima at this time of year. Due to the popularity of the event, all hotels are booked months in advance and those who are unable to secure a room in the city can choose to stay in Naruto (40 minutes away by train) or Takamatsu (one hour away by train).

Awa Odori Kaikan is a museum dedicated to Awa Odori, located at the base of Mount Bizan. There is a gift shop on the ground floor while the museum is on the third floor. The building also houses a hall where four daily performances of the Awa Odori are given. Like the actual event itself, the audience members are encouraged to participate in the dancing!

Points of Interest: Shikoku Region

Naruto Whirlpools Tokushima

Katsurahama Kochi

Marugame Castle Kagawa

Uwajima Castle Ehime

Kyushu Region

Introduction to Kyushu (九州)

Kyushu, which literally translates to "Nine Provinces", once consisted of nine ancient provinces: Chikuzen, Chikugo, Hizen, Higo, Buzen, Bungo, Hyuga, Osumi, and Satsuma. Today, Japan's third largest island includes seven prefectures: Fukuoka, Saga, Kumamoto, Nagasaki, Oita to the north, Kagoshima, and Miyazaki to the south.

By population, its largest city is Fukuoka with over 1.4 million citizens, followed by Kitakyushu and Kumamoto each with well over half a million inhabitants. Nagasaki is home to one of Japan's oldest international ports, which served as the only gateway to the outside world during the Edo period (1603-1867). It is also one of two cities in Japan, which suffered substantial damage from the atomic bombs toward the end of World War II.

The island is mountainous and home to Japan's most active volcano, Mount Aso. There are numerous onsens (hot springs), the most famous of which is Beppu. What sets Beppu apart from conventional hot water baths is that it offers sand baths where bathers are buried in the naturally heated sand. There are also steam baths that are heated by the steam from a hot spring and mud baths, which are basically muddy hot water baths.

Kyushu is also known for the various types of porcelain that have been produced in the region over the centuries including, Imari, Satsuma, and Karatsu.

The regional cuisine ranks right along with the area's other famous offerings. Among the dishes to sample are the mizutaki (a stewed dish consisting of chicken and vegetables eaten with ponzu dipping sauce), hakata ramen (noodles in a tonkotsu / pork bone stock soup topped off with beni shoga/ pickled ginger, sesame seeds and pickled greens), motsunabe (stewed beef or pork intestines); champon (a ramen-like dish consisting of seafood and vegetables), chicken namban (batter-fried chicken served with tartar sauce), dango jiru (wheat dumplings served in a miso or soy-based soup with vegetables and pork), kakuni (pork belly stewed in a sweetened soy broth), and toriten (tempura chicken that is typically dipped in a soy based sauce) that is popular in Oita.

Finally, if you still have room for dessert, try the castella (a sweet, rectangular sponge cake that was introduced in Nagasaki by the Portuguese). This item is also popular as a souvenir for anyone visiting Kysushu to bring home to their friends and loved ones.

The Fukuoka International Airport serves the Kyushu area and it is Japan's third busiest commercial airport.

You can also try the Sanyo Shinkansen line, which runs from Osaka to Fukuoka. Another option is the Kyushu Shinkansen that crosses the west side of the island to Kagoshima in the south. There are also numerous Limited Express trains serving many points of interest on the island.

Web Page: http://www.welcomekyushu.com/

Fukuoka Prefecture (福岡県)

Fukuoka-shi (福岡市): Fukuoka City

Canal City

There is a lot to see and do in Fukuoka Prefecture, but if you are just interested in a day trip, Canal City Hakata (Fukuoka City) is a great place to visit. Historically, Hakata and Fukuoka were two separate cities separated by a river, but as the two cities grew and developed they were merged into one, Fukuoka City. Hakata-ku is now merely one ward of Fukuoka City but most Japanese refer to Fukuoka as Hakata. Canal City is an enormous shopping and entertainment complex that bills itself as a city within a city. There are approximately 250 shops, cafés, restaurants, a theater, a game center, two hotels, and a canal that runs through the complex.

Located within a 10 to 15-minute walk from either Hakata Station or Tenjin Station, it is the largest private development in the history of Japan (US$1.4 billion for 234,460 m²). Its design utilizes unique colors and shapes to create a spacious atmosphere. The main feature of the complex is an artificial canal that runs from one end to the other. There is a fountain at the mid-point of the canal where water displays are presented every 30 minutes between 10:00 AM and 10:00 PM.

The complex is divided into five areas: Sea Court, Earth Walk, Sun Plaza Stage, Moon Walk, and Star Court. The Sun Plaza Stage, located in the center of the complex, offers a variety of performances. The stores include traditional Japanese companies like Uniqlo as well as U.S. chains such as GAP and Timberland. The restaurants range from fast food to fine dining. The fifth floor houses the Ramen Stadium with eight ramen

376

shops serving noodle dishes from all over Japan including the local specialty, Hakata ramen.

The theater has 13 screens including an IMAX screen and is the perfect place to catch the latest releases. The Canal City Theater (http://www.canalcitygekijo.com/), located on the fourth floor, runs various plays and musicals, but only in Japanese.

There are several duty-free shops and international ATMs within the facility, which makes it attractive to foreign visitors.

Location(s):   1-2, Sumiyoshi, Hakata-ku, Fukuoka-shi,
                Fukuoka

Web Page: http://canalcity.co.jp.e.jx.hp.transer.com/floor
                /b1f/

Kagoshima Prefecture (鹿児島県)

Chiran-cho ((知覧町)：Town of Chiran

Chiran Peace Museum for Kamikaze Pilots

Chiran is a small town in Kagoshima Prefecture known for its well-preserved samurai houses and gardens, which date back more than 250 years. During World War II, there was an airfield located on the outskirts where the kamikaze pilots were stationed. The site, which once housed the air base and flying school, is now home to the Chiran Peace Museum for Kamikaze Pilots, which documents the history of these men.

The kamikaze (divine wind) was the name given to the suicide attacks on Allied naval vessels during the closing stages of World War II. It was determined that this method of attack would destroy warships more effectively than utilizing conventional methods. During the campaign, 3,860 kamikaze pilots were killed but only about 19 percent of kamikaze attacks managed to hit a vessel.

The aircraft used for these attacks were basically pilot-guided missiles laden with explosives, bombs, torpedoes and full fuel tanks. The pilots would attempt to crash their aircraft into enemy ships, in what was called "taiatari" (body attack). The goal of crippling or destroying large numbers of Allied ships was considered to be a just reason for sacrificing pilots and aircraft. The tradition of death instead of defeat, capture, and perceived shame has long been deeply entrenched in Japanese military culture. It was one of the primary traditions in samurai life and the Bushido code: loyalty and honor until death.

The airbase at Chiran had two runways and served as the

departure point for hundreds of attacks during the Battle of Okinawa. During this battle 1,036 kamikaze pilots died, of which 439 were from the town of Chiran, many just young boys.

The museum was originally constructed in 1975 and expanded in 1986. It has four planes on display: a Nakajima Ki-43 Hayabusa, a 1943 Kawasaki Ki-61 Hien, a 1944 Nakajima Ki-84 Hayate, and a Mitsubishi Zero, which was recovered from the sea in 1980. The museum also exhibits the photographs of 1,036 pilots who were killed in the order in which they died. There are also countless letters, poems, essays, testaments, and other artifacts associated with these pilots and a piano on which it is said that two of the pilots played "Moonlight Sonata" the night before their final mission. The exhibits here are the most extensive of any war museum in Japan. In addition to the main exhibition hall, there are three other exhibition rooms that contain miscellaneous items and uniforms from the war not directly connected to the pilots.

There are touch panel displays where visitors can access a large selection of the pilots' writings in both Japanese and English. The English translations attempt to convey the meaning of the original letters, but since they were translated by someone whose first language was not English, they have some obvious errors and a few sections that are difficult to understand.

On average, the museum receives over 2,000 visitors per day. Busloads of visitors, mostly school children, come to view the museum's photos, exhibits, and films in an effort to learn more about these brave young men who willingly gave their lives in order to establish peace and prosperity for Japan.

After you are done touring the museum, take a walk around this historic town if you have time. Stone lanterns dedicated to the fallen pilots line the town's main street and the road leading up to the museum. There are several statues and memorials throughout the town as well.

Location(s):   17881 Chiranchokori, Minamikyushu, Kagoshima

Web Page: http://www.chiran-tokkou.jp/english/index.html

Kagoshima-shi (鹿児島市): Kagoshima City

<u>Senganen Garden (仙巌園) / Isoteien (磯庭園)</u>

Approximately one mile north of central Kagoshima, you will find the former summer villa of the Shimazu clan. The history of Kagoshima is largely shaped by the Shimazu family, with scholars, politicians, warriors, reformers, and modernizers among their generations. Constructed in 1658 as the family villa, Isoteien is incorporated into Senganen, a beautiful Edo-period garden occupying 5 hectares (12 acres) of land and utilizing Sakurajima and Kinko Bay as borrowed scenery.

The garden layout includes shrines, ponds, running streams, stone bridges, bamboo, plum, and early-blooming cherry blossom trees.

The main entrance gate is approximately 150 years old and was featured in the NHK drama, "Atsuhime" (2008). There is a large cannon nearby that is said to have been used to defend Kagoshima from a British fleet that attacked the town in 1863, demanding reparation for the murder of a Shanghai merchant, Charles Richardson, by the Shimazu clan samurai near Yokohama the year before. Behind the 150-pound cannon is the site of a former reverberating furnace that was used to cast that particular piece of artillery.

There is a separate garden that was built in 1702 by the 21st Shimazu lord. It is called Kyokusui Garden (meandering stream garden) and served as the setting for various poetry parties. The guests at these parties were seated along the banks of the stream and a lacquered sake cup was set afloat in the water from the highest point of the stream. As the cup floated downstream, the guests were required to write and read aloud a five line Tanka poem before the cup reached them. Failure to do so meant that the sake had to be drunk.

The garden is home to a cat shrine that is visited by thousands of cat lovers throughout the year. The 17th Shimazu lord was a general during the war with Korea at the end of the 16th century. It is said that he brought seven cats with him to serve as clocks. In China and Japan, it was believed that the irises of a cat's eye responded to changes in light. Therefore, it was easy to gauge the current time by the shape of the cat's irises. Only two of the seven cats returned to Japan after the war. After the cats had passed away, they were entombed in their own shrine at the castle. When the family moved to the estate at Senganen, they brought the cat shrine with them and it has remained there ever since. Annually on June 10, watch and clock makers gather at the shrine for a ceremony. There is a gift shop next to it that sells cat-related souvenirs and plaques, which can be hung at the shrine.

Located just outside of the entrance to the gardens, on the site of the former Shimazu Family School, you will find the Tsurugane Shrine. Built in 1869, it was moved to the present site in 1917. Generations of the Shimazu family are enshrined there. In recent times, one of the family members in particular, Kamujuhime, the youngest daughter of Yoshihisa Shimazu, has become popular. Yoshihisa Shimazu was the 16th leader of the Shimazu clan. He was famous for almost unifying Kyushu. Kamujuhime was renowned for her remarkable beauty; consequently, the shrine draws women from all over Japan who come to pray for beauty.

Included with the cost of admission to Senganen is entry to the Shoko Shuseikan Museum. The museum houses a vast collection of Shimazu clan heirlooms including scrolls, weapons, maps, documents, Satsumayaki ceramics, kiriko (cut glass), dolls, and tools. The museum showcases the Shimazu clan's efforts to modernize and industrialize Japan. For an extra ¥500, you can go on a 20-minute guided tour of the residence, Isoteien. The tour is in Japanese but you will be provided with a guide sheet in English.

Senganen is open from 8:30 AM to 5:30 PM daily. Last entry is at 5:00 PM. There are a number of buses, that make stops at the Senganen-mae bus stop including the Kagoshima City View Bus from Kagoshima Chuo Station, Kagoshima Aquarium, and the Shiroyama Observatory. From Kagoshima Airport, Senganen is approximately a 40-minute car ride.

Location(s):   Yoshino-cho 9700-1, Kagoshima

Web Page: http://www.senganen.jp/en/top/

Kumamoto Prefecture (熊本県)

Kumamoto-shi (熊本市): Kumamoto City

Kumamoto is the capital city of Kumamoto Prefecture. The city's most famous landmark is Kumamoto Castle, a large and extremely well-fortified Japanese castle in its day. Originally constructed in 1467, the castle was burned after a 53-day siege during the famous Satsuma Rebellion. Today, the central keep is a concrete reconstruction built in the 1970s, but several secondary original wooden buildings remain.

During the Satsuma Rebellion, the tradition of eating basashi (raw horse meat) originated. Basashi remains popular in Kumamoto and, to a lesser extent, elsewhere in Japan, though these days it is usually considered a delicacy.

Kumamoto has a prefectural mascot, Kumamon. He was first created in 2010 for a campaign called Kumamoto Surprise to draw tourists to the region after the Kyushu Shinkansen line opened. The character subsequently became nationally popular, and in late 2011, was voted first in a nationwide survey of mascots, collectively known as Yuru-kyara.

Mount Aso, which is located 30 miles (48 km) north of Kumamoto City, is a symbol of Kumamoto Prefecture. It is the largest active volcano in Japan, with its peak, Taka-dake, measuring at 5223 ft. (1,592 m) above sea level. Apart from Taka-dake, Mount Aso has four other peaks: Eboshi-dake, Kishima-dake, Neko-dake, and Naka-dake, all of which exhibit regular volcanic activity.

The fourth peak, Naka-dake can be reached by car, on foot, via a helicopter ride, or via the Mount Aso Ropeway cable cars.

However, it is not always open to visitors due to the regular emissions of ash and fumes. When open, the crater can be visited at night, when one can see the lava seeping out of its fissures creating fiery streaks in the dark.

The outer rim of Naka-dake, in contrast, is very peaceful like that of the other craters. It is coated with grassy plains where cows and horses graze and visitors can take a relaxing stroll or have a family picnic. There are designated camping grounds in the area as well.

Finally, located about 12 miles (19 km) north of Mount Aso, you will find Kurokawa, one of Japan's most attractive hot spring towns. The town's landscape is dominated by natural colors and materials, wooden buildings, earthen walls, and stone stairs. The town center, located in a forested valley, is compact and can easily be explored on foot. Kurokawa is known for its outstanding rotenburos (outdoor baths) and its ryokans (inns). Visitors not only have the opportunity to enjoy their own ryokan's baths as often as they would like, but also, along with many day trippers, they can explore other baths in town during the daytime hours and engage in Rotenburo Meguri (tour of outdoor baths).

Whether it's just a day trip or an overnight stay at Kurokawa, Kumamoto is definitely worth a visit if you're looking for a place to relax, enjoy great food, and just get away from it all.

Web Page: http://kumanago.jp/en/

Miyazaki Prefecture (宮崎県)

Miyazaki-shi (宮崎市): Miyazaki City

Heiwadai Park

Located on the southeastern coast of Kyushu, Miyazaki City enjoys one of the warmest climates in Japan. The town, dotted with beaches, resorts, and sports facilities, was considered a top honeymoon destination for Japanese couples until the 1980s. However, after the 1980s, tourism in Miyazaki declined until a popular comedian named Higashikokubaru Hideo became the governor of Miyazaki Prefecture in 2007 and used his celebrity to draw attention to Miyazaki once again.

Today, one of the main attractions in Miyazaki is Heiwadai Park, situated just 30 minutes on foot from Miyazaki Shrine. Constructed in 1940, the park sits 200 feet (61 m) above sea level and offers impressive views of the surrounding area. It draws many visitors for its wide lawns, immaculately kept flower beds, and cool forest atmosphere. Within the park, standing at 121 feet (37 m) high, is the Peace Tower, the most recognizable symbol of Miyazaki. Constructed of stones gathered from all over Asia, it was originally intended to be a symbol of Japanese imperialism. However, following the events of World War II, the tower became a monument for peace and a united world. On the front of the tower, you will find the phrase "Hakko Ichiu," which means "United under one roof."

At the far end of the park, you will find Haniwa Garden. The garden is famous for its collection of 400 replica haniwa (burial statues) depicting animals, warriors, boats, and houses, all arranged around a walking path. During the Kofun period, more than 1,500 years ago, clay statues like these were placed on burial mounds as a tribute to the deceased.

If you get hungry after walking around or if you just want to relax, there is a rest area in the park with a souvenir/snack shop and an organic restaurant serving dishes prepared with healthy organic ingredients provided by Miyazaki's local farmers. The snack shop offers light snacks, organic coffee, ice cream, and cold drinks.

The ideal outing is to combine a trip to the park with a visit to the Miyazaki Shrine and the Prefectural Museum. Admission to the park is free. There are direct buses each hour departing from Miyazaki Station to Heiwadai Park.

Location(s):	1-1-1 Tachibana-dōri Nishi, Miyazaki-shi, Miyazaki
Web Page:	http://h.park-miyazaki.jp/

Nagasaki Prefecture (長崎県)

Goto Islands (五島列島)

Nagasaki, Japan was heavily influenced by Portuguese and other European cultures from the 16th through the 19th century, and there are numerous churches and Christian sites today, that attest to this influence. But during the Sakoku period (1633-1853), Japan was closed off to foreigners and the teaching of the Roman Catholic religion was officially prohibited. Still, the Japanese Catholic Church had many followers (it is estimated that there were 30,000 converts throughout Japan) known as kakure Kirishitan (hidden Christian), who fled south to escape persecution, eventually ending up at the Goto Islands, where they continued to practice their faith in secret.

Goto Islands (translated means five islands) really consists of 140 islands off the western coast of Kyushu. The island chain spans 60 miles (97 km) and the total land area covers 266 square miles (689 km²). However, only one-third of the lands are inhabited. The five main islands of the chain include: Fukue, Hisaka, Naru, Wakamatsu, and Nakadori. The Japanese Agency for Cultural Affairs has submitted churches at these locations for consideration as UNESCO World Heritage sites and they have been included on a tentative list.

The largest of the chain of islands is Fukue. It is a three-hour ferry ride from Nagasaki. Here, you will find the Dozaki Church, a beautiful red brick building constructed in 1908, which served as the base for the revival of the Christian religion. It functioned as a mini-Vatican and symbolizes Goto Catholicism. There are 50 churches scattered throughout the islands, each imparting a sense of the area's long history.

Nakadori enjoyed a period of prosperity during the 13th century when trade with China flourished. Another period of prosperity followed with the whaling boom, which has long since ended. Today, it is a quiet place with camellias blooming everywhere. The camellia oil produced here used to be an important local product but now it serves primarily as a tourist omiyage (souvenir). The Tsuwazaki lookout point is quite scenic and includes the Tsuwazaki Lighthouse.

Hisaka was once the site of a prison where Christians were incarcerated. After the Meiji Restoration, many Christians who were hiding their faith decided to declare it publically and were imprisoned. They were released after word of their imprisonment spread overseas, raising a public outcry. Today, a chapel stands at the site of the former prison, serving as a monument to this period in history.

On Wakamatsu, you will find what is known as the eye of a needle, a cave-like crevice so-called because whichever way you look through it, you can see a sliver of sky on the other side. This was once a hiding spot where Christians congregated when they heard about coming raids. They were eventually caught when a local fisherman saw the smoke from their lunchtime fires and reported them to the local government. Today, a statue of the Virgin Mary stands next to the opening of the crevice and serves as a memorial to their ordeal.

Aside from their attachment to Christianity, Goto Islands are a mecca for marine sports and fishing. Since 2001, the islands have sponsored the Goto Nagasaki International Triathlon, a World Championship Qualifier event.

Whether you seek to immerse yourself in the history or simply want a quiet getaway where you can relax on the sandy beaches off the East China Sea, Goto Islands are a must-see.

Nagasaki-shi (長崎市): Nagasaki City

When you mention Nagasaki, Japan, most westerners immediately associate this port city situated on the island of Kyushu with the August 9, 1945, nuclear bomb that killed over 100,000 people, forcing Japan to surrender, officially ending World War II. But Nagasaki's history is far more extensive than this tragic event that has emblazoned its name in the minds of millions.

Nagasaki played an important role in Japan's emergence as a modern nation. Not only did it serve as a principal connection with the West, welcoming Dutch and Portuguese traders and missionaries, but the city also prospered greatly from the trade established with China and Korea due to its close proximity to the Asian mainland. Unfortunately, Japan's period of isolation significantly affected Nagasaki's prosperity and growth, restricting foreign contact in Nagasaki to a small Dutch enclave on the island of Dejima just off of Nagasaki Harbor. Through this small outpost, a trickle of Western science and culture found its way into Japan, and by 1720 the city emerged as a prominent scientific and artistic center. When Nagasaki reopened to the West in 1859, it quickly re-established itself as a major economic force, dominating in the area of shipbuilding, which made it an allied target on August 9, 1945.

Approximately 40 percent of the city's structures were completely destroyed or severely damaged by the nuclear bomb. The city has since been rebuilt and has become an important tourist center. There are several historic sites including the Sofuku-ji Chinese Temple dating back to 1629; the Glover Garden; the Peace Park, which was established under the point of detonation of the bomb; and the Roman Catholic

Cathedral of Urakami, which was rebuilt in 1959 to replace the original 1914 structure destroyed by the bomb.

Sofuku-ji was constructed by Nagasaki's Chinese residents in 1629 and is one of the best examples of Ming Dynasty architecture in the world. The temple is open to the public daily from 8:00 AM to 5:00 PM and admission is ¥300.

Glover Garden is Nagasaki's top tourist attraction, attracting nearly two million visitors a year. It features Japan's oldest western-style house, set in a beautiful garden overlooking Nagasaki Harbor. The house and garden were completed in 1863 by Hidenoshin Koyama for Thomas Blake Glover, who traveled to Nagasaki from Scotland in 1859 at the age of 21. Thomas Blake Glover prospered through his knowledge of ship building, coal mining, and other economically valuable trades he used to help modernize these industries in Japan. The design of Glover Garden reminded many people of the scenes in the opera "Madame Butterfly" by Puccini and the Glover House came to be known as the Madame Butterfly House. Consequently, statues of Puccini and diva Miura Tamaki, who played Cio-Cio-san, were erected in Glover Garden. The garden is open to the public from 8:00 AM to 6:00 PM and admission is ¥600.

Established in 1955, the Nagasaki Peace Park commemorates the atomic bombing of the city in 1945 and is situated next to the Atomic Bomb Museum and the Peace Memorial Hall. At the park's north end is the 32-foot (10 m) Peace Statue created by sculptor Seibo Kitamura. The statue's right hand points to the threat of nuclear weapons while the extended left hand symbolizes eternal peace. The mild face symbolizes divine grace and the gently closed eyes offer a prayer for the bomb victims' souls. The folded right leg and extended left leg signify both meditation and the initiative to stand up and rescue the people of the world. Installed in front of the statue is a black marble vault containing the names of the atomic bomb victims and survivors who died in subsequent years.

Urakami Cathedral, also known as St. Mary's Cathedral, was once the largest Catholic Church in Asia. It was completely destroyed when the bomb detonated just 1,640 feet (500 m) away. The Cathedral was filled with Catholics celebrating mass as the Feast of the Assumption of Mary (August 15) was near. The resultant collapse and heat-wave incinerated and buried all those present in the Cathedral that day. Statues and artifacts damaged in the bombing, including a French Angelus bell, are now displayed on the grounds. The nearby Peace Park contains remnants of the original cathedral's walls. What remained of the cathedral is now on display in the Nagasaki Atomic Bomb Museum.

Another Nagasaki attraction worth visiting is the Site of the Martyrdom of the 26 Saints of Japan. This monument and museum stand on the location where 20 Japanese Christians and six European missionaries were crucified in 1597. The martyrs were canonized as saints in 1862. The small museum, which stands behind the monument, contains one of the best collections of Christian artifacts and paraphernalia in East Asia, including many original letters and documents dating from the time of St. Francis Xavier. The site is only ten minutes on foot from Nagasaki Station.

If you want to see Japan's sole contact with the west during the isolation period, visit Dejima, the site of the former Dutch factory located near Nagasaki Port Terminal. Dejima was built to keep the West away from the locals in order to prevent the spread of Christianity. While only a few pieces of the original building foundations remain, many of the buildings have been recreated according to what is known about them. You can walk inside the warehouses, quarters, kitchen, and other rooms. The island also contains some 20 or so shops including restaurants.

For you James Bond fans, the 2012 movie Skyfall featured Nagasaki's next attraction, Gunkanjima (Battleship Island). It was once a mining city, which was abandoned in 1974. Regarded as the most densely populated place on earth, it is now a ghost town, showing the decay of what society left behind. Prior to 2009, no one was permitted on the island, but the ban has since been lifted and the island is now reachable by ferry from Nagasaki Port.

Finally, there is a little known attraction on an uninhabited islet about 196 feet (60 m) wide that is starting to garner more attention and attract more visitors. It is the Kojima Shrine, a Shinto holy site on Maekojima that is only reachable during low tide. Visitors approach the island on foot and then climb a path that leads through trees to the rear of the island, where the unmanned shrine stands. Shinto believers consider the island to be a sacred spot and visitors are asked to refrain from taking any leaves, twigs or pebbles as souvenirs.

Whether you are interested in seeing the influence of Dutch, Portuguese, and Chinese cultures in Japan, witnessing the devastation created during World War II or just familiarizing yourself with and enjoying another region in this wonderful country, Nagasaki should definitely be on your bucket list.

Web Page: http://www.visit-nagasaki.com/

Nagasaki-shi (長崎市): Nagasaki City

Kunchi Festival

Nagasaki City became the center of foreign influence from the 16th through the 19th centuries. It is home to one of Japan's three Chinatowns and Portuguese and Dutch influences can still be seen throughout the town.

Today, visitors to Nagasaki can witness a 400-year-old festival that incorporates different aspects of both the Chinese and Dutch cultures. The three-day event is known as the Nagasaki Kunchi Festival and was originally a celebration of the autumn harvest in the late 16th century. Later on, the festival was associated with the Suwa Jinja.

The Kunchi Matsuri features dance performances known as Hono-Odori. These dances are performed by various groups, each representing a specific Odori-cho (district) within the city. There are 59 groups who perform on a rotation basis once every seven years. In addition to the dances, the festival includes floats shaped like boats, gorgeous costumes, and a fireworks display. One of the boat-shaped floats features a boy who represents the son of the merchant, Araki Sotaro.

Sotaro was a samurai who relocated to Nagasaki from Kumamoto in 1588. He sailed to distant places like Vietnam, Thailand, and Cambodia, eventually returning to Japan with a Vietnamese wife. Sotaro and his wife later established a trading emporium in Nagasaki. The couple are buried in Nagasaki at the Daion-ji temple and their gravesite has been designated as a City Cultural Property.

The focal point of the festival is the Chinese Dragon Dance. It was originally performed on New Year's Eve by Nagasaki's Chinese residents and today maintains all the mesmerizing movements and energy from the past that brings the dragon to life. The festival music known as Shagiri is played on traditional Chinese musical instruments.

Four venues play host to the festival including: Suwa Jinja, Otabisho, Yasaka Shrine, and Kokaido. The event is free of charge; however, paid seating can be secured at each of the event venues. Be sure to get there early as tickets sell out quickly and the venues become very crowded.

Reaching Nagasaki from Tokyo is relatively easy via the JR Tokaido/ Sanyo Shinkansen; exit at Hakata Station in Fukuoka. From there, transfer to the JR Kamome Limited Express train to Nagasaki.

Location(s):   18-15, Kaminishiyama-machi, Nagasaki-shi, Nagasaki

Web Page: https://www.nagasaki-tabinet.com/mlang/english/guide/event.php

Nagasaki-shi (長崎市): Nagasaki City

Peiron Boat Races

One event where you can clearly see the influence of Chinese culture in Nagasaki City is during the annual Nagasaki Peiron Boat Races. The 361-year-old event was started by the Chinese people residing in the city as a way of offering prayers to the sea god.

In 1655, a severe storm struck Nagasaki Harbor sinking the Chinese vessels docked there. The Chinese locals borrowed boats and began racing them to appease the angry sea god. The boat races reached their pinnacle in mid Edo period. During that time, the race boats ranged in size from 65 feet to 148 feet (20 to 45 m). Today, the race boats are only 46 feet (14 m) long and carry a team of 33 rowers.

Spurred on by taiko drums and gongs, the rowers propel the boats using three-foot oars along a course that measures 3,773 feet (1,150 m) roundtrip. The Peiron Boat Races are held every year on the last weekend in July at the Matsugae Kokusai Kanko Futo Pier in Nagasaki Port. Various teams assemble from all over Japan to compete, including middle school students, workplace teams, and even all-women teams.

As with all festivals in Japan, an array of food vendors are available and at the end of each day, there is a fireworks display.

Nagasaki Port's Matsugae Kokusai Kanko Futo Pier is accessible via the JR Nagasaki Line. Exit at Nagasaki Station and take the municipal streetcar to Oura Tenshudo. The port is just a two-minute walk from that point.

Sasebo-shi (佐世保市): Sasebo City

Huis Ten Bosch

Although Japan once segregated the Dutch, today it embraces their culture. In fact, the Japanese have painstakingly recreated the Netherlands in a 152-hectare (376 acre) theme park located in Sasebo, Nagasaki. The park is called Huis Ten Bosch and was named after Huis ten Bosch, a royal palace in The Hague, which serves as one of three official residences of the Dutch Royal Family.

Opened in March 1992, the park features numerous Dutch-style buildings including hotels, villas, theaters, museums, shops, and restaurants, along with canals, windmills, amusement rides, and seasonal flowers throughout. Established as a tribute to the shared history and culture of the Netherlands and Nagasaki, it took five years to build on reclaimed land. Huis Ten Bosch is home to over 400,000 trees, 300,000 flowers and six kilometers (3.7 mi) of canals. The park consists of two areas: the Theme Park Zone, requiring paid admission, and the Free Zone.

The Theme Park Zone houses various amusements, many of which are modern theaters featuring 3D technology. There is also a Michael Jackson museum, haunted house, mirror maze, ferris wheel, and a replica of the Domtoren (Dom Tower) of Utrecht offering panoramic views from its observation deck. The original Dom Tower in the Netherlands is a Gothic-style tower, 368 feet (112 m) high. It was a part of the Cathedral Saint Martin whose unfinished nave collapsed in 1674 leaving the Dom Tower free standing.

The Free Zone's main attractions are a theater and boat ride related to the hit comic series, "One Piece" and a replica of the

Huis ten Bosch Palace, which houses an art museum.

There are several European themed hotels including the Watermark Hotel and Hotel Nikko. Guests staying at these hotels are advised to check at the counter for discount tickets to the Theme Park Zone.

Huis Ten Bosch is currently managed by H.I.S., a travel agency that invested ¥2 billion to revitalize the park. The park hosts various events throughout the year, including a tulip festival in the spring and a fireworks competition during the summer.

Park hours are from 9:00 AM to 9:30 PM daily (9:00 AM to 8:30 PM from December to February). A day passport ticket, covering entry and a number of attractions costs ¥6,100 for adults and ¥3,800 for children.

Location(s):   Hausutenbosu-machi, Sasebo, Nagasaki

Web Page: http://english.huistenbosch.co.jp/

Oita Prefecture (大分県)

Beppu-shi (別府市): Beppu City

A quaint, touristy, and hospitable city, Beppu is located in Oita Prefecture on the island of Kyushu. Upon seeing the steam rising from various vents throughout the city, one immediately recognizes why this is such a popular tourist destination. Beppu City produces more onsen (hot spring) water than any other area in Japan!

This long, thin city is framed by the coast on one side and mountains on the other, making walking to various onsens and tourist destinations relatively easy. However, if you plan to visit the Jigoku (Hells), you are better off arranging for transportation.

The Jigoku are seven multi-colored volcanic pits of boiling water and mud, which reach temperatures of 122-210°F (50-99°C), and as a result, are designated for viewing rather than bathing. A geyser called Tatsumaki-Jigoku is also a part of the popular Hells. It erupts every 30 to 40 minutes and the eruptions last about five minutes.

Viewing hours for the Jigoku are between 8:00 AM and 5:00 PM. The Tatsumaki-Jigoku will remain open a little past 5:00 PM. One can easily view all eight Jigoku at a leisurely pace in about two and a half hours.

Each Jigoku bears its own name: Umi-Jigoku (Sea Hell), Oniishibozu-Jigoku (Shaven Monk's Head Hell), Yama-Jigoku (Mountain Hell), Kamado-Jigoku (Boiling Hell), Oniyama-Jigoku (Demon Mountain Hell), Shiraike-Jigoku (White Pond Hell), Chinoike-Jigoku (Blood Pond Hell), and Tatsumaki-Jigoku

(Geyser Hell).

The Beppu Jigoku Association (Tel. 0977-66-1577) maintains the Hells. The admission charge is ¥400 per ticket for each individual Hell and ¥2,000 for a combination ticket for all seven Hells and the geyser. Note: If you purchase an unlimited bus ticket at the Foreign Tourist Office at the Beppu train station, you will receive a coupon book that includes a ¥200 discount coupon for the purchase of combination tickets. The combination ticket is a much better deal even without the discount coupon.

Also while in Beppu, make sure to try the Kintetsu Beppu Ropeway (Tel. 0977-22-2278). The ropeway will take you 2,600 feet (792 m) up to the top of Mount Tsurumi, where you can enjoy a full view of the city and Beppu Bay. Once you exit the last ropeway station on the top, it's about a ten-minute walk uphill to reach the summit of Mount Tsurumi. There are several small temples and shrines you can visit along the way.

Hours for the ropeway vary by season, but it typically stops running around dusk. The cost to ride the ropeway is ¥1,400 round-trip.

Whether you are here to relax in the soothing onsen waters or to be mesmerized by the Hells, Beppu City has something for everyone.

Web Page: http://www.city.beppu.oita.jp/seikatu/gaikokuji
             nmuke/ei/

Himeshima (姫島村): Princess Island

Just off the northeast corner of Kyushu on the Kunisaki Peninsula, you will find a tiny remote island called Himeshima (Princess Island). The island is part of Oita Prefecture and accessible by ferry.

At slightly over 4 miles (6.4 km) long, the island is known for its onsens (hot springs), delicious kuruma ebi (tiger prawns), and an Obon dance festival, Kitsune Odori Matsuri (Fox Dance Festival), that takes place annually from August 14 to 17. This is the one time of year when this tiny island gets crowded with visitors, but it is a quiet retreat the remainder of the time and a great place to get away from the hustle and bustle of daily life.

Exploring the island, you feel as though you have been transported to a bygone era. The quiet alleys are lined with beautiful old buildings that are preserved in excellent condition.

The best way to explore Himeshima is on a bicycle. There are several that are available to rent on the island. Once the sun starts to set, ride off to the Kannonzaki Peninsula, which forms the northeast point of Himeshima. There you will find Sennin-do, a tiny temple building situated on a rock overlooking the sea. The temple grounds offer the best scenery found on the island. In the distance, you can see the mountains of Kyushu, Honshu, and Shikoku and the fishing boats sailing out at sea. On the eastern tip of the island, there is a beautiful lighthouse with fantastic views as well.

The island's inhabitants earn their income from the famous kuruma ebi. They are farmed off the island, but wild prawns are also available in several restaurants, which dot the island. During October, the main season for prawns, the island hosts the Kuruma Ebi Festival.

The onsen water on Himeshima is cold, clear, and mineral rich. However, once it comes in contact with the air, it turns a milky brown. The water is heated in the onsen baths to make it more enticing for the bathers.

Himeshima is a 20-minute ferry ride from Imi Port. The first ferry departs at 5:50 AM and the last one at 7:10 PM. In between, boats run on the hour.

Web Page: http://www.visit-oita.jp/event/event0272.e.html

Kunisaki Peninsula (国東半島)

Located in the northern part of Oita Prefecture in Kyushu, is the Kunisaki Peninsula. Characterized by numerous hills and valleys, several inactive volcanoes, forests, and sparsely populated farmlands, Kunisaki is a veritable Japanese holy land, said to contain more than half of Japan's stone Buddhist statuary as well as some of its oldest.

The peninsula is home to a unique local Buddhist culture, called Rokugomanzan, which combines elements of Buddhism, Shinto, and mountain worship. The culture revolves around the peninsula's numerous temples and the Usa Shrine. The stone statues are a defining characteristic of the Rokugomanzan culture.

During the early 8th century, a priest named Ninmon founded 28 temples on this peninsula and created thousands of Buddha statues throughout the course of his life. The temples were constructed in six districts in the valleys radiating out from Mount Futago. (Rokugou means six districts in Japanese.) Another 37 temples were added during the 12th century, bringing the total number to 65.

A local lord named Atomo Sori, a Christian, did his best to deface the area's Buddhist heritage. As a result, only 33 temples remain today and they, along with the Usa Shrine, form a pilgrimage route.

The area is not very accessible even to this day, necessitating renting a car or utilizing a tour bus. Further, one needs a certain level of fitness to negotiate the steep stone steps to the sacred sites deep in the Kunisaki Peninsula for they have buckled and been deformed by time.

If you are fortunate enough to visit this mysterious land, the following points of interest should not be ignored.

Futago-ji Temple: Futago means twins in Japanese and the temple receives visits from the families of twin children, which is a rather rare occurrence in Japan. The temple is located at the center of the Kunisaki Peninsula near the top of Mount Futago. At the entrance of the temple, a pair of Niou (the guardians of the temple) keep watch. There is a path through the temple, which leads to the top of the mountain.

Usa Shrine: Dates back over 1,000 years and is dedicated to the God of War, Hachiman. The shrine is the oldest Hachiman shrine in Japan.

Fuki-ji Temple: Is the oldest wooden temple in Kyushu and one of the oldest wooden structures in Japan. The original temple dates back to 718. The main hall contains a seated image of Buddha, which was designated as a National Important Cultural Property.

Kitsuki City: Is home to what is claimed to be the smallest castle in Japan, two samurai districts, and one merchant district.

The two samurai districts are somewhat similar to those in Hagi in Yamaguchi Prefecture. As in Hagi, a number of former samurai residences are open to the public including the Isoya Residence, the Sano Residence, the Nomi Residence, and the Ohara Residence.

The Hitotsumatsu Residence is the former home of Sadayoshi Hitotsumatsu (1875-1973), a Showa era politician, which is also open to the public. The mansion was considered to be the height of technology in its day.

The area is also known for two major festivals. The first is the Kitsune Matsuri (Fox Dance Festival). It takes place from August 14 to 17 on the island of Himeshima off the coast of Kunisaki. It is a traditional Obon festival honoring the deceased ancestors, which draws considerable crowds to the normally tranquil and picturesque island.

The second is an interesting festival that takes place in the small village of Ota during the month of October. The Shirahige Tahara Doburoku Matsuri is dedicated to sampling doburoku, the early fermented mash resulting from the sake brewing process.

Without a doubt, there is plenty to see and do in this seemingly serene region that many tend to overlook during their travels to Japan. Whether you are inclined to take part in the fun and excitement afforded by the festivals or simply want to relax and enjoy the beautiful scenery, the Kunisaki Peninsula is worth visiting. It is accessible via the Chuo Expressway and the Sanyo Expressway from Tokyo. The trip will require over thirteen hours and includes traveling by ferry. Otherwise, you can fly to Oita from Tokyo utilizing either the Narita or Haneda Airport. Total flight time is 90 minutes, non-stop.

Web Page: http://www.gokunisaki.com/kunisaki-sightseeing/

Nakatsu-shi (中津市): Nakatsu City

Fukuzawa Residence & Memorial Museum

When visiting Nakatsu Castle in Oita Prefecture, it is a worthwhile idea to combine a visit to the Yukichi Fukuzawa Residence and Memorial Museum as well. The property is close to the castle and only a 15-minute walk from JR Nakatsu Station.

Although not a well-known figure outside of Japan, Yukichi Fukuzawa was undoubtedly one of the most important and influential thinkers during Japan's modernization period. Born in Osaka in 1835, he was the second son of a low ranking samurai from the Nakatsu Domain in the present day Oita Prefecture. Fukuzawa never really knew his father, who died when Yukichi was less than two years old. Raised by his mother, he credits her in his autobiography with having had a profound influence on his attitude. He especially noted her benevolence and kindness towards those in the lower classes. Fukuzawa himself was deeply resentful of the disdain and discrimination he suffered. While the class system of Tokugawa Japan is well known, less well known is that within the samurai class there were deep divisions and distinctions between lower and upper ranking samurai.

The family's poverty also meant that he was not able to go to school until the relatively late age of 14. Fortunately, his father had collected a sizable number of books, so Yukichi was able to study by himself and was, therefore, able to escape the rigidity of thought that characterized the schools.

In 1853, when Fukuzawa was 19, Commodore Perry arrived in Japan for the first time and demanded that Japan open up to the West. Fukuzawa was sent to Nagasaki to study Dutch and Western gunnery, but only stayed a short time before making his own way to Osaka, where he enrolled in the Tekijuku, a school of Dutch learning. During his three years there, he studied physics, chemistry, physiology, and, of course, Dutch.

In 1858, he was appointed the teacher of Dutch to the Nakatsu Domain and moved to Edo (present day Tokyo). The following year, Yokohama opened as a treaty port but upon visiting the foreign settlement, Fukuzawa was shocked to discover that Dutch was not the language of the world; rather it was English. So, with little more than a Dutch-English dictionary, he set about the task of learning a new language.

In 1860, he was invited to join the first mission sent by the Shogunate to the United States, and while there for three weeks, he was able to get what he considered his most valuable asset, a Webster's dictionary. Upon his return, he was employed by the government to translate diplomatic documents and in the next year, he was invited to join a year-long mission to Europe.

Fukuzawa Yukichi is variously described as a writer, translator, newspaperman, journalist, teacher, educator, and entrepreneur. He was the founder of the prestigious Keio University. He was the man who coined the phrases "Civilization and Enlightenment" (bunmei kaika) and "leave Asia, join the West" (datsu-a, nu-o). These slogans drove Japan's modernization program in the Meiji period. Today, his likeness graces the front of the ¥10,000 Japanese banknote.

He passed away in 1901 in Tokyo at the age of 66. His grave is in Azabu-san Zenpuku-ji Temple, Minato ward, Tokyo.

Fukuzawa lived in the house in Nakatsu until he was 19 years old. It is a registered National Cultural Heritage Site and next to it is the Fukuzawa Memorial Museum. The museum contains manuscripts, first editions, and other artifacts from Fukuzawa, including the first edition of Gakumon no Susume (Encouragement of Learning).

In the yard, you will find a storehouse that Fukuzawa himself remodeled to serve as his study space. The Inari Shrine that Fukuzawa experimented with as a youth is also on the grounds.

So when in Oita, take a moment to learn about the man who appears on the ¥10,000 Japanese banknote that is in your wallet. I am certain you will find it an enlightening experience!

Location(s):   586 Rusui-machi, Nakatsu-shi, Oita

Web Page: http://www.visit-oita.jp/spot/spot0347.e.html

Nakatsu Castle

Any visit to Oita Prefecture should include a stopover at one of the main attractions in the area, Nakatsu Castle. Easily accessible, the castle is located just 15 minutes on foot from JR Nakatsu Station on the Nippo Main Line between Kokura City in Kitakyushu and Kagoshima.

Classified as one of the three great water castles of Japan, Nakatsu Castle is located on the edge of the beach and in its time utilized the sea as part of its defensive structure. Construction of Nakatsu Castle was begun in 1587 by Kuroda Yoshitaka and was completed by his replacement Hosokawa Tadaoki, who also built Kokura Castle. The castle switched hands several times in the course of history until its abandonment in 1871 with the establishment of the Meiji Government.

The castle was burned down by local samurai in 1877 in what became known as the Satsuma Rebellion. The current concrete reconstruction of the five-storied keep was built in 1964. As no images or plans of the castle existed, Nakatsu was modeled after Hagi Castle, also known as Shizuki Castle, located in Yamaguchi Prefecture.

Located on the top floor of Nakatsu Castle is an observation deck with excellent views of the town and the coast. The remainder of the castle houses a museum with a sizeable collection of armor, weapons, roof tiles, photographs, and rangaku items.

Rangaku is the term used to identify a body of knowledge developed by Japan through its contacts with the Dutch traders who were the only European foreigners tolerated in Japan from

1639 to 1853 due the Tokugawa shogunate's policy of national isolation. Through rangaku, Japan learned many aspects of the scientific and technological revolution that was taking place in Europe at that time.

Today, Japan welcomes visitors from all over the world and Oita, particularly the Yufuin and Beppu resorts, attracts over 10 million visitors a year! Furthermore, Oita is ideal for those looking to get away from the crowds by seeking out nature, hot springs, and regional delicacies as well as the landscapes reminiscent of the Edo period.

Location(s):   1273 Ninocho, Nakatsu-shi, Oita

Web Page: http://www.nakatsujyo.jp/

Takasakiyama Monkey Park (高崎山自然動物園)

Another great attraction to include during your visit to Oita Prefecture is the Takasakiyama Monkey Park. Located just outside of Beppu City, the forested Mount Takasaki is home to over 1,500 wild monkeys. Yes, wild monkeys! The Mount Takasaki Monkey Park does not function as a zoo. There are no fences or boundaries, no off-limits areas for the Japanese Macaques. Human visitors are cautioned to keep their distance, avoid aggressive behavior, and refrain from touching or feeding the monkeys. In return, they are given the opportunity to observe these animals up close.

A few decades ago, the area's Macaques were wreaking havoc on farmer's fields and foraging for food in neighborhood trash cans. A local official decided to alleviate the problem by luring the monkeys to the mountain with a whistle and some food. The ruse worked and Mount Takasaki has been home to these monkeys ever since.

The monkeys are fed regularly by park wardens so that they will not destroy crops on the nearby farms. Three troupes of monkeys regularly descend from the peak to eat, play on the equipment the park staff has constructed, and groom themselves and their babies. Feeding occurs several times a day around the central play area. If you miss the announcement, just watch the monkeys. It's always a crazy rush when the feed is scattered.

The Mount Takasaki Monkey Park is a ten-minute bus ride from central Beppu (Beppu Station or Beppu Kitahama). Be sure to get off at the Takasakiyama bus stop. A visit to the Monkey Park is best when combined with a visit to the nearby Umitamago Aquarium. The Monkey Marine Ticket costing ¥2,260 includes round-trip transportation from Beppu to the Monkey Park, admission to the Monkey Park, and the Umitamago Aquarium.

Location(s):   3098-1 Tanoura, Oita-shi, Oita

Web Page: http://www.takasakiyama.jp/

Yufuin-cho (湯布院町): Town of Yufuin

Nestled in the picturesque valley below the double-peaked Mount Yufu-dake and about 75 minutes by train from Beppu City via the Kyudai Line, is the small town of Yufuin. Yufuin is a popular hot spring resort with a wealth of art museums, cafés, and boutiques that line its main street. The ryokans and hotels are spread out across town and not clustered along the main street as in many other resort towns. The area is rather rural and upon leaving the main walkway, visitors will encounter the rice paddies and farm houses that make up a considerable part of the town.

Yufuin can easily be explored on foot as the majority of the town's attractions are located along the main walking path between Yufuin Station and Lake Kinrinko. Walking the entire route takes 20 to 30 minutes. Bicycles are a convenient method for traveling to the more remote baths or for seeing the town swiftly. Rental bicycles can be obtained at Yufuin Station between the hours of 9:00 AM and 5:00 PM for ¥200 per hour or ¥1,000 per day.

Lake Kinrinko is a small lake located at the end of the town's main walking route. Walking paths lined with small shops and cafés surround the lake. There is a small shrine located at the lake's southern end.

When you are in Yufuin, you will soon realize that the town lives for tourism. It is a good place to see contemporary Japanese crafts such as ceramics, clothing, woodworking, and to sample interesting foods offered in one of its many cafés. But do note that Yufuin gets pretty crowded during the holidays and weekends. If you plan to stay overnight, make every effort to arrive before dusk.

Web Page: http://yufuin.or.jp/global/index.php?easiestml_
            lang=en

Saga Prefecture ((佐賀県)

Arita-cho (有田町): Town of Arita

Arita Porcelain Park

Arita, a small town in Saga Prefecture, is known throughout Japan for its pottery called Arita-yaki. As a matter of fact, Arita was the first place in Japan where porcelain was produced. Arita's pottery was popular both domestically as well as in China and Europe. Because the pottery was exported from the nearby Imari Port, Arita-yaki would also become known as Imari-yaki, particularly when describing the products manufactured for foreign markets.

Today, travelers to Arita can visit a small theme park called the Arita Porcelain Park and see first-hand the porcelain wares that this town is famous for. Located just outside of the town center, the park is a recreation of a traditional German village. The focal point of the park is the Zwinger Palace, a replica of the palace located in Dresden, Germany. Incidentally, Dresden is also famous for its local porcelain known as Meissen. Zwinger Palace at Arita Porcelain Park serves as a museum with an impressive collection of both Arita-yaki and European porcelain. Behind the museum, there is a gorgeous European-style garden that affords excellent photo opportunities.

After touring the museum and garden, you may be interested in seeing the Tengudani Kiln. There is a workshop nearby, where you can create your own porcelain cups or bowls for a cost of between ¥800 and ¥4,000. If you are not interested in getting your hands dirty, there are many shops within the park and around town that sell porcelain wares. The main shop in the park also offers sake tasting for those inclined to cap off your day in this fashion.

The park operates between 9:00 AM and 6:00 PM. Although no entrance fee is charged to enter the park, there is a nominal ¥500 admission fee for the museum.

Accessing the park is relatively easy via JR Arita Station on the Sasebo Line. The park is a 10-minute taxi ride from the station.

Location(s):   340-28 Otsu Toya, Nishimatsura-gun, Arita-cho, Saga

Ogi-shi (小城市): Ogi-City

Kiyomizu Take Akari: Kiyomizu Bamboo Light Festival, Kiyomizu Waterfall

Only a 15-minute train ride from Saga City in Kyushu is the rural town of Ogi. It is pretty much off the beaten path as far as international tourism is concerned but this town, nicknamed Little Kyoto, is a great place to visit any time of the year. Ogi Park, with over 3,000 cherry trees, is considered one of the top 100 places to view the cherry blossoms in Japan during sakura season. During the winter, Tenzan Resort in Saga City offers excellent skiing and snowboarding for people of all skill levels.

The Kiyomizu Waterfall is the symbol of the town and is a beautiful place to visit year-round. Next to the waterfall is Kenryu-ji, a Buddhist temple constructed in 1627. There are incredible Buddhist statues and shrines throughout the area set against an amazing, lush background of vegetation. At the base of the waterfall, there is a gazebo where you can relax and enjoy a picnic if so inclined.

The waterfall also affords an excellent place to view the autumn foliage. The brilliant crimson and gold leaves are illuminated with flood lights at night and between November 15-23 the Kiyomizu Take Akari Lantern Festival further enhances the beauty of the area. Ten thousand bamboo lanterns are placed along the promenade leading up to the waterfall and arranged in artistic patterns, which must be seen to be believed. Ogi is also known for its hotaru (fireflies) and the light emitted by these stunning insects combined with the lit lanterns when the sun goes down creates a scenery that you will find difficult to forget.

The festival takes place between 6:00 PM and 9:00 PM and the entrance fee is only ¥500. You can reach the falls via the JR Karatsu Line, exit Ogi Station. From there your destination is a 15-minute taxi ride.

Location(s):   Kiyomizu Ogimachi, Ogi-shi, Saga

Web Page: https://www.city.ogi.lg.jp/main/6226.html

Takeo-shi (武雄市): Takeo City

Mifuneyama Rakuen (御船山楽園): Mount Mifune Park

If you happen to be in Saga Prefecture on the island of Kyushu, you really should make a point of visiting Takeo City in the western part of the prefecture. Here, you will find the sprawling 170-year-old park on the western foot of Mount Mifune (御船山), called Mifuneyama Rakuen.

Built over a period of three years, it was completed in 1845. The park was the second residence of Shigeyoshi Nabeshima, the 28th ruler of the Takeo Region. It sprawls over 15 hectares (37 acres or 10 Tokyo Domes) and is home to 200,000 azalea bushes, 5,000 cherry blossom trees and a 170-year-old Japanese wisteria tree. Mifuneyama Rakuen was listed as one of 30 reasons to go to Japan before you die by Tsunagu Japan and it is truly amazing. During the autumn months the momiji or Japanese maple presents a dramatic explosion of color, which is further enhanced by the night time illumination during the month of November.

Mount Mifune Park hosts a variety of events throughout the year including tea parties and photo sessions. The tsutsuji (azaleas) bloom from mid to late April.

The park is a 30-minute walk from Takeo Onsen Station (via the JR Sasebo Line). There is an admission charge of ¥600 for adults and ¥300 for children. Do not forget to bring your camera!

Location(s):   4100, Takeocho Takeo-shi, Saga

420

Yoshinogari-cho (吉野ヶ里町): Town of Yoshinogari

<u>Yoshinogari Historical Park (吉野ヶ里 遺跡)</u>

Located just seven miles from the Ariake Sea in the Kanzaki District, you will find the town of Yoshinogari. The town dates back to before 400 BC when the Jomon culture flourished in Japan. The Yayoi period followed the Jomon period (400 BC to 300 AD) and spanned about 700 years. The archaeological site at Yoshinogari has been continuously excavated by a number of different agencies since 1986. It was designated as a "Special National Historic Site" in 1991 due to the quality of artifacts unearthed there and its significance to Japanese prehistory. The Yoshinogari Historical Park was created in 1992.

Dozens of pit dwellings, elevated store houses and over 2,000 tombs were unearthed at the Yoshinogari Historical Park. It is considered to be the largest and most important Yayoi period site in Japan. The settlements are believed to have been some of the largest moat-encircled villages of their time and are speculated to have been the seat of one of the earliest forms of state government found in Japan. Today, the ancient villages have been reconstructed for tourists and some even contain mannequins used to reenact various duties and ceremonies associated with that period in history.

The park spans over 117 hectares (289 acres) and is divided into three main sections. The Entrance Zone houses a mini theater, restaurant, and souvenir shop. Here, visitors can participate in hands-on activities such as stone carving and building a fire with a bow drill. The Moat-Encircled Zone, or Minami Naikaku, at the center of the park is one of the most important areas. Enclosed by defensive walls and moats, the Yayoi period rulers governed the village from this location. Another important enclosed settlement called Kita Naikaku is located just a short distance north and contains a large shrine and dwellings used for ancient ceremonies. Finally, the Ancient Field Zone, which covers about 20 hectares (49 acres), provides space for various recreational activities such as picnics.

The park is currently developing a fourth area that it plans to call the Ancient Forest Zone. When completed, this area will recreate the forest habitat of ancient Yayoi.

Park hours are from 9:00 AM to 5:00 PM (January 1 to May 31 and September 1 to December 30) and 9:00 AM to 6:00 PM (June 1 to August 31). Admission is ¥400 for adults and ¥80 for children over six years of age.

Location(s):	Saga, Kanzaki-gun, Yoshinogari-machi Tade 1843
Web Page:	http://www.yoshinogari.jp/en/

Points of Interest: Kyushu Region

Huis Ten Bosch Nagasaki

Beppu Blood Pond Hell Onsen Oita

Nakatsu Castle Oita

Yoshinogari Historical Park Saga

Nagasaki Peace Park

Ryukyu Region

Introduction to Ryukyu (琉球諸島)

The Ryukyu Islands are a chain of islands stretching nearly 620 miles (998 km) southwest from Kyushu to Taiwan and include Osumi, Tokara, Amami, Okinawa, Miyako, Yaeyama, and Yonaguni. The largest of the islands is Okinawa.

Osumi and Tokara Islands fall under the Kyushu region, where the people are ethnically Japanese and speak a variation of the Kagoshima dialect. The Amami, Okinawa, Miyako, and Yaeyama Islands have a native population collectively called the Ryukyuans, named after the former Ryukyu Kingdom. The Ryukyuan language is traditionally spoken on these islands. However, Japanese is the primary language with the Okinawan Japanese dialect prevalently spoken.

With the average annual temperatures hovering around 22.4 C (72.3 F), the area is a major tourist destination for the Japanese.

In addition to having a language/ dialect of their own, the Okinawans also have their own customs that set them apart from mainland Japanese. For instance, on the rooftops and at the gate of almost every house in Okinawa, you will find the omnipresent Shisa (Guardian lion dog). They are usually placed in pairs, one with its mouth open to catch good fortune and another with its mouth closed to keep in good fortune. Okinawan music is also distinctive and the instrument of choice is the sanshin, a three-stringed banjo-like instrument that is a distant cousin of the mainland's shamisen.

Throughout Okinawa, numerous historical sites related to World War II can be found including the Peace Memorial Park in Naha, the capital of Okinawa, and the Himeyuri Monument. The Himeyuri Monument was built in April 7, 1946, to commemorate those who had died during the Battle of Okinawa.

The Himeyuri Corps was a group of 222 students and 18 teachers from the Okinawa Daiichi Women's High School and the Okinawa Shihan Women's School, who formed a nursing unit. They were mobilized by the Japanese army on March 23, 1945. During the three-month-long Battle of Okinawa, the students served on the front lines, performing surgery and attending to the medical needs of the injured. On June 18, 1945, an order of dissolution was given to the unit. In the week following the dissolution order, approximately 80 percent of the girls and their teachers were killed. Survivors committed suicide in various ways because of fears of systematic rape by US soldiers. Some threw themselves off cliffs while others killed themselves with hand grenades given to them by the Japanese soldiers.

Traces of the former Ryukyu Kingdom are also present, such as the rebuilt Shuri Castle in Naha and Taketomi Village located on the Yaeyama Islands.

Okinawan cuisine is also distinct from that of mainland Japan, with notable Taiwanese influences. Some dishes worth sampling are the goya champuru (a bitter melon that is stir fried with pork and tofu), gurukun (a small fish, considered the official fish of Okinawa that is prepared in various ways), hirayachi (a savory pancake similar to okonomiyaki but thinner), rafti (a dish consisting of stewed pork), sata andagi (deep fried dough also known as Okinawan donuts), and soki soba (noodles in soup stock with cubed pork pieces).

For those that are more adventurous, there are also several exotic dishes worth looking into including chiraga (the skin from a pig's face), mimiga (sliced pork ears in vinegar), umibudo (seaweed that is eaten raw, dipped in vinegar or soy sauce), and sukugarasu (fermented fish pressed into tofu).

There are many American restaurants in Okinawa too, opened to serve the military stationed there. Consequently, you will find several hybrid Okinawan-American dishes including the nuuyaru burger (using Spam) and taco rice (rice served with Mexican-style taco meat, cheese, lettuce, and tomatoes). Since Spam is abundant in Okinawa, you will find many restaurants serving poku tamago (pork eggs) consisting of fried slices of Spam served with scrambled eggs and plenty of ketchup!

The Naha Airport is Japan's seventh busiest airport and the primary air terminal for passengers and cargo traveling to and from Okinawa Prefecture. The airport also handles scheduled international traffic to Taiwan, Hong Kong, Korea, and China. It is home to the Naha Air Base, now utilized by the Japan Air Self-Defense Force and formerly under the control of the United States Air Force.

Web Page: http://www.pref.okinawa.jp/english/

Okinawa Prefecture (沖縄県)

Many Americans probably know Okinawa by its association with the 1945 Battle of Okinawa, which was fought on the Ryukyu Islands of Okinawa Prefecture. It was World War II's largest amphibious assault in the Pacific War. When World War II ended, Okinawa was placed under U.S. administration for 27 years. It wasn't until 1972 that the islands were finally returned to the Japanese. The U.S. still maintains a large military presence in Okinawa; 27,000 military personnel and 22,000 family members are stationed there.

Okinawa Prefecture consists of hundreds of islands known as the Ryukyu Islands, which span a distance of 620 miles (998 km). Okinawa Island is the largest, encompassing 464 square miles (1,201 km²). The inhabited islands are divided into three groups. They are the Okinawa Islands (Iejima, Kume, Okinawa Island, and Kerama Islands), Miyako Islands (Miyako-jima) and Yaeyama Islands (Iriomote, Ishigaki, and Yonaguni). Naha, Okinawa's capital, is located in the southern part of Okinawa Island. With its warm weather and sandy beaches, Okinawa is often considered the Hawaii of Japan.

During the Ryukyu Kingdom era, from the 15th century to the 19th century, various cultures were integrated into the Okinawan culture. There are traces of Chinese, Thai, and Austronesian (Indonesia, Malaysia, Philippines, Brunei, Micronesia, and Polynesia) influences. Although standard Japanese is almost always used in formal situations, the actual traditional Okinawan language is still used in traditional folk music and dance.

Home to people from over 30 different countries, Okinawa hosts an International Carnival each year, bringing together

429

people from all walks of life. The second day of the International Carnival is called Gate 2 Fest. On this day, motorcycle riders from all over the country assemble on Gate 2 Street and ride together in force, showing off their motorcycles and gear.

Situated in the Nakagami District, just 17 miles (27 km) north of Naha is Yomitan Village. Fierce fighting took place here during World War II. Yomitan is mainly an agricultural and crafts village, with its economy supported by crops such as chrysanthemums, sugar cane, and sweet potatoes. The village attracts many tourists with its beautiful and largely unspoiled beaches as well as its folk arts, which include pottery and glass blowing.

Yachimun pottery has existed in Okinawa for over 300 years. There are two categories: the unglazed Arayaki ware and the glazed Joyaki ware. Once a year, Okinawa's most famous pottery fair takes place where handmade Yomitan Village shisa, pots, vases, cups, sake jars, and more are on display and for sale.

The Okinawan art of glass blowing, known as Ryukyu glass, is famous and popular with both Japanese and foreigners alike. The origin of Ryukyu glass can be traced back to the Meiji era. In those days, people used the art of glass blowing to construct glass bottles for medicine and parts for lamps. After World War II, glass craftsmen began to produce glass products for American soldiers in Okinawa. Today, it is a very important part of Okinawan culture.

Yomitan is also home to multiple UNESCO World Heritage Sites including Zakimi Castle, which was constructed between 1416 and 1422. It is in ruins, but the foundations and walls have been restored. Before and during World War II, the castle was used as a gun emplacement by the Japanese. After the war, U.S. forces utilized the castle as a radar station, destroying some of the walls in the process of installing the equipment. There is a small museum next to the parking lot with displays of local art and folk craft. The museum does not focus on the castle in particular, but rather gives a general perspective on the local community, including exhibits of archaeological relics, dwellings, funerary customs, and the war.

Sharing the UNESCO designation is Nakijin castle, which is located on northern Okinawa's Motobu Peninsula. It was constructed between the late 13th century and the beginning of the 15th century. The castle was strategically built on a hill, where it was well defended by natural elements such as the river, cliffs, and a deep valley. It was the residence of the Ryukyuan Kingdom governor and currently lies in ruins. Nearby is the Nakijin Village History and Culture Center with a small museum displaying items unearthed on the castle grounds such as Chinese pottery, coins, and documents. There are also exhibits about everyday life and culture of Nakijin Village.

Cape Zanpa in Yomitan Village is the first of many spectacular capes that dot the eastern coastline. The Cape Zanpa Lighthouse sits on the corner of the cape on acres of beautifully manicured land. The walking paths around the lighthouse border the China Sea and provide great scenic views. The cape is a popular fishing spot and the rocks along the water are usually crowded with fishermen. A huge shisa guards the entrance to the Zanpa Misaki Recreation Plaza, where you will find a playground, restaurants, shops, and barbecue pits.

Nakadomari Beach, located on the west side of Okinawa,

overlooking the East China Sea is registered as a National Seashore. Here, visitors can enjoy parasailing, horseback riding, fishing, scuba diving, snorkeling, and surfing. There are stairs carved from rock at Maeda Point, the entrance to the bay, which allows easy access to the water for surfers and divers.

Located in the suburbs of Nago City, just a short drive from the Okinawa Churaumi Aquarium, is the Kanucha Resort Hotel. Set amidst the sea and surrounding mountains of northern Okinawa, the hotel offers a championship-caliber golf course called the Kanucha Golf Course. Given its ideal location, guests at this resort can partake in many different types of water sports and activities including diving, jet skiing, snorkeling, banana boat rides, and glass bottom boat excursions, to name a few.

In 1975, Okinawa hosted the World's Exposition at its Ocean Expo Park. Unfortunately, over the years, the park saw a decrease in visitors, prompting the construction of the Okinawa Churaumi Aquarium in 2002 in an effort to help boost tourism. Churaumi in Okinawan Japanese means beautiful ocean. The aquarium has four floors with tanks containing deep sea creatures, sharks, coral, and tropical fish. It is one of only a few aquariums that keep whale sharks in captivity and is currently trying to breed them. Over 20 million visitors have walked through its doors since its opening.

Ufuya, which translates to big house, is a great restaurant in the Nago area just south of the Churaumi Aquarium. They do not accept reservations on weekends and tend to get very crowded. The waiting room outside of the restaurant has a water fountain, a wooden swing, and a pineapple field, which help its patrons pass the time while they wait to be seated.

432

Located just north of Nago City is Kouri Island. Visitors must cross two bridges to access the island. The first bridge connects the main island of Okinawa with Yagaji Island. The second, the Kouri Big Bridge, is Japan's longest toll-free bridge, spanning 1.2 miles (1.9 km). It connects Yagaji to Kouri Island. Once you reach Kouri Island, you can take advantage of the beautiful beach and all it has to offer including swimming, snorkeling, kayaking, and diving. Kouri is famous for producing delicious sea urchins, a delicacy in Japan.

Nirai Kanai in Okinawan Japanese means "closest place to heaven", and it is the name given to a mythical island where the gods are said to reside. According to Okinawan legend, the gods travel from the island each year to bless their people. An hour south of Nago City is Nanjo City where there is a bridge called the Nirai Kanai Bridge. The view from the bridge is breathtaking. There is an observation spot just above the tunnel that leads to the entrance of the bridge but finding a parking spot can be a challenge.

Japan National Route 58 is an unusual highway that runs along the coast of Okinawa and continues to other islands. It starts at the Meiji Bridge in Naha and ends in Kagoshima. Unfortunately, sections of the highway running from island to island are not connected in any manner other than the name.

Hotel Moon Beach is approximately 60 minutes by car on Route 58 and offers great views of the crescent-shaped private, white sand beach known as Moon Beach. The beach extends 160 yards (146 m) along the water and is often densely populated with beach goers. There are areas for beach umbrellas, volleyball nets, and a designated swimming area.

If your travels take you to the Okinawa Prefecture, take the time to immerse yourself in the unique Ryukyu culture and partake in all that the region has to offer. The experience will be both educational and enjoyable.

Itoman-shi (糸満市): Itoman City

<u>Okinawa Prefectural Peace Memorial Museum</u>

The year 2015 marked the 70th anniversary of the dropping of atomic bombs on Hiroshima and Nagasaki. A uranium gun-type atomic bomb was dropped on Hiroshima on August 6 and Nagasaki was decimated by a plutonium implosion-type bomb on August 9, 1945. Japan surrendered on August 15. On September 2, Japanese Foreign Affairs Minister, Mamoru Shigemitsu, signed the Japanese Instrument of Surrender on board USS Missouri, effectively ending World War II. In Japan, August 15 is known as Shusen-kinenbi (終戦記念日)/ shusen no hi (終戦の日), a day of mourning for the war dead and praying for peace.

Toward the end of World War II, Okinawa became the site for one of the war's bloodiest battles. It is estimated that 200,000 people including more than 100,000 civilians and 12,500 US soldiers perished during the battle, which lasted from April to June 1945. The devastating effects of the war had a profound impact on the Okinawans and there are a number of monuments and museums relating to the period throughout Okinawa. The worst fighting took place in the south and that is where some of the larger monuments have been erected.

The Peace Memorial Park, located in Itoman City, is the main memorial dedicated to the Battle of Okinawa. This park stands on the site where the Battle of Okinawa came to a bitter end and where the most bloodshed ensued. The Okinawa Prefectural Peace Memorial Museum established on June 11, 1975, serves as the main attraction.

Divided into five separate areas, the museum's main purpose is to promote an idea of everlasting peace to the world. The first area contains exhibits that cover the history of Okinawa leading up to World War II. The second area is devoted to the progress of the battle itself and the harsh realities of war as described from a people's perspective. The third area covers the atrocities faced by the Okinawans during the battle, everything from hiding out in caves to wandering the killing fields. The forth area displays personal testimonies preserved in print and video recordings. The fifth area focuses on postwar Okinawa, drawing attention to the refugee camps and the 27-year US military occupation. There is also an exhibit designed specifically for children to teach them about the importance of human life and to cultivate a desire for peace in the future.

An important stopping-off point for visitors is the Cornerstone of Peace (Flame of Peace), which is fed by flames from both Hiroshima and Nagasaki as well as a flame from Zamami, where US forces first landed on Okinawa in 1945. The flame is in the center of a circular pond and it is where visiting heads of state often come to pay their respects to the dead.

The Okinawa Prefectural Peace Memorial Museum is open Tuesday through Sunday from 9:00 AM to 5:00 PM. It is closed between December 29 and January 3, in observance of the New Year holiday.

The museum is a 40-minute journey by car from Naha Airport (via highway) and a three-minute walk from the nearest bus stop (Heiwa Kinendo Iriguchi). You can also take one of the readily available taxis from Naha Airport.

Location(s):   614-1, MabunI, Itoman, Okinawa

Web Page: http://www.peace-
museum.pref.okinawa.jp/english/index.html

Naha-shi (那覇市): Naha City

Shuri Castle (首里城) / Shinshun no Utage: New Year's Banquet

Shuri-jo or Shuri Castle was once the center of the Ryukyuan Empire (1429–1879) and has played a significant role in shaping Okinawan culture. Today, even though Okinawa has been assimilated into the nation of Japan, the spirit of the Ryukyus is still very much alive and reflected in the music, arts and crafts, language, and lifestyles of the locals.

Not only is the castle of great historical importance, but it is also quite magnificent and beautiful. The original structure was destroyed in the final days of World War II during the Battle of Okinawa. However, it was rebuilt and reopened to the public in 1992.

The castle grounds come alive from January 1 to 3, during New Year's ceremonies called Shinshun no Utage. Primarily, this is a costumed reenactment of the New Year's Day rituals held at the castle during the Ryukyu Dynasty. The king and the queen emerge from behind castle walls on January 1 and 2 to pray for peace and prosperity. On January 3, the Ryukyu no Utage or Banquet of the Ryukyus is held.

The festivities begin at 8:30 AM and last until 5:00 PM on the first two days. The celebrations begin with an uzagaku (live musical performance), which lasts from 8:30 AM to 8:50 AM. The actual ceremony (chohaigokishiki) follows and has three parts. The first part, known as the kokorehogohai, runs from 10:00 AM to 10:25 AM. During this time the king prays and asks for peace. The second part is called the chonuunufe. The king prays for prosperity as his various subjects swear their loyalty to the king. The second part of the ceremony takes place from 10:50 AM to 11:00 AM. The third part, known as otori, takes place from 11:25 AM to 11:50 AM and involves drinking awamori, a distilled beverage native to Okinawa. The custom involves one person, the oya (master of ceremonies), making a short speech related to the celebration or ceremony being observed. He then drinks and pours awamori for the next person. The oya usually moves counterclockwise around in a circle, repeating the ritual for each individual.

Following the rituals, there are Ryukyu dancing and entertainment. A booth is set up offering visitors their choice of tea or a sweet alcoholic drink made from sake kasu (the lees leftover from sake production).

On January 3, the final day of the ceremony, the king and queen appear twice, from 10:00 to 10:20 AM and again from 11:00 to 11:20 AM. There are traditional musical performances on this day and visitors have an opportunity to have a souvenir photo taken with the king and queen.

If you want to participate in the celebrations, you must pay an admission fee. The charges are ¥820 for adults and ¥620 for high school students. Elementary and junior high students are admitted for ¥310 while there is no charge for children six years old or under.

The castle is easily accessible from Naha Airport via National Highway No. 331 or you can take the Yui Rail from Naha Airport Station to Shuri Station. The castle is a 15-minute walk from this point.

Location(s):   1-2 Shurikinjocho, Naha-shi, Okinawa

Web Page: http://oki-park.jp/shurijo/en/

http://oki-park.jp.e.ms.hp.transer.com/shurijo/event/180
(Shinshun no Utage)

Naha-shi (那覇市): Naha City

Underground Caves

Okinawa is often referred to as Japan's Hawaii, but with average yearly temperatures hovering around 22.4 C (72.3 F) and with rainfall averages of 78 inches (198 cm) per year, the island can be a very hot and humid location to visit. Not to fear, there are several popular caves to explore to get away from the heat and humidity of the summer months.

Located just six miles (10 km) south of Naha Airport you will find the Gyokusendo Cave, which is the second largest cave system in Japan, with over 0.5 miles (0.8 km) of passageways open for exploration. Discovered in 1967, this 300,000-year-old cave stretches three miles (5 km) from end to end. Here, the temperatures are a cool 69°F (20°C) year-round and visitors can comfortably take in the small streams, waterfalls, stalactites, and stalagmites. The cave is actually located beneath a theme park about Okinawan culture called Okinawa World. A craft village, a snake museum, and the cave itself are the park's main attractions. The cave is strategically lit so that the crystal clear pools of water give off a rich, blue glow and the stalactites overhead display a psychedelic show of colors, courtesy of motion detector-controlled pinwheel lighting. The cave served as the backdrop for several movies including the 1974 film, *Godzilla vs. Mechagodzilla*.

Between July and September Okinawa World offers daily tours that take you beyond the walkway into parts of the cave that are normally off-limits. The tour lasts about 90 minutes and involves a fair amount of climbing and wading into the river, which runs beneath the walkway. Anyone over the age of five is allowed to participate.

For drink connoisseurs, a special type of awamori (an alcoholic beverage indigenous to Okinawa) is distilled here. The beverage is made from long grain indica rice and fermented for five years. The consistent temperature of the cave provides an ideal environment for the fermentation process. If you are feeling adventurous, there is a drink called habushu. It is awamori bottled with a small pit viper.

The next cave is located in the town of Kin next to the Kin Kannon-do Temple, just down the road from the front gate of the US Marine Corp base, Camp Hansen. The Kin Kannon-do Temple is one of the eight famous temples in Okinawa and has a rich history. It is said that in 1552, a Buddhist priest named Nisshu washed ashore during a typhoon as he was traveling back from China. He stayed in Kin Village and expressed his gratitude to the people for their help and generosity by praying for the destruction of the large Habu snakes that lived in the cave and attacked the villagers' domestic animals. Nisshu created three statues: one of Buddha, one of Yukushi (God of Medicine), and one of Kannon (God of Mercy) to be placed in front of the cave. Later a temple was erected near the cave and is still used for wedding ceremonies and funeral services.

After descending down a steep flight of stairs leading into the cave, you discover the sheer beauty of the colorful stalagmites and stalactites. On one level there is a smiling golden Buddha statue and on the next, unimaginable treasures. Like Gyokusendo Cave, the cave at Kin is used to store thousands of bottles of Tatsu Awamori (Dragon Awamori). The bottles are stored for five to ten years and are often tagged with the owner's name and the date on which the bottle went into storage. Some bottles have baby photos or wedding photos. They are retrieved by the owner when the special occasion for which they planned arrives. The bottles typically cost ¥10,000 and are safely locked away behind a gate.

So, when you visit Okinawa, take in the beaches, sunshine, windsurfing, and other activities this tropical island has to offer and for a change of pace, descend to subterranean Okinawa and experience the secrets that lie below. It is an experience you will remember for a lifetime.

Web Page: http://www.okinawa-information.com/content/gyokusendo-caves-okinawa-world

Points of Interest: Ryukyu Region

Shuri Castle Okinawa

Churaumi Aquarium Okinawa

Cape Manzamo

Kouri Island

Kouri Bridge Okinawa

Nakijin Castle

Cape Zanpa

Cape Zanpa

American Village Okinawa

Photo Credits

1. Cover photo: iordani/Shutterstock.com

2. Akan Kokuritsu Koen: Akan National Park: Izumi Walker

3. Akan Kokuritsu Koen: Akan National Park: Izumi Walker

4. Shikisai no Oka: Hills of Seasonal Colors: Izumi Walker

5. Shiretoko Goko: Izumi Walker

6. Oshinkoshin Falls: Izumi Walker

7. Oshinkoshin Falls: Izumi Walker

8. Sapporo TV Tower: Sean Pavone/Shutterstock.com

9. Snow Festival in Sapporo: Dr_Flash/ Shutterstock.com

10. Aomori City: Sean Pavone/Shutterstock.com

11. Okama Crater Lake: Norikazu/Shutterstock.com

12. Yamadera: CDRW/Shutterstock.com

13. Kakunodate: Norikazu/Shutterstock.com

14. Tashirojima: Cat Island: Yoshihiko Tanaka/ Shutterstock.com

15. Mount Shirouma Hakuba: Kamikochi/Shutterstock.com

16. Ueda Castle: Piti Sirisriro/Shutterstock.com

17. Lake Ashi, Mount Fuji Hakone: Wiennant M./Shutterstock.com

18. Lake Suwa: Vitoony35/Shutterstock.com

19. Kitano Tenmangu Shrine: Moritoshi Inaba

20. Fushimi Inari Taisha: Sean Pavone/Shutterstock.com

21. Sagano Bamboo Forest: Sean Pavone/Shutterstock.com

22. Kiyomizu-dera: Chen Min Chun/Shutterstock.com

23. Gion District: Sergii Rudiuk/Shutterstock.com

24. Osaka Castle: Cowardlion/Shutterstock.com

25. Dotonbori Hotel: twoKim Images/Shutterstock.com

26. Osaka Bay: littlewormy/Shutterstock.com

27. Kobe Port Tower: Peera_stockfoto/Shutterstock.com

28. Heijo Palace: Sean Pavone/Shutterstock.com

29. Byodoin Temple: Sean Pavone/Shutterstock.com

30. Himeji Castle: S.R.Lee Photo Traveller/Shutterstock.con

31. Shirahama: Sean Pavone/Shutterstock.com

32. Kurashiki City: Moritoshi Inaba

33. Korakuen Garden: Moritoshi Inaba

34. Bitchu Matsuyama Castle: Moritoshi Inaba

35. Hiroshima Genbaku Dome: Hayato Kobayahi

36. Miyajima: ESB Professional/Shutterstock.com

37. Kintai Bridge: tuklopburi/Shutterstock.com

38. Naruto Whirlpools: Hayato Kobayashi

39. Katsurahama: Ktomy/Shutterstock.com

40. Marugame Castle: Mokokomo/Shutterstock.com

41. Uwajima Castle: Masakichi/Shutterstock.com

42. Huis Ten Bosch: Monkeyfoto/Shutterstock.com

43. Beppu Blood Pond Hell Onsen: Sean Pavone/Shutterstock.com

44. Nakatsu Castle: Rocky Andoh

45. Yoshinogari Historical Park: kan_khampanya/Shutterstock.com

46. Nagasaki Peace Park: Tomo/Shutterstock.com

47. Shuri Castle: Torasun/Shutterstock.com

48. Churaumi Aquarium: Moritoshi Inaba

49. Cape Manzamo: Moritoshi Inaba

50. Kouri Island: Eiji Umezawa

51. Kouri Bridge: Eiji Umezawa

52. Kouri Bridge: Eiji Umezawa

53. Nakijin Castle: Moritoshi Inaba

54. Nakijin Castle: Moritoshi Inaba

55. Cape Zanpa: Moritoshi Inaba

56. Cape Zanpa: Moritoshi Inaba

57. American Village: Moritoshi Inaba

References

Bitchu-Takahashi Travel: Bitchu-Matsuyama Castle. (n.d.). Retrieved from http://www.japan-guide.com/e/e5777.html

CHUGOKU - Go Japan Go. (n.d.). Retrieved from http://www.gojapango.com/travel/chugoku.htm

Hanshin Tigers - Wikipedia, the free encyclopedia. (n.d.). Retrieved from https://en.wikipedia.org/wiki/Hanshin_Tigers?oldid=0

Hiroshi Senju Museum Karuizawa | Ryue Nishizawa - Arch2O. (n.d.). Retrieved from http://www.arch2o.com/hiroshi-senju-museum-karuizawa-ryue-nishizawa/

Karuizawa Picture Book Forest Museum - Atlas Obscura. (n.d.). Retrieved from http://www.atlasobscura.com/places/karuizawa-picture-book-forest-museum

Koraku-en - Wikipedia, the free encyclopedia. (n.d.). Retrieved from https://en.wikipedia.org/wiki/Koraku-en

Lafcadio Hearn - Wikipedia, the free encyclopedia. (n.d.). Retrieved from https://en.wikipedia.org/wiki/Lafcadio_Hearn

Matsue Castle - Shimane - Japan Travel - Tourism Guide ... (n.d.). Retrieved from http://en.japantravel.com/shimane/matsue-castle0/3946

Naha Air Base - Wikipedia, the free encyclopedia. (n.d.). Retrieved from https://en.wikipedia.org/wiki/Naha_Air_Base

New Chitose Airport (Shin- Chitose Airport, CTS). (n.d.). Retrieved from http://www.japan-guide.com/e/e2435.html

Okayama Castle - Wikipedia, the free encyclopedia. (n.d.). Retrieved from https://en.wikipedia.org/wiki/Okayama_Castle

Ryogoku Kokugikan Sumo Hall / Official Tokyo Travel Guide ... (n.d.). Retrieved from http://www.gotokyo.org/en/tourists/topics_event/topics/1209 03/topics.html

Ryukyu Islands - Wikipedia, the free encyclopedia. (n.d.). Retrieved from https://en.wikipedia.org/wiki/Ryuku_Islands

Saiho-ji (Kyoto) - Wikipedia, the free encyclopedia. (n.d.). Retrieved from https://en.wikipedia.org/wiki/Saih%C5%8D-ji_(Kyoto)

Sendai - Wikipedia, the free encyclopedia. (n.d.). Retrieved from https://en.wikipedia.org/wiki/Sendai

Senganen Garden Kagoshima | JapanVisitor Japan Travel Guide. (n.d.). Retrieved from http://www.japanvisitor.com/japan-parks-gardens/senganen-garden

Shikoku - Wikipedia, the free encyclopedia. (n.d.). Retrieved from https://en.wikipedia.org/wiki/Shikoku

Sumo - Wikipedia, the free encyclopedia. (n.d.). Retrieved from https://en.wikipedia.org/wiki/Sumo

Tohoku, Japan | Backpacking Asia Travel Guide. (n.d.). Retrieved from http://www.backpackingasia.com/Location/Asia/East_Asia/Japan/Tohoku/54

Where Are the Ryukyu Islands? - WorldAtlas.com. (n.d.). Retrieved from http://www.worldatlas.com/articles/where-are-the-ryukyu-islands.html

Yokote Kamakura Snow Festival - Japan National Tourism ...
(n.d.). Retrieved from
https://www.jnto.go.jp/eng/spot/festival/kamakurasnow.html

Lightning Source UK Ltd.
Milton Keynes UK
UKHW051341281122
412966UK00011B/115